The Splendor of the
Church in Mary

The Splendor of the Church in Mary

Henri de Lubac, Vatican II, and
Marian Ressourcement

Sr. Theresa Marie Chau Nguyen, OP

FOREWORD BY PAUL MCPARTLAN

The Catholic University of America Press
Washington, D.C.

Cataloging-in-Publication Data is available at the Library of Congress
ISBN : 978-0-8132-3691-9
eISBN : 978-0-8132-3692-6

For my dear parents
and my fellow sisters in community
MTJD

The soul and the Church are the twofold aspect
of one single lover, whose ceaseless flux of
changing countenance is tinted with the rays
of the Immaculate One.

—Paul Claudel, L'Épée et le miroir

The conception of Jesus in Mary's womb is the
prelude to the birth of every Christian
in the womb of the Church. We understand, then,
how the relationship which unites Mary and the Church
is so deep: by looking at Mary, we discover the most
beautiful and most tender face of the Church; and by
looking at the Church, we recognize the
sublime features of Mary.

—Pope Francis, 3 September 2014 General Audience

CONTENTS

Very soon after his election, explaining his choice of name, Pope Francis said that he, like Francis of Assisi, would love a Church that was poor and for the poor. Jean Corbon says that Jesus "in his person" is "the mystery of poverty," living for his Father with nothing of his own, and living for us too, giving us the Spirit, who proceeds from the Father and reposes upon him. The Spirit draws us into the poverty of Jesus, and love "streams forth" from the kenosis of his death. The "most intense movement of the Spirit in our hearts" enables us to say "'Yes' with our whole being to the love that gives us life," and opens us to what Corbon calls "knowledge of the divine compassion." Dramatically focusing this profound reflection, and surely recalling her *fiat* at the Annunciation and the song of joy she sang when visiting her cousin Elizabeth, he says that the Virgin Mary "is the mirror of this knowledge, its vital space." Moreover, it is henceforth in that very space that the Church lives, as we may deduce from Corbon's wonderful phrase: the holy Virgin is "the Church as she dawns in a single person."[1]

Thanks to the work of Henri de Lubac and other great scholars, the twentieth century truly was "the century of the Church," in which ecclesiological reflection broadened and deepened immensely. After many centuries in which Catholic teaching, in particular, had concentrated on the outward, institutional aspects of the Church, the Second Vatican Council spoke of the Church as a mystery, "a complex reality," with inner and outer, earthly

---

1. Jean Corbon, *The Wellspring of Worship*, trans. Matthew J. O'Connell (San Francisco: Ignatius Press, 2005), 246, 249.

and heavenly, human and divine aspects (*Lumen Gentium*, LG 8), indeed
as "the universal sacrament of salvation" (LG 48), "at once manifesting and
actualizing the mystery of God's love" (*Gaudium et Spes* 45). De Lubac pi-
oneered the recovery of that sacramental idea in the 1930s and expounded
it more fully in his *Méditation sur l'Église* in 1953, translated as *The Splendor
of the Church*, which both in content and in structure remarkably foreshad-
owed the Council's dogmatic constitution on the Church, *Lumen Gentium*
(1964). Both texts start with a chapter on the Church as mystery and both
notably conclude with a chapter on the Blessed Virgin Mary, reinforcing the
message that the Church must primarily be understood in personal rather
than institutional terms.

First and foremost, of course, that means that the Church is the body of
Christ, by the power of the Holy Spirit; but the Church is also that which—
or rather she who—responds to Christ, the bride of Christ, and to understand that aspect of the mystery we must turn to Mary. Such a reference is
at once both essential and elusive. Mary herself seems to deflect attention,
referring us always to her Son: "Do whatever he tells you" (Jn 2:5), but that
is precisely the point: we turn to her to learn how to do that. In a somewhat similar way, neither for the fathers nor for the great scholastics was the
Church a separate topic of study. Not until the fourteenth century did works
on the Church itself appear, significantly institutional, juridical, and external in their preoccupation, as de Lubac himself lamented. In earlier times,
the Church was simply the vital matrix within which the whole Christian
mystery was lived and explored; not itself the focus of attention, but implicit
to all reflection. What Pierre Teilhard de Chardin, with a seeming nod to
Gerard Manley Hopkins, says of Mary in his astonishing poem, "The Eternal
Feminine," thus seems apt for the Church, too: she is the very air we breathe
in the presence of God. Indeed, just a few lines earlier, Teilhard himself identifies the dual subject of his poem as "the Church, the bride of Christ" and
"Mary the Virgin, mother of all humankind."[2]

One of the many contributions of this fine book is to consider the influence of Teilhard's mystical insights on the thought of de Lubac, who wrote
an extensive commentary on his friend's poem. Somewhat similarly, in his
famous book, *The Orthodox Church*, Sergius Bulgakov said that while the
Mother of God is of course not a substitute for the one mediator who intercedes for us, we nevertheless ceaselessly pray for her intercession: "Love

---

2. Pierre Teilhard de Chardin, *Writings in Time of War*, trans. René Hague (New York: Harper
& Row, 1966), 200–201.

and veneration for the Virgin is the soul of Orthodox piety, its heart, that which warms and animates its entire body." There comes a point where mystics must guide theologians to the heart of the mystery, where analysis must yield to poetry and prayer, and system to song.

To her great credit, Sr. Chau respects both system and song in this important study. It is a careful and rigorous work of systematic theology infused with a sense of wonder and joy. She first of all analyzes de Lubac's own Mariological thought, situating it within the wider context of Mariological reflection prior to the Council. She then considers the conciliar debates and decisions regarding Mary and the Church, and the immense significance of the fact that the Council determined that Mary herself should not be treated separately. Seeing Mary in relation to the Church also means seeing the Church in relation to Mary, though it is a curious fact that there has been little effort since the Council to consider ecclesiological issues through a Marian lens, perhaps because of uncertainty as to what exactly that might mean. Boldly venturing into that territory and cleverly deploying her background knowledge of de Lubac, Sr. Chau examines the particularly complex issue of the relationship between the universal and particular churches through that very lens, with illuminating results. Her proposal that, since de Lubac undoubtedly influenced the Council's decision to treat Mary in *Lumen Gentium*, his own understanding of the relationship between Mary and the Church can help in the reception and application of the Council's teaching, is both compelling and full of potential for further results.

For the light it casts and the promise it offers, this book is to be warmly welcomed.

Paul McPartlan

PREFACE

At the twenty-third International Mariological Congress in 2012, Pope Benedict XVI stated: "The singular figure of the Mother of God must always be developed and studied from diverse and complementary perspectives: while the *via veritatis* is always valid, we do not forsake the *via pulchritudinis* and the *via amoris* to discover and contemplate still more profoundly Mary's crystalline and solid faith, her love for God, her indestructible hope." I was in the middle of my doctoral studies at the time, and these words struck a chord deep within me. As far back as memory serves, I have been captivated by the splendor of the Blessed Virgin Mary. In my youth, I was drawn to the gaze of this beautiful and beloved mother in the *via pulchritudinis*. In my religious life, I've sought to conform my heart to hers in the *via amoris*. In my scholarship, I've contemplated her pondering heart in *via veritatis*. But a moment of reckoning brought me to the realization that somewhere in the rigor of my doctoral studies, the *via pulchritudinis* and *via amoris* had taken a back seat to the *via veritatis*; I had completed all of my coursework without any mention of Mariology.

As I set out to address this lacuna in my theological formation, I discovered the final chapter of Henri de Lubac's *Méditation sur l'Église* in which the threefold paths of reason, beauty, and love dovetail exquisitely. *The Splendor of the Church in Mary* is the result of this discovery. It exhumes the vision of a Marian ecclesiology espoused by one of the most renowned theologians of the twentieth century. De Lubac's *ressourcement* on the topic of Mary and the Church is a theological compass providing orientation and direction in today's ideological forests; it brings us to the heart of the "great mystery" to which the Sacred Scriptures testify (Eph 5:32; Rev 19:7).

Admittedly, *The Splendor of the Church in Mary* does not seek to rest its gaze on the glories of the Virgin Mary as an end in itself. Just as the Church possesses no radiance of her own but only a reflection of the radiance of Christ, so too our contemplation of Mary as the personal realization of the Church directs our gaze to the effulgence of God's grace perfected in her—in truth, in beauty, and in love. All that is good, all that is beautiful, all that is true—in essence, everything—in Mary proclaims *soli Deo gloria*.

This work has been a labor of love. Many a friend and mentor have accompanied me along the way, and a debt of gratitude is owed to each and every one of them. In particular, I wish to express my deepest gratitude to my parents, Teresa and Hung Nguyen, who planted the seeds of my faith and were the first to teach me love of the Church. Their ardent prayers, endless support, and generous sacrifices for me are beyond measure. I am profoundly grateful to my Doktorvater Msgr. Paul McPartlan, whose virtuous scholarship, profound wisdom, and immense kindness have been an unfailing source of inspiration and encouragement. An immeasurable debt of gratitude is owed to my superiors and fellow Dominican Sisters of Mary Immaculate Province for their sororal support and care. With them, I concretely experience the bridal aspect of the communion of the Church and the quotidian joys of consecrated life. In particular, I want to thank Sr. Bernadette and Sr. Catherine Teresa for their willingness to read drafts of my writing. I am also very grateful to Father Richard Hinkley, Father Aaron Pidel, SJ, Father John Sica, OP, Father Jared Wicks, SJ, and Jon Kirwan, D.Phil., for their support and invaluable feedback, which has improved this work in substantial ways. All remaining errors and infelicities are my own. A heartfelt thank you to Rev. Ján Dolný, whose friendship continues to provide me a most fruitful context for religious life and stimulating theological reflection. My gratitude also extends to my students and colleagues at the University of St. Thomas (Houston) and to the academic community of the Catholic University of America (Washington, D.C.), where this study first began.

I wish to express my sincere appreciation to John, Brian, Trevor, and the entire team at CUA Press for their editorial support and encouragement throughout the process of preparing this manuscript for publication. Acknowledgement is also due to the Mariological Society of America (MSA) for granting permission to reproduce, in the appendix of this work, Father James T. O'Connor's English translation of the 1962 schema on the

Blessed Virgin Mary, which was first published in volume 37 of *Marian Studies* (1986). Additionally, portions of chapter 1 and chapter 8 of the present work were developed at the MSA meetings in 2013 and 2018 and subsequently published in *Marian Studies*, volumes 64 and 69. Similarly, portions of chapters 4 and 6 have appeared in articles published in *Maria: A Journal of Marian Studies*, volumes 1 and 2. I am grateful to the editors of *Marian Studies* and *Maria* for permission to reuse these materials.

Above all, I offer praise and thanksgiving to God, echoing the words of the Blessed Virgin Mary: "*My soul magnifies the Lord and my spirit rejoices in God my Savior.*"

Feast of the Visitation, 2022

LIST OF ABBREVIATIONS

Acta   *Acta Synodalia Sacrosancti Concilii Oecumenici Vaticani Secundi.*
Six volumes corresponding to the four sessions; each with multiple
parts. Vatican City: *Typis polyglottis Vaticanis,* 1970–2000.

ASC   de Lubac, Henri. *At the Service of the Church: Henri de Lubac Reflects
on the Circumstances That Occasioned His Writings.* Translated by
Anne Elizabeth Englund. San Francisco: Ignatius Press, 1993.

CCCM   *Corpus Christianorum Continuatio Mediaevalis.* Edited by Rhaban
Haacke. Turnhout: Brepols, 1974.

CSEL   *Corpus Scriptorum Ecclesiasticorum Latinorum.* Vienna: Imperial
Academy of Sciences, 1864–.

CPM   de Lubac, Henri. *The Church: Paradox and Mystery.* Translated by
James Dunne. Shannon: Ecclesia Press, 1969.

DH   Denzinger, Heinrich, and Peter Hünermann. *Enchiridion Symbolorum:
A Compendium of Creeds, Definitions, and Declarations on Matters of
Faith and Morals.* English edition: Robert Fastiggi and Anne Englund
Nash, eds. San Francisco: Ignatius Press, 2012.

EF   de Lubac, Henri. *The Eternal Feminine: A Study on the Poem by
Teilhard de Chardin Followed by Teilhard and the Problems of Today.*
Translated by René Hague. London: William Collins, 1971.

LG　　*Dogmatic Constitution on the Church, Lumen Gentium.* Solemnly Promulgated by His Holiness, Pope Paul VI. 21 November 1964.

MC　　de Lubac, Henri. *The Motherhood of the Church: Followed by Particular Churches in the Universal Church and an Interview Conducted by Gwendoline Jarczyk.* Translated by Sr. Sergia Englund. San Francisco: Ignatius Press, 1982.

MM　　de Lubac, Henri. "Mysticism and Mystery." In *Theological Fragments,* 35–69. San Francisco: Ignatius Press, 1989.

PG　　Migne, Jacques Paul, ed. *Patrologiae Cursus Completus, Series Graeca.* 162 vols. with Latin translation. Paris, 1857–66.

PL　　Migne, Jacques Paul, ed. *Patrologiae Cursus Completus, Series Latina.* 221 vols. Paris, 1844–64.

SC　　*Sources chrétiennes.* Paris: Éditions du Cerf, 1942–.

WTW　　Teilhard de Chardin, Pierre. *Writings in the Time of War.* Translated by René Hague. New York: Harper & Row, 1966.

The Splendor of the
Church in Mary

Introduction

The Second Vatican Council (1962–65) was an event of far-reaching consequences in both ecclesiastical and secular history. Over half a century later, the Catholic Church continues to reap the fruits of that momentous gathering that achieved lasting reforms of the liturgy, instituted fresh ecumenical initiatives, and renewed the structures of the Church. Yet one of the most fundamental achievements of the Council has been largely neglected: *Lumen Gentium*'s integration of Mariology and ecclesiology in its concluding chapter. This cornerstone, once hailed by Pope Paul VI as the "crown and summit" of the Dogmatic Constitution on the Church, had initially prompted a heated controversy. The question of whether the Council should treat Mary within its discussion of the Church or in a separate document divided the fathers, seemingly indicating that the Blessed Virgin Mary, under whose patronage Pope John XXIII had placed the Council,[1] had become a source of division, a sign of contradiction and discord, at the heart of the great assembly. Perhaps an even greater irony is that the synthesis of Mariology and ecclesiology that the Council eventually agreed upon and set as the keystone

---

1. On 25 December 1961, Pope John XXIII issued a bull convoking the Second Vatican Council, in which he stated, "Trusting therefore in the help of the Divine Redeemer, the Beginning and the End of all things, in the help of His Most Excellent Mother and of St. Joseph—to whom we entrusted from the very beginning such a great event—it seems to us that the time has come to convoke the Second Vatican Ecumenical Council"; Floyd Anderson, ed., *Council Daybook: Session I* (Washington, DC: National Catholic Welfare Conference, 1965), 8. He also announced on 5 February 1962 that the Council would open on 11 October, the feast of the Divine Maternity of Mary, thus linking the Vatican Council to the Council of Ephesus (431 AD), which upheld belief in Mary as the Mother of God.

of its discussion on the nature and mission of the Church has been largely neglected by postconciliar theology. This neglect is evidenced in contemporary ecclesiology's continuing to grapple with its various issues without any reference to Mary.[2] Had the Council not elected to incorporate the discussion of Mary within its discussion on the Church—namely, had it proceeded to present Mariology *apart* from the treatise on the Church—one might expect the present dearth of attention to the Marian dimension of the mystery of the Church. However, the Council did otherwise; it indeed achieved an integral Marian-ecclesiological synthesis of which, unfortunately, postconciliar ecclesiology has yet to take full cognizance. Ecclesiologist Christopher Ruddy argues that this "relative neglect of the ecclesiological substance and the implications of this chapter's teaching" remains "one of the greatest losses in the interpretation and reception of Vatican II."[3]

A Historical Sketch

The impoverished state of Marian theology in the years after the Council had not always been the case. The waxing and waning of Marian devotion and theology in the life of the Church has been described as a rhythmic process comparable to a rising tide, an ocean wave, that comes to a crest, rolls back, and then is followed by another wave that carries the waters further.[4] The Church's doctrinal reflection on the Virgin's role in salvation history has similarly developed over time with a rhythm reflecting the pulse of the Church's own life. The following swift and brief historical survey of the development of Mariology serves to provide the necessary context for an understanding of the state of Mariology at the time of Vatican II. Particular attention is given to the maximalist tendencies that characterized the broader Marian movement and the subsequent Marian *ressourcement* which emerged in the mid-twentieth century.

2. An exception to this general trend can be seen in the work of *mujerista* theologians such as Ada María Isasi-Díaz and Natalia Imperatori-Lee on the import of devotion to Our Lady of Guadalupe as a locus for ecclesiological renewal and feminist empowerment. However, a *full* cognizance of the Council's Marian-ecclesiological synthesis within mainstream ecclesiology has yet to be achieved.

3. Christopher Ruddy, "'In my end is my beginning': *Lumen Gentium* and the Priority of Doxology," *Irish Theological Quarterly* 79, no. 2 (2014): 160. Gilles Routhier, correspondingly, notes that "ecclesiologists have not contributed in a significant way to Mariology"; see "Quarante ans après Vatican II, qu'est devenu le Mouvement marial?" *Istina* 50 (2005): 326.

4. This sketch relies principally on René Laurentin's *Court Traité sur la Vierge Marie* (Paris: P. Lethielleux, 1968); English translation: *A Short Treatise on the Virgin Mary*, trans. Charles Newmann (Washington, DC: Ami Press, 1991), 3. See also Denis Farkasfalvy, *The Marian Mystery: The Outline of a Mariology* (New York: St. Paul, 2014).

Two Scriptural passages provide the foundation for reflections on Mary's relationship with the Church. First is John 19:27 in which the crucified Christ gives his mother to the Beloved Disciple. Second is Acts 1:14, the Pentecost event in which Mary is present with the disciples at the coming of the Spirit in Jerusalem. Both point to the constitution of the Church with Mary present, confirming her integral place in the mystery and mission of the Church. Though little else is recorded of Mary's role in the early Church, her abiding presence was crucial to the fledgling community, and all subsequent theological reflection must build on these foundations.

Marian devotion and an incipient Marian doctrine took shape in the patristic era, with the earliest extra-biblical allusions to the Blessed Virgin Mary found in the apocryphal *Book of James* and the letters of Ignatius of Antioch (d. 110 AD).[5] Another early development is the Fathers' consideration of the link between Mary and Eve,[6] a topic discussed in Justin Martyr's *Dialogue with Trypho* (c. 160 AD) and expounded in Irenaeus of Lyon's theological treatise, *Adversus haereses* (c. 180 AD).[7] For Irenaeus especially, this typological link between Mary and Eve was an integral part of understanding redemption as regeneration by way of *recapitulation* in Christ, the New Adam. In the fourth century, Ambrose of Milan (337–397) identified Mary as the *typus ecclesiae*,[8] and Augustine of Hippo (354–430) developed the idea further, describing the Virgin Mary as the ideal image and exemplary member of the Church.[9] Another foundational milestone of the patristic era was the recognition of Mary as *Théotokos* by the Council of Ephesus in 431 AD. These represent some of the key patristic ingredients of *ressourcement* on Mary.

The early Middle Ages witnessed the flowering of Marian devotion in the monasteries with liturgical developments that focused on the mysteries of Mary's life and death. For example, the Carolingian liturgy added the

---

5. Ignatius of Antioch's *Letter to the Ephesians*, ch. 7.2; 18.2; 19.1; *Letter to the Smyrnaeans*, ch. 1.1; *Letter to the Trallians*, ch. 9 in J. B. Lightfoot, ed. and trans., *The Apostolic Fathers: Clement, Ignatius, and Polycarp*, 2nd ed., vol. 2 (Grand Rapids, MI: Baker Book House, 1981). See also Bertrand Buby, *Mary of Galilee*, vol. 3: *The Marian Heritage of the Early Church* (New York: Alba House, 1997), 4–10; Luigi Gambero, *Mary and the Fathers of the Church: The Blessed Virgin Mary in Patristic Thought* (San Francisco: Ignatius Press, 1999); and Tina Beattie, "Mary in Patristic Theology," in *Mary: The Complete Resource*, ed. Sarah Jane Boss (London: Continuum, 2007), 75–105.

6. Cf. Luigi Gambero, "Patristic Intuitions of Mary's Role as Mediatrix and Advocate: The Invocation of the Faithful for Her Help," *Marian Studies* 52 (2001): 78–101.

7. Justin Martyr, *Dialogus cum Tryphone Judaeo* (PG 6:709–12); Irenaeus, *Adversus haereses libri quinque* (PG 7:1175–76).

8. Ambrose, *Expositio evangelii secundum Lucam II*, 7 (CSEL XXXII, 4, 45).

9. Augustine, *De sancta virginitate 6* (PL 40, 399); *Sermo XXV*, 7 (PL 46, 938).

feasts of the Assumption and the Nativity of the Virgin—transported from the East—to the Frankish calendars, and this gave rise to the composition of corresponding liturgical texts for the Divine Office and the proliferation of Marian readings of Scripture in the commentary tradition.[10] In subsequent centuries, the founding of cathedral schools and then universities established a new intellectual climate that initiated a shift from the previous liturgical outlook "to a subjective and personal one, expressed in the proliferation of newly created forms of devotion."[11] New focus was given to Mary's personal cooperation in the work of Redemption at the cross and consequently, also, to her role as mother and intercessor of the Church: "This is your mother" (Jn 19:27) was interpreted as spoken not only to the Beloved Disciple but also to every Christian person.[12] With this subtle shift toward an emphasis on *subject* over object, a preference for the *mystic* over the mystery, Mary's role in the events of salvation history would recede into the background, with greater attention paid to her effective intercession for Christians in the present day. Mary was increasingly portrayed as a mediator between God and humankind, an aqueduct of all graces, and a special recipient of the singular divine privileges of God.[13] As Marian piety continued to develop along these lines, its objective connection to the central mystery of Christ and the Church expanded and focused on the person of Mary alone.[14] A hint of the encroaching pious sentimentalism is detectable in *Mariale super missus est* (c. 1503),[15] an influential theological treatise falsely attributed to St. Albert the Great, which emphasized Our Lady's privileges apart from the Church.[16] Another work, uncritically attributed to St. Bonaventure, re-directed the praises of God, such as those of Psalm 96, to Mary: "Sing to Our Lady a new song: for she hath done wonderful things. In the sight of the nations she hath revealed her mercy; her name is heard even to the ends of

---

10. Cf. Luigi Gambero, *Mary in the Middle Ages: The Blessed Virgin Mary in the Thought of Medieval Latin Theologians* (San Franscisco: Ignatius Press, 2005).

11. Elizabeth Johnson, "Marian Devotion in the Western Church," in *Christian Spirituality: High Middle Ages and Reformation*, vol. 2, ed. Jill Raitt (New York: Crossroad, 1987), 394.

12. Laurentin, *Short Treatise on the Virgin Mary*, 109–10, 112.

13. Brain E. Daley, "Sign and Source of the Church: Mary in the *Ressourcement* and at Vatican II," in *Mary on the Eve of the Second Vatican Council*, ed. John Cavadini and Danielle Peters (Notre Dame, IN: University of Notre Dame Press, 2017), 35.

14. Laurentin, *Short Treatise on the Virgin Mary*, 122.

15. *Alberti Magni Opera*, ed. Borgnet (Paris: Vivès, 1898), t. 37, 1–362; as quoted in Laurentin, 117.

16. *Mariale: super missus est* gained status principally because it had been attributed to St. Albert the Great. It was not until the 1950s that this attribution was proved incorrect; cf. B. Korosac, *Mariologia sancti Alberti Magni eiusque coaequalium* (Rome: Pontificia Academia Mariana Internationalis, 1954).

the earth."[17] When Protestant Christians, armed with the principles of *sola Scriptura* and justification by faith alone, disparaged Mary's role in salvation history, Catholics countered with an ardent defense and even greater exultant praise of Our Lady.

By the early seventeenth century, the Catholic Counter-Reformation flourished under the banner of Mary. A plethora of literature on Mary was produced between the seventeenth and nineteenth centuries, with more than three hundred works on the Immaculate Conception by Jesuits alone.[18] The first treatise on Mary's role in salvation history was produced by Chirino de Salazar, SJ (1575–1646), who is described as having "dominated the entire problematic of seventeenth century Mariology."[19] His and other such works represented the heightened Marian spirit of the times and gave special prominence to the glories of Mary.

In his sociological analysis of the Church in the modern era, Joseph Komonchak examines how Marian piety stood in strong opposition to the liberal and secular culture and served to fortify Catholic faith in its project of rechristianizing society. He describes how "modern Roman Catholicism took the form of a counter-society, legitimated by a counter-culture, as a response to and in opposition to the emerging liberal culture and society."[20] The Catholic culture of the nineteenth and twentieth centuries, according to Komonchak, was characterized by the flourishing of Catholic associations, the centralization of Catholic life on Rome, authoritative Roman control over Catholic thought, and the rapid spread of new devotions. Marian devotion played an essential role in all of this, fortifying Catholic identity with a burgeoned Marian piety.

Furthermore, the many religious orders and societies destroyed or dissolved in and after the French Revolution were replaced by newly founded religious congregations. These new foundations often invoked the explicit patronage of the Blessed Mother and became powerful vehicles for the promotion of ever greater veneration of Mary. Most significantly, the proclamation of the dogma of the Immaculate Conception in 1854 augmented the widespread Marian exuberance, carrying that fervor into the twentieth century together with a long series of Marian apparitions. Early ones recognized

---

17. Bonaventure, *The Mirror of the Blessed Virgin Mary and the Psalter of Our Lady,* trans. Sr. Mary Emmanuel (St. Louis: Herder, 1932), 254.

18. See Laurentin, *Short Treatise on the Virgin Mary,* 134.

19. Laurentin, 128n7a.

20. Joseph Komonchak, "Modernity and the Construction of Roman Catholicism," *Christianesimo nella Storia* 18 (1997): 356.

by the Vatican included Mary's appearances to Catherine Labouré in Paris in 1830, and in 1846 to the two children of La Salette-Fallavaux, Maximin Giraud and Mélanie Calvat. These were followed by appearances to Bernadette Soubirous at Lourdes in 1858, which served as confirmation of the dogma of the Immaculate Conception proclaimed by the Church four years prior; then, to the young Eugène Barbedette in Pontmain, France, in 1871; and to two women in Knock, County Mayo, Ireland, in 1879. The twentieth century witnessed the great "Miracle of the Sun" in a series of apparitions to Sts. Lucia, Jacinta, and Francisco of Fatima between May 13 and October 13, 1917.[21] These Marian apparitions further gave rise to an era of international Marian congresses. The first was in Lyon in 1900, and it catalyzed a movement leading to the definition in 1950 of Mary's Assumption. Between 1947 and 1958, a total of eighty-nine Marian congresses—regional, national, and international—were held.[22]

Marian devotion also flourished under the modern pontificates. Pope Leo XIII (1810–1903), also known as the "Rosary Pope," was the first to embrace and formally teach the idea that divine grace comes through the mediation of Mary as Mediatrix.[23] His twenty-five-year pontificate produced eleven encyclicals addressing topics related to Mary and sixteen major documents promoting devotion to the rosary.[24] It is, however, the pontificate of Pope Pius XII (1876–1958) that has been called the "official zenith of the Marian movement."[25] His statements, encyclical addresses, and sermons on Mary total more than those of his five predecessors combined.[26] Pius announced the first ever Marian year in 1954, in commemoration of the centennial of the dogma of the Immaculate Conception. He also instituted the feast of the Immaculate Heart of Mary in 1944 and introduced anew the feast of the Queenship of Mary in 1954. Above all, the proclamation of the dogma of Mary's Assumption into heaven in 1950 was Pius's crowning

---

21. Cf. Chris Maunder, *Our Lady of the Nations: Apparitions of Mary in Twentieth-Century Catholic Europe* (Oxford: Oxford University Press, 2016); and Sandra Zimdars-Swartz, *Encountering Mary: From La Salette to Medjugorje* (Princeton, NJ: Princeton University Press, 1991).

22. Laurentin, *Short Treatise on the Virgin Mary*, 138.

23. See Pope Leo XIII, Papal encyclical *Iucunda Semper Expectatione, On the Rosary* (1894), no. 2: "The recourse we have to Mary in prayer follows upon the office she continuously fills by the side of the throne of God as *Mediatrix of Divine grace.*"

24. Komonchak, "Modernity and Construction," 365.

25. Laurentin, *Short Treatise on the Virgin Mary*, 140. "Marian movement" is a reference to the height of Marian piety in the nineteenth and twentieth centuries, also refered to as "Marian maximalism." It should not be confused with the subsequent "Marian movement" which centered on a *ressourcement* of the tradition on Mary.

26. Alberic Stacpoole, *Mary and the Churches* (Collegeville, MN: Liturgical Press, 1990), 95.

contribution to the development of doctrine and veneration of the Virgin Mary.[27] At this peak of the development of Marian doctrine, fresh theological currents of *ressourcement* had also begun to emerge in the life of the Church. It is this coalescence of theological *ressourcement* with the reigning Marian devotion that critically shaped the Marian movement of the mid-twentieth century.

The Marian Movement at the Center of the Twentieth Century

Catholic Marian devotion burgeoned in the twentieth century, and the heightened Marian exuberance extended also to the realm of theology and Mariological research. The dogmatic manuals of the era embodied many maximalist characteristics in its exposition of Mary's eminent dignity as the Mother of God.[28] This emphasis, valid in itself, only became problematic as it increasingly focused on Marian titles and privileges alone, considered from the perspective of God's eternal decrees and apart from the mystery of the Church in time. These Mariological tracts tended to be speculative, ahistorical, and decontextualized—deducing atemporal principles on the basis of divine predestination. Disconcertingly missing from the manual tradition is the ecclesial context of Mariology and its foundations in Scripture and the economy of salvation. The problem of Marian maximalism was not so much that it maximally expounded Mary's divine maternity and plenitude of grace but that it tended to do so in an *isolated* doctrinal context.

This began to change, however, as the emergent biblical, patristic, and liturgical movements introduced a new theological current. Mariological literature published in and after the 1950s began to exhibit a fresh, new approach that was decisively more historical and less scholastic in style. In contrast to the earlier manuals of dogmatic theology, these works revived and fruitfully expounded biblical and patristic perspectives. Following the Church Fathers who never spoke of Mary apart from the Church, the scholarship that emerged midcentury on Mary also focused on Mary's intrinsic relationship to the Church. For example, Otto Semmelroth's work, *Urbild*

27. Pius XII, Apostolic Constitution *Munificentissimus Deus* (1950); preceded by Papal Encyclical *Deiparae Virginis Mariae* (1946).

28. See, for example, Réginald Garrigou-Lagrange, *The Mother of the Saviour and Our Interior Life* (St. Louis: Herder, 1948); Edouard Hugon's *De B. Virgine Maria Deipara* (Tractatus Theologici, 1926); Gabriele M. Roschini's multivolume *Mariologia* (Rome, 1941–48); and José Antonio de Aldama's *Sacrae Theologiae Summa*, vol. 3 (Madrid: Editorial Católica, 1953).

der Kirche, Oranischer Aufbau des Marienge-heimnisses (1950), proffered a historically grounded theology for the renewal of Marian studies within an ecclesiological context. Semmelroth's revival of Ambrose's notion of Mary as the *typus Ecclesiae* argues for Mary as the embodiment or "personification" of the essence and mystery of the Church in whom the mystery of the divine economy of salvation is both enclosed and perfectly expressed.[29] For Semmelroth, Mary's relationship to the Church is typological: As "archetype," she is "in closest union with the Church, because she bears within herself the pleroma of grace that will be poured from her into the Church that unfolds in time and space."[30] In 1951, Hugo Rahner published his famous work, *Maria und die Kirche,* in which he lamented that the "strong Marian movement of our day seems to have little connection with the theology of the Church, and even perhaps run counter to it."[31] In response, his work aimed to "show from the warm-hearted theology of the great Fathers and Doctors that the whole mystery of the Church is inseparably bound up with the mystery of Mary … [and thus] to learn once more what was so treasured by the early Church: learn to see the Church in our Lady, and in our Lady the Church."[32] Yves Congar also developed the Mary-Church relationship in *Le Christ, Marie, et l'Église* (1952). His approach was to root the tradition of Mary and the Church in a Chalcedonian understanding of the humanity of Christ and its role in the economy of salvation: Mary and the Church are "intimately connected" because of their close association with the sacred humanity of Christ.[33] Similarly, René Laurentin's *Court traité de théologie mariale*—which first appeared in 1953—presented Mary within the context of Scripture, the Church, and salvation history.[34] Laurentin, known for his critical edition of documents related to the Marian apparition at Lourdes, also contributed biblical perspectives on Mary with his exegetical studies of Luke's infancy narratives. His works exemplify the positive fruits of the biblical movement for the renewal of Mariology.

29. Otto Semmelroth, *Urbild der Kirche, Oranischer Aufbau des Mariengeheimnisses* (Würzburg: Echter, 1950); English translation, *Mary, Archetype of the Church,* trans. Jaroslav Pelikan (New York: Sheed and Ward, 1963).

30. Semmelroth, *Mary Archetype,* 648.

31. Hugo Rahner, *Maria und die Kirche* (Innsbruck: Marianischer, 1951); English translation, *Our Lady and the Church,* trans. Sebastian Bullough (New York: Pantheon, 1961), 2.

32. Rahner, *Our Lady and the Church,* Foreword, 5–6.

33. Yves Congar, *Le Christ, Marie, et l'Église* (Bruges: Desclée de Brouwer, 1952); English translation, *Christ, Our Lady and the Church: A Study in Eirenic Theology,* trans. Henry St. John (London: Longmans, Green, 1957), 31.

34. René Laurentin, *Luc I–II* (Paris: Gabalda, 1954), and *Jésus au Temple. Mystère de Pâques et foi de Marie en Luc 2: 48–50* (Paris: Gabalda, 1966).

The impetus for these new horizons—what I am calling a "Marian *ressourcement*"—was provided by the movements of renewal in liturgical, biblical, and patristic scholarship, movements that had begun to foment in the nineteenth century. Ironically, these movements both triggered and challenged the new developments in Mariology. To better understand their role and impact in shaping twentieth century Mariology, we first examine *ressourcement* in broad perspective.[35]

The term *"ressourcement"* was first coined by Charles Péguy (1873–1914) who described political, cultural and intellectual revolutions as "the appeal of a less perfect tradition to a more perfect tradition, an appeal from a less profound tradition to a deeper tradition, a search for the deepest sources— in the literal meaning of the word, re-sourcing."[36] The notion of "source" bears the connotation of provenance or origin, as a fountain or spring is a living source of water. To return to a source is not only to return to that which springs from the source but to the very origins of its vitality. In the context of theology, this involves a dynamic engagement, not simply with the tradition but with the mysteries at the source of Christian faith and theological reflection. The foremost proponents of this "renaissance in Catholic theology" were Jesuits of Lyon-Fourvière such as Jean Daniélou, Hans Urs von Balthasar, and Henri Bouillard, together with their teacher, Henri de Lubac; French Dominicans of Le Saulchoir such as Marie-Dominique Chenu, Yves Congar, Dominique Dubarle, and Henri-Marie Féret; and other influential thinkers such as Emile Mersch, Odo Casel, Romano Guardini, Karl Adam, and Anselm Stolz. This wide range of scholars shared a common inspiration to engage the modern world with a reinvigorated theology by reviving contact with the vital sources of theology and spirituality. As Péguy had suggested, *ressourcement* was "a new and deeper sounding of ancient, inexhaustible, and common resources."[37] It was a call *ad fontes*, a reengagement with the living sources of Christian thought.

---

35. For a comprehensive study on the theology and history of the *ressourcement* movement, its antecedents, and its continued relevance, see Gabriel Flynn and Paul Murray, eds., *Ressourcement: A Movement for Renewal in Twentieth-Century Catholic Theology* (Oxford: Oxford University Press, 2012). See also Jon Kirwan, *An Avant-garde Theological Generation: The Nouvelle Theologie and the French Crisis of Modernity* (Oxford: Oxford University Press, 2018).

36. Charles Péguy, *Cahiers de al Quinzaine* (March 1904), as quoted in Yves Congar in *Vrai et fausse réforme dans l'église* (Paris: Cerf, 1950), 602; English translation, *True and False Reform in the Church*, trans. Paul Philibert (Collegeville, MN: Liturgical Press, 2011), 370; emphasis added and translation altered.

37. Charles Péguy, preface to *Cahiers de al Quinzaine* (March 1904), reprinted in *Oeuvres complètes* (Paris: N.R.F., n.d.), 12: 186–92; cf. Congar, *Vraie*, 602; *True and False Reform*, 369.

The biblical, liturgical, and patristic movements from the mid-1800s prepared the grounds for the work of *ressourcement.* The biblical movement began in Germany and spread abroad. It bore fruit with the founding of the *École biblique* in 1890 in Jerusalem by the French Dominican Marie-Joseph Lagrange (1855–1938) and Pope Leo XIII's encyclical *Providentissimus Deus* in 1893. The liturgical movement, which began with Dom Prosper Guéranger (1805–1875), took root and flourished under the spirit of Dom Lambert Beauduin (1873–1960), the Belgian liturgist and founder of the Abbey of Amay, now at Chevetogne. And with this, the patristic movement joined forces, with the production of Migne's *Patrologiae Cursus Completus* and *The Library of the Fathers* associated with the Oxford Movement.

"Marian *ressourcement*"—understood as the theological effort to return to biblical and patristic sources on Mary in order to bring the Church's Marian belief into conversation with the various movements renewing the Church's intellectual life in the early twentieth century—benefited directly from these movements of renewal. The groundwork for it had been laid by two precursors, John Henry Newman (1801–1890) and Matthias Scheeben (1835–1888). John Henry Newman discovered the Eve-Mary patristic parallel while still an Anglican,[38] and he later expounded it, in his Catholic years, in support of the doctrine of the Immaculate Conception. In the realm of Thomism, Matthias J. Scheeben's theological masterpiece, *Handbuch der katholischen Dogmatik,* provided a formidable Marian-ecclesiological synthesis, in which the same Eve-Mary parallel held an integral place, illumining the Adam-Christ parallel of the New Testament.[39] Both Newman and Scheeben revived an understanding of Mary's role in the order of salvation and within, not above, the Church.

The proclamation of the dogma of Mary's Assumption in 1950 also prompted a surge in scholarship specifically on the Virgin Mary in relationship to the Church.[40] The French Mariological Society (*Societé francaise d'études mariales*) devoted three years to the study of this topic from 1951

38. See *The Splendor of the Church,* trans. Michael Mason (San Francisco: Ignatius Press, 1999), 314n1; 315n4; 317n11; 319n24, and 335n110 for de Lubac's references to John Henry Newman, *Mary, the Mother of Jesus* (New York: Catholic Book Exchange, 1894). See also Newman, *Mary: The Second Eve* (Rockford, IL: Tan Books, 1982).

39. See *Splendor of the Church,* 327–28, 333, for de Lubac's references to Matthias Scheeben; see also Scheeben, *Mariology,* vol. 1, trans. J. M. J. Geukers (St. Louis: Herder, 1946); *Handbuch der katholischen Dogmatik,* 7 vols. (Freiburg, 1873–87); and Laurentin, *Short Treatise on the Virgin Mary,* 137.

40. The section relies on the work of Thomas Thompson's "Recovering Mary's Faith and Her Role in the Church," in *Mary on the Eve of the Second Vatican Council,* 55–78.

to 1953, and the German Mariological Society (*Mariologische Arbeitsgemeinschaft deutscher Theologen*) undertook a two-year study of Mary in salvation history. The decisive, new perspective was a patristic one, and publications on the Mary-Church relationship thus abounded, such that one scholar comments: "Under the double influence of patristics and biblical scholarship, almost every Catholic theologian of name and fame in the decades preceding Vatican II, regardless of how he was recognized or classified later, felt prompted to publish a book on Mary."[41] Yves Congar, Karl Rahner, Edward Schillebeeckx, Otto Semmelroth, Louis Bouyer, and Hugo Rahner are but a few of the authors whose Mariological writings anticipate the Marian ecclesiology of the Second Vatican Council.

De Lubac's Contribution

Unlike Congar, Laurentin, and Semmelroth who all had book-length Marian writtings prior to the Council and would later make their mark as esteemed *periti* involved in the drafting of what would become chapter 8 of *Lumen Gentium*,[42] Henri de Lubac (1896–1991) neither published any book-length treatise on Mariology nor was he directly involved in the composition of the Marian chapter of *Lumen Gentium*. And yet, his principal work on Mary and the Church, the final chapter of *Méditation sur l'Église* (1953), is incomparably significant for understanding the historical and theological zeitgeist that shaped the Council's Mariology.[43]

Méditation sur l'Église was profoundly influential upon the generation of ecclesiastics present at the Council. In fact, the chapter on Mary and the Church represents de Lubac's own attempt to recover the breadth of tradition regarding Mary, and, like the Church Fathers whom he explored, de Lubac did not write about Mary in isolation but always in relationship to Christ and his body, the Church. De Lubac's exposition in *Méditation sur l'Église* appears to anticipate the synthesis the Council worked so hard to define, and his work thus provides insight into the intention of the Council in

41. Farkasfalvy, *The Marian Mystery*, 221.

42. Most noteworthy is Gerard Philips, the principal redactor of the final Marian schema; he, too, had studied and written on the relationship of Mary and the Church prior to the Council. See G. Philips, "Marie et l'Église: Un thème théologique renouvelé," in *Maria: Études sur la Saint Vierge*, vol. 7, ed. Hubert du Manoir (Paris: Beauchesne, 1964), and "Mariologische Perspectieven: Maria en de Kerk," *Mariale Dagen*, vol. 12 (1953): 9–78.

43. *Méditation sur l'Église* (Paris: Aubier, 1953); English translation: *The Splendor of the Church*, trans. Michael Mason; hereafter cited as *Splendor*.

returning to Tradition as the vital source of renewal and in presenting Mary at the culmination of its Dogmatic Constitution on the Church.

Although de Lubac did not have a direct hand in the drafting of the Marian chapter of *Lumen Gentium*, it is quite certain that he exerted a profound influence on the text. De Lubac's biographer, Rudolf Voderholzer, writes: "Even more than by his direct collaboration on the conciliar texts, de Lubac influenced the Council through the voluminous theological studies that he published in the years leading up to the Council, through which he had contributed to a renewal of theology based on the sources, that is, Sacred Scripture and the writings of the Church Fathers."[44] As will be seen in the first chapter of this study, the structure of *Lumen Gentium* notably mirrors the structure of de Lubac's *Méditation sur l'Église*, written ten years before the Council. Both works espouse a sacramental/Eucharistic ecclesiology, both begin with a chapter on the Church as mystery, and both notably end with an extensive discussion on Mary. These evident parallels indicate, as one scholar has suggested, that "the chapter on Mary in *Lumen Gentium* proceeds from an understanding of the Church as the sacrament of salvation."[45] As will be shown in chapter 6, de Lubac's work, in which he favored a sacramental understanding of the Church, can help to explain that suggestion and to show why the final chapter on Mary is not a mere addendum but the apex and culmination of the Church's self-understanding. Mary can indeed be seen as a key to understanding the Church as a sacrament, a major theme of the Council's ecclesiology.[46]

De Lubac's contribution to this topic not only casts fresh light on his understanding of the Church but also provides a solid theological framework for the integration of Mary and the Church that the Council sought. De Lubac himself anticipated the Council's work to rein in the excesses of the Marian movement by reference to the Church Fathers, and *Méditation sur l'Église* can be considered a seedbed for a genuine renewal of the Church in relationship to Mary. Only when the Council's full intention is understood and embraced will its teachings fully bear fruit in ecclesial renewal. De Lubac's works contribute greatly to this endeavor.

44. Rudolf Voderholzer, *Henri de Lubac begegnen* (Augsburg: Sankt Ulrich Verlag, 1999); English translation: *Meet Henri de Lubac*, trans. Michael J. Miller (San Francisco: Ignatius Press, 2008), 20.

45. Johann Auer, *The Church: The Universal Sacrament of Salvation*, trans. Michael Waldstein (Washington, DC: The Catholic University of America Press, 1993), 480.

46. Cf. *Sacrosanctum Concilium*, nos. 5 and 26; *Lumen Gentium*, nos. 1, 9, 48; and *Gaudium et Spes*, nos. 42 and 45. All church documents are taken from the Vatican website, www.vatican.va.

Aims and Method

This is the first book-length study of de Lubac's theology of Mary and the Church and its aim is threefold. First, it seeks to retrieve de Lubac's legacy of *ressourcement* by examining his principal works on Mary and the Church: first and foremost is *Méditation sur l'Église* (1953), followed by *Paradoxe et Mystère de l'Église* (1967) and *L'Éternel féminin* (1968). Although de Lubac never produced a systematic treatment of Mary, what he did write exemplifies the Council's twofold aim of *ressourcement* and *aggiornamento* and serves as a reminder of the enduring significance of the Marian dimension of the Church as found in Tradition. Second, it looks to de Lubac as a guide to exploring the texts and debates of the Council in order to seek out the Council's genuine spirit and to contribute to a fuller reception of the Council's teaching. De Lubac's inclusion of Mary in the final chapter of *Méditation sur l'Église*, published a decade before the Council, greatly influenced the principal architects of *Lumen Gentium*. Third, with a clear grasp of de Lubac's unique contribution to the Council, we can further employ his Marian ecclesiology in order to address contemporary questions and help advance postconciliar ecclesiological discourse.

To this end, our plan of study comprises eight chapters divided into two parts. The first part, consisting of chapters 1 through 4, focuses on de Lubac and his preconciliar Marian *ressourcement*. Chapter one provides an introduction to the man and his works, showing how de Lubac embodied the dynamic of *ressourcement* and lived the ideals of a true *homo ecclesiasticus* who sought to engage the modern world with a reinvigorated theology in contact with its vital sources. The next three chapters present a close reading of de Lubac's preconciliar thought on Mary and the Church, taking inventory of de Lubac's retrieval of the tradition. Chapter 2 studies the final chapter of de Lubac's *Méditation sur l'Église*, "L'Église et la Vierge Marie," which is his principal Marian *ressourcement*. The chapter underscores de Lubac's patristic outlook on Mary and the Church as both mother and virgin bride. Chapter 3 extends the discussion with a study of de Lubac's biblical *ressourcement* in a Marian reading of the Song of Songs. It also offers an appraisal of de Lubac's work on patristic and medieval exegesis. Chapter 4 studies two figures with whom de Lubac engaged in scholarly exchange: Pierre Teilhard de Chardin and Jules Monchanin. Attention is accorded to the Mariology found in the poems they respectively wrote: Teilhard's "*L'Éternel féminin*" and Monchanin's "*La Vierge aux Indes*." The ideas we find here provide important elements for de Lubac's own Marian thought, especially regarding the idea of a "concrete universal." The chapter contextualizes this concept within a framework of mystery, examining the Marian allusions in de Lubac's essay on "Mystique et Mystère" and drawing out the implications of the idea of Mary as a "concrete universal" for de Lubac's study of Amida Buddhism. The essential common thread is de Lubac's emphasis on the *mystical* dimension in which Mary—and the Church in Mary's likeness—are both "concrete universals."

These first four chapters aim to retrieve de Lubac's legacy and to appreciate his own voice and historical context. They show that de Lubac's Mariology is not rooted in a wistful, nostalgic return to the sources but in a *ressourcement* that seeks an authentic renewal of the Church. In this way, they prepare the foundations for the constructive analyses of the final chapters.

The second part of the book focuses on conciliar and postconciliar developments. Chapter 5 delves into the Marian debates at Vatican II, tracing how the Council hammered out a synthesis of Mariology and ecclesiology in chapter eight of *Lumen Gentium*. It also explores the patristic *ressourcement* in *Lumen Gentium*. This chapter concludes with a survey of the patristic sources employed in the Marian chapter and an assessment of the key achievements of Vatican II on Mary and the Church. Chapter 6 explores the sudden decline in Mariological scholarship in the decade after Vatican II and then offers a corrective perspective, reading the Council's sacramental ecclesiology and its revival of episcopal collegiality in light of an integrated Mariology.

Our exploration of postconciliar developments continues in chapter 7 with a test case of the potential of the Marian mystery of the Church to assist in the treatment of contemporary theological questions. This chapter argues that the perennial ecclesiological issue of the relationship of the particular churches to the universal Church, especially as it played out in the celebrated debate between Walter Kasper and then-Cardinal Joseph Ratzinger, can be disentangled in light of de Lubac's Marian theology and his conception of "concrete universals." Based on the metaphysical unity of the-one-and-the-many—exemplified in the "concrete universal," chapter 8 expounds the correlation between Mary's maternal mediation and the Church's sacramental mediation, suggesting that, in view of de Lubac's understanding of the sacraments, one could posit a distinctly "Marian subjectivity" of the Church.

The story of conciliar Mariology is one of yet unrealized promises. Although Vatican II offered an objectively better and more balanced Mariology than the maximalism of the nineteenth and twentieth centuries, it was actually followed by a collapse of Marian devotion and theology, and the integrated treatise of Mary and the Church has had relatively little impact on ecclesiological scholarship today. As a pioneer of *ressourcement*, Henri de Lubac can help to reenchant contemporary theology with an authentic Marian *ressourcement* grounded in the patristic sources on which the Council relied for its Marian ecclesiology. At a time when the universal Church is reflecting on synodality, de Lubac's theology of Mary and the Church, informing the configuration of the universal and particular churches, offers a fresh perspective.

It is said that de Lubac initially expressed concern at the English translation of the title of *Méditation sur l'Église*. "The Splendor of the Church" seems to reek of pompous triumphalism and to associate de Lubac's ecclesiology with the institutional conceptions of the Church that he wished to overcome. With this in mind, I have rendered every reference to the work in its original French title. Still, I have taken up an echo of the English title for this work with hopes that by the end, it will become clear to the reader that a genuine *méditation sur l'église* with de Lubac as our guide should truly bring to mind the "splendor of the Church in Mary." The Church is resplendent because of the radiance of Christ that shines forth in full force in the Church's most eminent member: its radiance is manifested *in Mary*.

PART I

Henri de Lubac and Preconciliar Marian *Ressourcement*

CHAPTER 1

Henri de Lubac

Pioneer of *Ressourcement*

In an essay entitled "An Imagined Unity: Henri de Lubac & the Ironies of Ressourcement," Robin Darling Young, a scholar of Christian spirituality and early Christian studies, asserts that de Lubac's personal disillusionment with the modern world led him to seek refuge in his own creation of "a mythology of the 'patristic age.'"[1] In an extended work, she argues that de Lubac's evocation of patristic ecclesiology and its sense of ecclesiastical mystery failed to acknowledge the sea of conflict and the bitter polemics that characterized the early Church.[2] Young thus considers de Lubac's incomplete, if not superficial, vision to be a futile prescription for a premodern antidote to the disoriented postwar predicament, namely the specious unity he perceived in the Fathers.[3]

Did the Jesuit Cardinal who died at ninety-five and survived two World

1. Robin Darling Young, "An Imagined Unity: Henri de Lubac & the Ironies of Ressourcement," *Commonweal* 15 (2012): 15.

2. Robin Darling Young, "A Soldier of the Great War: Henri de Lubac and the Patristic Sources for a Premodern Theology," in *After Vatican II: Trajectories and Hermeneutics*, ed. James L. Heft with John O'Malley (Grand Rapids, MI: Eerdmans, 2012), 136–44.

3. Young, "An Imagined Unity," 17.

Wars, sustaining a major combat injury in the first and actively leading an intellectual resistance in the second, producing over forty volumes of more than ten thousand pages of theological writing, give way to a despairing view of the Church in the modern world following the Ecumenical Council for which he participated as an esteemed *peritus*? It is my contention that de Lubac's return to the sources of the early Church Fathers constitutes a striving—not for the unity of the patristic era in itself but for the inspiration that animated their work and that constitutes the unity of the Christian faith in every era. The blessed Virgin Mary embodies this unity. She concretely realizes the faith of the Church, and de Lubac's *ressourcement* of the Marian tradition brings one to not a sea of conflict but an ocean of mystery centered on Christ. It is theology's contact with this mystery that empowers its renewal and its meaningful engagement with the contemporary world. In view of such a critique from as formidable a scholar as Robin D. Young, the following biographical sketch, drawn from de Lubac's memoirs as well as his theological writings and secondary sources, serves to contextualize de Lubac's work and to highlight the Marian dimensions implicit therein. As the main contours of his portrait emerge, the reader will be better equipped to judge for himself the integrity of de Lubac's life and legacy.

A Life-long Love of the Fathers

Henri-Marie Joseph Sonier de Lubac was born in 1896 in Cambrai, Northern France, to Maurice Sonier de Lubac (1860–1936) and Gabrielle de Beaurepaire (1867–1963).[4] He entered the Society of Jesus at age seventeen, but his early formation was interrupted by the start of the First World War. Drafted in 1914 and stationed with the Third Infantry Regiment, de Lubac suffered a head injury on All Saints' Day in 1917, a wound that earned him the Croix de Guerre but also caused him life-long suffering. Discharged from the military in 1919, de Lubac resumed his studies and professed simple vows on Easter day of 1920. De Lubac describes his formative years as filled with intellectual exhilaration: "I had a great thirst for knowledge, and I read everything I could."[5] De Lubac voraciously devoured Augustine's *Confessions*, Irenaeus's

---

4. The biographical details of this chapter rely primarily on de Lubac's memoir, *At the Service of the Church* (ASC) and Voderholzer's *Meet Henri de Lubac*. For an extensive multivolume, annotated biography, see Georges Chantraine, *Henri de Lubac. Tome I, De la naissance à la démobilisation, 1896–1919* (Paris: Éd. du Cerf, 2007); *Tome II, Les années de formation, 1919–1929* (Paris: Éd. du Cerf, 2009). See also Jean-Pierre Wagner, *Henri de Lubac* (Paris: Éd. Du Cerf, 2001).

5. Henri de Lubac, in an interview with Patrick Granfield, OSB, *Theologians at Work* (New York: MacMillan, 1967), 172.

Adversus haereses, and John Henry Newman's translated works. He also devoted himself to studying Saint Thomas Aquinas, who, with Saint Augustine, "constituted my basic nourishment."[6]

De Lubac's love of the Church Fathers is manifest in his own "clandestine teaching ministry" after he was appointed as chair of fundamental theology in the Faculty of Theology at the Catholic University of Lyons and took up residence at the Jesuit College in Lyons-Fourvière.[7] Although he was not an instructor to the Jesuit scholastics, his presence exerted a formative influence and his erudition fascinated the younger generation of Jesuits. Xavier Tilliette (1921–2018) describes how "professors and students both visited his room regularly [even though he] himself was never concerned about having 'disciples'—'One is your Master'—but rather about inspiring them to be diligent theologians."[8] Similarly, Hans Urs von Balthasar recounts how, while others were out playing soccer, he, Jean Daniélou, Henri Bouillard, and a number of other students would gather around de Lubac who "referred [them] beyond Scholasticism to the Church Fathers."[9] Under de Lubac's tutelage, these young and gifted minds imbibed patristic thought; the gathering became known as the "Fourvière school."

One of the concrete fruits of the Fourvière gathering was the founding of *Sources chrétiennes,* a series of critical editions of patristic texts, complete with facing translations.[10] The idea originated from Father Victor Fontoynont, SJ (1880–1958) but with complications arising from the Second World War, the project fell to de Lubac and flourished with the help of Jean Daniélou (1905–1974).[11] The first volume was launched in 1942, and it presented Gregory of Nyssa's spiritual interpretation of *The Life of Moses.*[12] De Lubac was also instrumental in founding a second series, *Théologie,* that sought to provide critical thematic studies as a supplement to the patristic and medieval texts. One sees in these initiatives the first seeds of

6. ASC, 65.

7. Voderhozer, 42.

8. Xavier Tilliette, "Henri de Lubac achtzigjährig," *Internationale Katholische Zeitschrift Communio* 5, no. 12 (1976): 187.

9. Hans Urs von Balthasar, *Test Everything, Keep What Is Good* (San Francisco: Ignatius Press, 1986), 11–12.

10. Patristic critical editions were always in the original languages. *Sources chrétiennes* (SC), however, went a step further in providing a French translation on each facing page, thus opening up the Fathers' writings to a vast audience.

11. Cf. Étienne Fouilloux, *La collection "Sources chrétiennes," Éditer les Pères de l'Église au XXe siècle* (Paris: Cerf, 1995).

12. Gregory of Nyssa, *La vie de Moïse,* trans. Jean Daniélou, in SC series 1 (Paris: Éditions du Cerf, 1942).

ressourcement, a revival of the Church Fathers and patristic exegesis, which will continue to inform de Lubac's theological writings. Three major works are surveyed in following: *Catholicisme: Les aspects sociaux du dogme* (1938), *Surnaturel* (1946), and *Méditation sur l'Église* (1953).[13]

Catholicisme and Related Works

De Lubac's first book publication, *Catholicisme: Les aspects sociaux du dogme* (1938), was a "major breakthrough" in theology. In it, de Lubac argues for the Church as the "common destiny of man" based on a principle of sacramentality as developed by the early Church Fathers. It is the patristic idea that divine grace permeates the world and is written into the social, historical, and interior dimensions of human existence—what John Henry Newman referred to as the "dispensation to the Gentiles."[14] De Lubac drew deeply from the wellspring of the Church Fathers as his principal inspiration, and their writings constitute the core of his argument. De Lubac's *ressourcment* is readily observed in the fifty-five texts that he includes in the appendix, of which two-thirds are patristic texts. For our purposes, it is the thirty-seventh extract that provides the germ of a Marian presence: Isaac of Stella's sermon on the Assumption relating Mary directly to the Church and to individual souls. De Lubac will later expound this text at length in his Marian chapter in *Méditation sur l'Église.*

Catholicisme is programmatic of de Lubac's entire theological career.[15] It provides an indispensable vantage point for grasping the main lines of his theology, as many of the themes that he develops later in life are already anticipated in *Catholicisme.* Following the tripartite structure of de Lubac's presentation on the social, historical, and interior dimensions of Catholicism, we explore these major themes to appreciate the unity and coherence of de Lubac's legacy.

First, in de Lubac's discussion on the eminently social character of the Church, one finds a common theme in his ecclesiology, a theme which comes to fruition in *Corpus Mysticum: L'Eucharistie et l'Église au Moyen Âge, Étude*

---

13. For full reference information for all works by de Lubac mentioned in this chapter, see the bibliography.

14. John Henry Newman, *Apologia Pro Vita Sua* (1865), 26–27.

15. Hans Urs von Balthasar, *The Theology of Henri de Lubac: An Overview,* trans. Joseph Fessio (San Francisco: Ignatius Press, 1991), 35. In the foreword to the 1998 English translation of *Catholicisme,* Joseph Ratzinger similarly describes his encounter with the book as "an essential milestone on my theological journey" (11).

historique (1944). The corporate identity, or the "common destiny of man," is achieved in the *Corpus Christi mysticum*—the Church as constituted by the Eucharist, the sacrament of Christian unity.[16] Furthermore, *Corpus Mysticum* contains important allusions to the Virgin Mary, as found in de Lubac's discussion of Ambrose's (and Augustine's) identification of the sacramental body of Christ with the historical "body *born of the Virgin*."[17] De Lubac also examines the medieval texts of Gottschalk of Orbais who, commenting on Ambrose and Augustine, distinguishes in order to unite the three species that make up the one flesh of Christ: "One is the body born of the Virgin and ascended into heaven, another is the body created and consecrated anew each day, and finally another is the body that we ourselves are, and that receives the sacrament.... [B]y nature the three bodies make up one single body alone: *different in species, and yet one in nature*."[18]

Second, de Lubac's focus on the historical character of Catholicism (in which God is simultaneously immanent and transcendent) is programmatic for his later work on the study of religions. He argues that because nonbiblical religions do not assign any salvific meaning to history, these religions can only offer "an individualistic doctrine of evasion."[19] In contrast, Christianity is "a unique phenomenon in the history of religious experience"[20] because of its core tenet that the Christian God has condescended and penetrated human history, and as a result, Christianity is historically embedded. Moreover, the fact that Mary also appears in de Lubac's studies of religion hints both of her unique participation in the "unique phenomenon" of Christianity and of her significance for de Lubac's theology. In his writings on Pure Land Buddhism, for example, de Lubac draws a striking comparison between the compassionate spiritual son of Buddha Amida, bodhisattva Avalokitesvara (known in China as the Kuan-yin and in Japan as Kannon), and the Blessed Virgin Mary.[21] We will embark on further exploration of this topic in chapter 4.

16. See *Catholicism*, 88–101; with reference to the subtitle of the book, *Catholicism: Christ and the Common Destiny of Man*.

17. *Corpus Mysticum*, 26–27; emphasis added.

18. Gottschalk of Orbais, *Oeuvres théologiques et grammaticales de Godescalc d'Orbais* (Spicilegium sacrum lovaniese, 1945), 326, 335–36; as quoted in *Corpus Mysticum*, 26; emphasis as found in the original.

19. *Catholicism*, 137.

20. *Catholicism*, 137.

21. "Faith and Piety in Amidism," *Theological Fragments*, 359–60. See also de Lubac's other works on Buddhism, especially chapter 5 of *Aspects du bouddhisme*, vol. 2: *Amida* and *La reconte du bouddhisme et de l'Occident*.

De Lubac also expounds the theological significance of history as a medium through which God achieves his plan of salvation.[22] This history is recorded in the Bible, and de Lubac's works on spiritual exegesis—*Histoire et esprit* (1950), the multivolume *Exégèse médiévale* (1959, 1961, 1963, 1964), *Pic de la Mirandole* (1974), and *La postérité spirituelle de Joachim de Fiore* (1979–1981)—all take their point of departure from a recognition of the historical dimension of Christianity. History is the medium by which "the New Testament is hidden in the Old Testament, and the Old is manifested in the New."[23] The mystical dimension of history, accessible in the spiritual sense of Scripture, also testifies to a Marian dimension. As will be our topic of study in chapter 3, de Lubac expounds the patristic and medieval exegesis of the Song of Songs, a tradition which interpreted the bridal figure anagogically as a figure of Mary.

Third, de Lubac's attention to the interior dimension of Christianity—as found in the third part of *Catholicisme*[24]—flowered in his works on the relationship between nature and the supernatural. Building on his earlier presentation of the social and historical dimensions of Catholicism, de Lubac argues that just as Catholicism incorporates an individual into a communal body of believers without negating his or her individuality, so too, the supernatural—namely grace—embraces, elevates, and transforms nature without contradicting or destroying it. And, just as the historical dimension of Catholicism tends toward a transcendent consummate point in the eschaton, so too, the creaturely nature of human beings tends toward a single supernatural end as ordained and endowed by God. Catholicism does not allow any "severance between the natural and supernatural."[25] The supernatural penetrates the natural sphere *from within*; the ordering of the natural to the supernatural is an *interior* ordering.

De Lubac's 1968 study of Teilhard de Chardin's eponymous poem, *L'Éternel Féminin* (also to be examined in chapter 4), not only provides us with a coup d'œil at significant contemporary influences on his thought but also introduces a central notion of his Mariology. For de Lubac, as for Pierre Teilhard de Chardin and Jules Monchanin, the Blessed Virgin is a "concrete-universal"—the eternal feminine figure who simultaneously embodies the social, historical, and interior dimensions of being. Much more

---

22. *Catholicism*, 165.
23. *Catholicism*, 176; quoting Augustine, *Q. in Heptat.*, lib. 2, q. 73 (PL 34, 623).
24. See, in particular, "Person and Society" in *Catholicism*, 326–50.
25. *Catholicism*, 313.

will be said of these adumbrations of Mary's significance for de Lubac in subsequent chapters.

In sum, de Lubac's triptych of the simultaneously social, historical, and interior dimensions of Christianity expounds "that character of universality and totality best expressed by the word 'catholicism.'"[26] Catholicity rests on the inner plenitude of the Spirit through whom individuals are drawn into the unity of the body of Christ, thereby serving the solidarity and common destiny of all human persons. For de Lubac, the Church, though small, was already "catholic" at Pentecost, and her universal scope of being for peoples of all times and in all places extends into eternity.[27] This understanding of the Church will have direct implications for de Lubac's contribution to the communion ecclesiology of the Second Vatican Council and further application to the relevance of Mary for contemporary ecclesiology, to be explored in later chapters.

Surnaturel

A second impactful work is *Surnaturel* (1946). Whereas *Catholicisme* represents de Lubac's most influential writing work, *Surnaturel* is his most controversial. When it first appeared in the summer of 1946, the book initially received many sympathetic reviews.[28] Gérard Philips of Louvain, who would later become the principal author of the Council's chapter on Mary, wrote a favorable review in the bibliographical journal *Erasmus*.[29] However, in challenging the long-standing authority of neo-Scholasticism, de Lubac's thesis, namely, that the notion of pure human nature lacking any proper desire for a supernatural end was a theological innovation by Cajetan and Suárez, was perceived by many as subversive. De Lubac appeared to have undermined the conventional wisdom that had, for centuries, passed under the authority of St. Thomas as the traditional teaching about nature and grace. Questions of de Lubac's orthodoxy subsequently arose and broke into a storm of controversy.[30]

26. ASC, 27.

27. Cf. *Catholicism*, 49.

28. Appendix II of ASC documents the reception of *Surnaturel* with extracts from letters received by de Lubac, 201–3 [2:10] and eight substantial reviews of the work, 203–23 [2:11]. N.b.: The bracketed numbers are taken from de Lubac's own text and refer to documents located in the Appendices. The number of the Appendix precedes the colon; the number of the document follows the colon.

29. ASC, 37.

30. De Lubac's interpretation of Saint Thomas has constituted a topic of continued debate.

De Lubac was never formally censured, nor was there ever any formal questioning of his theology. He even says that he received words of assurance and confidence from the Holy Father and from Father Janssens, his General Superior.[31] However, attacks against him increased, and, in 1950, de Lubac received a secret letter from the latter, asking him to leave his editorship of *Recherches de science religieuse* and to stop teaching altogether. Moreover, in anticipation of *Humani Generis*, Father Janssens, the General of the Society in Rome, had sought to deflect all potential accusations against the Society by ordering the removal of Fathers Émile Delaye, Henri Bouillard, Alexandre Durand, Pierre Ganne, and de Lubac from their duties and residences, without any further inquiry or explanation.[32] Expelled from Lyons and forbidden to teach, de Lubac thus found himself driven from place to place; his books—specifically, *Surnaturel, Corpus Mysticum,* and *De la connaissance de Dieu*—were all removed from the Jesuit libraries and banned from the market. "Lightning [had] struck Fourvière."[33]

When *Humani Generis* was officially promulgated in August of 1950, expressing concern at "false opinions threatening to undermine the foundations of Catholic Doctrine," many accusatory fingers pointed to de Lubac, believing that the encyclical contained a condemnation of his theology. However, when de Lubac read the text for the first time in *La Croix* on the very day he arrived in Paris at the end of August, he found that the encyclical "avoids all mention of that 'pure nature' so many established theologians wanted to canonize and accuse me [de Lubac] of not sufficiently appreciating."[34] *Humani Generis* made no explicit reference to de Lubac, and as de

---

Recent studies in agreement with de Lubac include: Denis Bradley, *Aquinas on the Twofold Human Good: Reason and Human Happiness in Aquinas's Moral Science* (Washington, DC: The Catholic University of America Press, 1997); Eric de Moulins-Beaufort, *Anthropologie et mystique selon Henri de Lubac: 'L'Esprit de l'homme' ou la présence de Dieu en l'homme* (Paris: Cerf, 2003); Stephen Wang, "Aquinas on Human Happiness and the Natural Desire for God," *New Blackfriars* 88 (2007): 322–34. In disagreement with de Lubac's position are: Georges P. Cottier, *Désir naturel de voir Dieu: Sur les traces de saint Thomas* (Paris: Parole et Silence, 2002); Stephen A. Long, "On the Possibility of a Purely Natural End of Man," *Thomist* 64 (2000): 211–37; Guy Mansini, "Henri de Lubac, the Natural Desire to See God, and Pure Nature," *Gregorianum* 83 (2002): 89–109; Lawrence Feingold, *The Natural Desire to See God according to St. Thomas Aquinas and His Interpreters* (Rome: Apollinaris, 2001); Reinhard Hütter, "*Desiderium Naturale Visionis Dei—Est autem duplex hominis beatitudo sive felicitas*: Some Observations about Lawrence Feingold's and John Milbank's Recent Interventions in the Debate over the Natural Desire to See God," *Nova et Vetera*, English edition 5 (2007), 81–132.

31. See ASC, 61 [4:4].

32. The only explanation given for the censureship referred to "the pernicious errors on essential points of dogma maintained by these professors"; ASC, 68.

33. This is de Lubac's own expression of the events, as he describes it in ASC, 67.

34. *A Theologian Speaks*, 4.

Lubac maintains, "Far from containing any rebuke in my regard, the passage borrows a sentence from me to express the true doctrine."[35] The line de Lubac is referring to seems to be *Humani Generis,* number 26, which rejects the position of those who refuse to recognize the natural desire of every human being for a supernatural end: "Others destroy the gratuity of the supernatural order, since God, they say, cannot create intellectual beings without ordering and calling them to the beatific vision."

The decade in which de Lubac was suspended from his theological work was a particularly difficult period. He reveals in his memoirs:

> During the whole affair ... that would last so many years, I was never questioned, I never had a single conversation about the root of the matter with any authority of the Church in Rome or the Society. No one ever communicated to me any precise charge.... [N]o one ever asked me for anything that would resemble a "retraction," explanation or particular submission. Even in that Spring of 1953, when I finally saw the Father General two times, the latter was still evasive both about the basis as well as about the facts.[36]

De Lubac suffered quietly. One understands from his memoirs how the ideal of obedience that had been planted in his spirit early on prevailed throughout his life. When de Lubac was still a young priest, Emmanuel Podechard, a renowned Old Testament scholar who had found himself with restricted academic freedom, had responded to de Lubac's suggestion that Podechard publish a critical study on the Servant of Yahweh, saying: "And why?" "It is based on critical positions that are not admissible today. You see, my Father, with respect to biblical questions, the church and I are not in agreement; so one of us must be silent, and it is only natural that it be I."[37] Decades later, de Lubac, too, would remain silent and submit himself to the judgment of Mother Church. Little known is the fact that the ensuing silencing of de Lubac in the 1950s in fact became the context—almost by accident, if not by providence—for the publication of *Méditation sur l'Église* (1953), which contains his principal writing on Mary.

35. *A Theologian Speaks.* An interview with Henri de Lubac by Angelo Scola (Los Angeles: Twin Circle Publishing), 4.

36. ASC, 78.

37. De Lubac recounts this conversation in ASC, 22.

Méditation sur l'Église

In view of the circumstances, *Méditation sur l'Église* (1953) is perhaps de Lubac's most remarkable work of this period. It is a collection of conference talks given to brother priests between 1946 and 1949 but assembled and published only after the outbreak of the Fourvière affair. In 1950, when the sanctions were imposed and de Lubac found himself in exile, he had chosen to respond with what has been called a "hymn of praise" to Mother Church. If *Méditation sur l'Église* is "the spirituality for the theology of *Catholicisme,*"[38] as described by Hans Urs von Balthasar, then this is so because the work reveals the spirituality of its author—a spirituality marked by steadfast loyalty to the Church of Christ.

De Lubac envisioned the work to be a meditation on the "radiant motherhood" of the Bride of the Lamb whose splendor is an existential center willed by God for the salvation of many.[39] In his exploration of "certain of the aspects of the mystery of the Church as an attempt to work [himself] into the very heart of that mystery,"[40] de Lubac discovered that the light shining forth from the Church evokes an exuberant joy that triumphs over sin and gives life to all.[41] The entirety of *Méditation sur l'Église* reverberates with a profound appreciation for "the pricelessness of that good which consists, quite simply, in belonging to the Church at all."[42] In the context of the suspicions regarding his orthodoxy, one sees how de Lubac was more deeply loyal to the Church than to any of his controversial positions.

In addition to the final chapter devoted to Mary and the Church, of particular significance is the seventh chapter, entitled *Ecclesia Mater.* Here, in an almost lyrical style, de Lubac champions what it means to be a "man of the Church" and offers us a glimpse of his own interior life. The *homo ecclesiasticus,* according to de Lubac, is one who has "fallen in love with the beauty of the House of God; the Church will have stolen his heart.... It will be from her that he learns how to live and die. Far from passing judgment on her, he will allow her to judge him, and he will agree gladly to all the sacrifices demanded by her unity."[43] The man of the Church is one who allows the

---

38. Balthasar, *Theology of Henri de Lubac,* 107.
39. *Splendor,* 10.
40. *Splendor,* 9.
41. Cf. *Splendor,* 12.
42. *Splendor,* 12.
43. *Splendor,* 241.

radiance of the Church and the truth of God to captivate his heart and direct his life:

> The truth which God pours into our minds is not just any truth made to our humble human measure; the life which he gives us to drink is not a natural life which would find in us the wherewithal to maintain itself. This living truth and this true life only find foothold in us by *dispossessing us of ourselves; if we are to live in them we must die to ourselves.*"[44]

Here, de Lubac identifies the essential dynamic of self-sacrifice and self-dispossession as the key that unlocks the way into the truth and life that is from God. For de Lubac, "this is perhaps the most secret point in the mystery of faith, and that which is hardest of access to a mind which has not been converted by the Spirit of God."[45] De Lubac knew by experience the "spiritual fruitfulness of sacrifice."[46]

> It is possible that there may be many things in the human context of the church that deceive us. And it is also possible that we may be profoundly misunderstood within her, without the things being our fault; we may even have to undergo persecution within the very heart of the Church.... In such a situation patience and loving silence will be of more value than all else; ... the Church never gives Christ to us better than on these occasions when she offers us the chance of sharing in the likeness of his Passion.[47]

In a personal letter to his friend, François Charmot, dated 1950, he describes his reliance on the "benefactions" of the Church in his suffering:

> Although the shocks that assaulted me from without also troubled my soul to its depths, they are still powerless against the great and essential things that make up every moment of our lives. *The Church is always there, in a motherly way,* with her Sacraments and her prayer, with the Gospel that she hands down to us intact, with her Saints who surround us; in short, with Jesus Christ, present among us, whom she gives us even more fully at the moments when she allows

44. *Splendor,* 258; emphasis added.
45. *Splendor,* 258.
46. *Splendor,* 266–67.
47. *Splendor,* 213.

us to suffer.... What does all the rest matter in comparison with such benefactions?[48]

The remarkable insight springing from de Lubac's experience is his deep appreciation of the Church as a *mother* who is ever-present to him with tender care. She is the mother who ultimately gives Jesus at all times, but especially in times of suffering. One cannot avoid seeing here the ever-abiding presence of Mary with Jesus at the foot of the cross, a presence that illumines the mystery of the Church also. De Lubac's reflections on *Mater ecclesia* in chapter 7 of *Méditation sur l'Église* culminate in that book's final chapter, "*L'Église et la Vierge Marie*" and suggest to us that his concrete experience of the maternal dimension of the mystery of the Church is intertwined with the Blessed Mother. Nestled in the bosom of both as his true "mothers,"[49] de Lubac is able to assert that "joy is still triumphant, breaking through the most somber of appearances and flourishing on everything which should, humanly speaking, snuff it out."[50]

The Second Vatican Council and Postconciliar Years

In June of 1959, Pius XII's successor, Pope John XXIII, granted de Lubac permission to resume teaching theology, a work from which he had been barred since 1950. In July of 1960, de Lubac discovered his name printed in *La Croix* among a list of theologians appointed by the Holy Father as consultors to the Preparatory Theological Commission for the Second Vatican Council.[51] Pope John XXIII, formerly the papal nuncio in Paris, had known of de Lubac and had thought favorably of him. He had also been aware of the controversy of Fourvière but was never consulted about it. Now, as pope, he was eager

48. Henri de Lubac, Letter to Rev. François Charmot, dated 9 September 1950, in "Deux lettres inédites," *Bulletin de Littérature Ecclésiastique* 94 (1993): 54; emphasis added. The other letter is addressed to Msgr. Bruno de Solages and is dated 26 April 1947.

49. *Mater Ecclesia* is a central concept in de Lubac's ecclesiology. In addition to chapter 7 of *Méditation sur l'Église*, de Lubac also has an extended discussion on the motherhood of the Church; cf. *Les Églises particulières dans l'Église universelle: suivi de la maternité de l'Église et d'une interview recueillie par G. Jarczyk* (1971); English translation: *The Motherhood of the Church: Followed by Particular Churches in the Universal Church and an Interview Conducted by Gwendoline Jarczyk* (1982). Hereafter cited as MC.

50. *Splendor*, 10.

51. An indispensable source for looking into Lubac's experience at the Council is his conciliar diary, published in two volumes: Henri de Lubac, *Carnets du Concile, tomes 1 et 2* (2007). English translation: *Vatican Council Notebooks*, 2 vols. (2015, 2016); hereafter cited *Notebooks*. De Lubac gives his reaction to this appointment in his journal, describing it as an "astonishing piece of news" (*Notebooks* vol. 1, 53; 25 July 1960 entry). See also ASC, 116, and Voderholzer, 84.

to show his good will, not only by reinstating de Lubac's teaching position but also with the appointment, first in 1960 as consultor to the Preparatory Theological Commission and later in 1962 as an official *peritus* to the Council itself.[52] De Lubac thus served as a *peritus* on the preparatory commission and at the four sessions of the Second Vatican Council. Except for a period of absence at the beginning of the second session of the Council due to health issues, he was present at and bore witness to the theological ferment of two years of preparation, four Conciliar sessions, and three periods of work by the Theological Commission between the sessions.

There are numerous points of contact between the teachings of the Council and de Lubac's theological work. For example, de Lubac's discussion of the relationship between nature and the supernatural in *Surnaturel* was significant for the Council's deliberations on the church in the modern world, as found in *Gaudium et Spes*. Undoubtedly, de Lubac was also the outstanding expert on the problem of atheism. His influence on the topic was brought to bear prior to the Council by means of *Le drame de l'humanisme athée* (1944), and at the Council, in the production of Schema 13.[53] Rudolf Voderholzer notes: "Articles 19 through 22 of *Gaudium et Spes*, which deal with modern atheism and the proper response of the church, clearly show that they were inspired by de Lubac, down to the formulation of individual sentences."[54]

De Lubac's extensive studies of Scriptural exegesis also prepared important foundations for *Dei Verbum*.[55] While de Lubac did not work on that schema, he had been outspoken against the affirmation of a *duplex fons* of revelation, as espoused in the original schema. His influence can thus be seen in the Council's eventual adoption of a *unus fons*, the key claim of de

52. ASC, 116. See also Voderholzer, 83–94, and Aaron Riches, "Henri de Lubac and the Second Vatican Council," in *T&T Clark Companion to Henri de Lubac*, ed. Jordan Hillebert (London: Bloomsbury T&T Clark, 2017), 121–56.

53. "Schema 13" refers to the draft text, which only entered the agenda of the Council near the end of its first session and eventually became the Pastoral Constitution of the Church in the Modern World, *Gaudium et Spes*.

54. Voderholzer, 85. The Christocentric anthropology of *Gaudium et Spes*, no. 22, frequently quoted by Pope Saint John Paul II throughout his pontificate, is almost identical to de Lubac's own words in *Catholicism*, 339: "By revealing the Father and by being revealed by him, Christ completes the revelation of man to himself."

55. Cf. *Histoire et esprit* (1950) and *Exégèse médiévale* (1959, 1961, 1963, 1964). In his commentary on *Dei Verbum*, B. Rigaux makes a point to acknowledge de Lubac's work in restoring to honor the spiritual meaning of the Scriptures; cf. Commentary in *Das II. Vatikanische Konzil* 2, 572; also noted in Neufeld, "In the Service of the Council: Bishops and Theologians at the Second Vatican Council," trans. Ronald Sway, in *Vatican II: Assessment and Perspectives*, vol. 1, ed. René Latourelle (New York: Paulist Press, 1988), 95.

Lubac's *Exégèse médiévale*, namely, that Jesus Christ, the Word Incarnate, is himself the unity and interpretation of the Testaments and of Tradition.[56] Additionally, on the question of the relation of the Church with non-Christian religions, *Nostra Aetate* contains ideas corresponding to *Catholicisme* as well as to de Lubac's works on Buddhism. And the Council's teaching in *Ad Gentes* on the Church's missionary activity coincides with the ideas in *Catholicisme* and *Le fondement théologique des Missions* (1946), in which de Lubac emphasized the Church's missionary responsibility to proclaim the gospel to all peoples.

Although it is not apparent that de Lubac had a hand in the drafting of *Lumen Gentium*, it is quite certain that he exerted a significant influence on the development of the text, a text he called the "backbone" of the Council. Many elements of the ecclesiology found in *Lumen Gentium* had been developed in de Lubac's early writings. For example, *Corpus Mysticum* laid the theological foundations for the Eucharistic ecclesiology proposed by the Council in *Lumen Gentium*, numbers 3, 7, 11, 26 (see also *Sacrosanctum Concilium*, numbers 10, 41). The tidy and much-quoted expression, "The Church makes the Eucharist; the Eucharist makes the Church," had been formulated by de Lubac.[57]

Méditation sur l'Église also revived the importance of considering the church as a mystery (chapters 1 and 2) and as the sacrament of Christ (chapter 6), two notions of principal importance in *Lumen Gentium*. It is no mere coincidence that the structure of *Lumen Gentium* mirrors the structure of de Lubac's *Méditation sur l'Église*, written ten years beforehand. For example, the Dogmatic Constitution endorses de Lubac's emphases on the idea of the church as a Christocentric mystery and as a sacrament rooted in the mystery of the Trinity. These themes are written into the parallel structure of the two works: The opening chapters of both *Méditation sur l'Église* and *Lumen Gentium* address the inner core of "the Church as mystery."[58] The Eucharistic Ecclesiology treated in the middle chapter of *Méditation sur l'Église* can also be found at the heart of *Lumen Gentium* and throughout

---

56. *Exégèse médiévale*, tome I, vol. 1, 322. See also de Lubac's commentary on *Dei Verbum*, *La Révélation divine* (Paris: Éditions du Cerf, 1968).

57. The formula was coined by de Lubac in *Splendor*, 133, and he had already developed the same theme at length in his book *Corpus Mysticum* (1944).

58. It is worthy of note that the original schema, *De Ecclesia*, began with a chapter on "*De natura Ecclesiae militantis.*" De Lubac's influence and his predilection for the notion of mystery can be seen in the revised title of the first chapter of LG, "*De Ecclesiae Mysterio,*" which echoes the first chapter of *Méditation sur l'Église*, "*L'Église est un mystère.*"

the Council's ecclesiology as a whole.[59] Moreover, the final chapters of both works address the relationship of Mary and the Church, and both texts conclude with a doxology to the Trinity. *Méditation sur l'Église* excerpts a prayer from the Great Vespers of the Byzantine Rite: "Come, O peoples, let us adore the Divinity in three Persons—the Father in the Son and with the Holy Spirit.... Holy Trinity, glory be to thee!"[60] *Lumen Gentium* similarly concludes with an invocation to Mary, the Mother of God that all peoples "may be happily gathered together in peace and harmony into one People of God, for the glory of the Most Holy and Undivided Trinity."[61] Altogether, "it was above all *Méditation sur l'Église* with which the Council fathers were familiar as a source of theological ideas and as inspiration for the spiritual life."[62] It is evident that the Council's teachings—*Lumen Gentium* in particular—rely to a good extent on de Lubac's preconciliar work.

Prior to the closing of Vatican II, de Lubac was appointed to the Vatican's Secretariat for Non-Christians and the Secretariat for Non-believers. In the years after the Council, he traveled extensively to promulgate conciliar teachings. In March of 1966, he spoke at the University of Notre Dame, and these lectures became the first three chapters of *Paradoxe et Mystère de l'Église* (1967).[63] Later that year, de Lubac went to Chicago where he spoke at the Saint Xavier Symposium and the Theological Congress. These lectures on the implications of the teaching of *Gaudium et Spes* on atheism were subsequently incorporated into de Lubac's *Athéisme et sens de l'homme* (1968).[64] Similarly, a lecture given at Saint Louis University was expanded under the title *L'Église dans la crise actuelle* (1969).[65]

De Lubac had suffered the assault of certain enemies of reform in the Preparatory Commission at the start of his involvement in the Council, and by its end, he found himself in no lesser anguish over the reductive tendencies which seemed to systematically reinterpret the Council's teaching on reform and renewal through a secular ideology. De Lubac referred to this

59. *Méditation sur l'Église* treats of the doctrine of the Eucharist in chapter 4, "The Heart of the Church," and a Eucharistic ecclesiology is evident in *Lumen Gentium*, nos. 3, 7, 11, 26.

60. *Splendor*, 379.

61. *Lumen Gentium*, no. 69.

62. Neufeld, "In the Service of the Council," 94.

63. See de Lubac's preface to *The Church: Paradox and Mystery* (English translation, Ecclesia Press, 1969); hereafter cited CPM, vii.

64. For an abridged English translation of *Athéisme et sens de l'homme: une double requête de Gaudium et Spes* (1968), see "The Total Meaning of Man and the World," trans. D. C. Schindler, *Communio* 35 (2008): 613–41.

65. For an abridged English translation, see "The Church in Crisis," *Theology Digest* 17 (1969): 312–25.

phenomenon as the "para-council," and he denounced its "false idea of 'openness to the world,' shamelessly preached as if it were the thought of the Council."[66] De Lubac refused to yield to any disillusionment. In *The Motherhood of the Church,* written in the midst of the postconciliar crisis, de Lubac asserts: "We are confident that the fruits of the Council will ripen in their time. Now is the time for patience, that is for hope, and hope does not deceive."[67] His postconciliar works and writings continued to champion a commitment to renewal through the rediscovery of tradition.

In 1968, de Lubac refused to sign the "Declaration on the Liberty and Function of Theologians in the Church," an open petition for greater academic freedom proposed by theologians associated with *Concilium,* a journal whose editorial board he had resigned from in 1965. In 1972, de Lubac joined Hans Urs von Balthasar and Joseph Ratzinger in founding *Communio,* a counterjournal aimed at fostering theological scholarship expressly from within the heart of the Church and critically reappropriating Tradition in the way of *ressourcement.*

In 1969, Pope Paul VI appointed de Lubac to the newly created International Theological Commission as one of its thirty founding members. *Petite catéchèse sur Nature et Grâce* (1980) grew out of a presentation to the Commission on the topic of nature and grace. De Lubac continued to produce scholarly monographs up to the last decade of his life; his final works include *Pic de la Mirandole* (1974) and *La postérité spirituelle de Joachim de Fiore* (1979–1981). In 1983, he was created a cardinal by Pope John Paul II.

In October of 1986, de Lubac suffered a stroke. A second followed in 1989, leaving him with impaired speech. At the end of his journey, the "theologian of friendship" whose particular vivacity came in conversation was now buried in silence.[68] Yet the eloquence once exhibited in his writings now found its manifestation in contemplative joy and silent prayer. Georges Chantraine recounts a Eucharist celebrated with de Lubac three months before his death: "In his wheelchair, clothed with his priestly vestments, he appeared more alive than ever. In the sobriety of the liturgical gestures our Catholic communion found its expression. Simpler still and as full of meaning were the prayers he recited ... which always concluded with a

---

66. ASC, 150. See also de Lubac's lecture at Saint Louis University in 1969, *L'Église dans la crise actuelle* (referenced above) as well as his essay directly on the topic of "The Council and the Para-Council," in Appendix C of *Petite catéchèse sur Nature et Grâce.*

67. MC, 28.

68. Xavier Tilliette, "Henri de Lubac: The Legacy of a Theologian," *Communio* 19 (1992): 341. Voderholzer also describes de Lubac's "genius for friendship," in *Meet Henri de Lubac,* 21.

resounding 'Amen' that welled up out of his heart. Reduced to silence and inaction, he was immersed in joy."[69] De Lubac passed into that eternal joy on September 4, 1991.

Responding to the Charge of Antiquarianism

The legacy of Henri de Lubac is extensive. His intense literary productivity was the fruit of a unified and singular vision, a vision de Lubac possessed from the very early years of his theological career, as evidenced by *Catholicisme*. The coherence of this organic vision, despite the confrontation and controversy to which it gave rise, "grows and broadens and branches out under the impulse of a truth that is generative of a design."[70] The vision of unity that de Lubac sought in the revival of the Church Fathers did not terminate in the patristic writings per se. As this survey of his works has shown, de Lubac's work addressed the entire scope of the Church's tradition as a living tradition, and his pioneering work of *ressourcement* consistently sought an authentic reading of this tradition throughout the ages.[71]

Aidan Nichols proposes that de Lubac's writings constitute a mosaic depicting the theme of unity.[72] Each piece of the mosaic represents some aspect of the Christian mystery: the unity of God with man is the central thesis of *Le drame de l'humanisme athée*; the unity of human beings with one another in and through the Church is the concern of *Catholicisme*; the unity of nature and grace is explored in *Surnaturel*; the unity of Scripture is presented in *Exégèse médiévale*; the unity of philosophy and theology is discussed in *Pic de la Mirandole*; and the unity of salvation history is the underlying argument of *La postérité spirituelle de Joachim de Fiore*. From this point of view, whether de Lubac's understanding of unity is real or simply "imagined" is not a question of the unity of the patristic era in itself. It is, rather, about the unity of the experience of Christians of every age in every encounter with God—an experience to which the early Church had a unique and privileged witness. The Trinity, the ultimate transcendent reality of Unity, grounds the hope on which Christian faith—and de Lubac's legacy—holds fast.

Robin D. Young concludes her critiques of de Lubac stating that "de

---

69. Georges Chantraine, "Cardinal Henri de Lubac (1896–1991)," *Communio* 18 (1991), 298.

70. Tilliette, "Henri de Lubac: Legacy," 334.

71. The controversy around *Surnaturel*, for example, grew from his endeavor to vindicate the genuine teachings of Saint Thomas.

72. See Aidan Nichols, "Henri de Lubac: Panorama and Proposal," *New Blackfriars* 93 (2012): 31–33.

Lubac's fabrication of a patristic theology for the purposes of renewal actually failed the renewal it envisioned because it could not anticipate or give space to the discordant elements that have comprised Christianity from its beginnings, elements that seem to take the lead whenever reform is the order of the day."[73] While it is true that de Lubac grew increasingly concerned with the "para-council" and what he considered a distortion of the Council's teachings, *ressourcement* was not intended by de Lubac to be the magical cure of all modern ills. He was not naïve about the bitter polemics of the patristic era. Nor was he nostalgic for some romantic theology of the early Church. To say that de Lubac had become disenchanted by the modern, postconciliar Church and sought refuge in his own concoction of an idealized past is to stop short of the full range of his perspective and the depths of his hope. I contend that de Lubac's outlook was not simplistically anchored in the Church Fathers. Rather, the locus of his vision and his hope for renewal was anchored in Jesus Christ. De Lubac understood what the Congregation for Catholic Education later says about the study of the Church Fathers:

> Tradition, as it was known and lived by the Fathers, is not like a monolithic, immovable block, but a multiform organism pulsating with life. It is a practice of life and doctrine.... To follow the living Tradition of the Fathers does not mean hanging on to the past as such, but adhering to the line of faith with an enthusiastic sense of security and freedom, while maintaining a constant fidelity towards what is foundational.[74]

That which "is foundational" is the mystery of Christ. De Lubac's insistent recourse to the wellspring of the Fathers was anchored in Jesus Christ who alone stands as the source and end of *ressourcement.* De Lubac immersed himself in both patristic and medieval theology because he intuited in these sources their direct contact with the profundity of the mysteries of salvation, and he sought to weave that theology into the common fabric of ecclesial life. The privileged witness of the Church Fathers provided but a means to an end, and that end is union with Christ in his Church.

---

73. Young, "Soldier of the Great War," 162–63.

74. Congregation for Catholic Education, *Instruction on the Study of the Fathers of the Church in the Formation of Priests,* 10 November 1989, published in *L'Osservatore Romano* (English edition), 15 January 1990, no. 22. Robin Darling Young's criticism of de Lubac as having sought "to revive an apparently lively, less problematic, even mythologically archaic form of language and liturgical life" ("Soldier of the Great War," 137) makes for an interesting contrast to the Congregation's appraisal of patristic thought.

The depths of de Lubac's perspective is intimated in what he writes about ecclesial reform. In a work on "Particular Churches in the Universal Church," he explains that "the subject of institutions" was never of principal interest for him because he believed that institutional, structural reforms were always secondary in importance to spiritual renewal, *"the only true renewal."*[75] The goal of ecclesial renewal, for de Lubac, was never expected to be achieved by a simplistic reinstitution of some bygone era or the replication of ancient structures. Rather, renewal is principally a spiritual work which must be animated by the Holy Spirit who blows as he wishes in his time (cf. Jn 3:8). Perhaps this is the fundamental element that is missing from Young's otherwise incisive analysis.

Reflecting on his work, de Lubac says in his memoirs:

Without claiming to open new avenues to thought, I have sought rather, without any antiquarianism, to make known some of the great common areas of Catholic tradition. I wanted to make it loved, to show its ever-present fruitfulness. Such a task called more for a reading across the centuries than for a critical application to specific points; it excluded any overly preferential attachment to one school, system, or definite age; it demanded more attention *to the deep and permanent unity of the Faith*, to the mysterious relationship (which escapes so many specialized scholars) of all those who invoke the name of Christ, than to the multiple diversities of eras, milieux, personalities and cultures.[76]

De Lubac assiduously read "across the centuries" in search of "the deep and permanent unity of the Faith." For him, *ressourcement* was never an end in itself but fundamentally an essential re-orientation to vital contact with *the source* of unity, Jesus Christ, so as to bear witness to him in the modern world. As one Lubacian scholar has argued, de Lubac's mystical outlook is a "mysticism of the incarnate rather than an escape to something otherworldly or disembodied."[77]

With regard to *Marian ressourcement,* moreover, the witness of the Church Fathers laid important foundations for all subsequent generations of the Christian faithful. The testimony of Ignatius, Justin, Irenaeus, Ambrose, and Augustine bring us to the heart of the *regula fidei* and to the Incarnation

---

75. De Lubac, introduction to MC, 33; italics as found in the original; also quoted in ASC, 133.
76. ASC, 143–44; emphasis added.
77. Susan Wood, *Spiritual Exegesis and the Church in the Theology of Henri de Lubac* (Grand Rapids, MI: Eerdmans, 1998), 211.

of the Word *ex Maria.* Mary is the access point to the saving mysteries of Christ, and any substantive renewal of the Church is bound to find itself gazing on the countenance of this Virgin Mother. The patristic witness should not be relegated to a distant, moribund past or set aside as idiosyncratic or obsolete.

De Lubac's *ressourcement* enabled "the voice of the fathers of our faith [to] speak so that we hear the voice of the origin in all its freshness and astonishing relevance."[78] So too, might his own words provide us with a fundamental orientation:

> That voice of Tradition has continually called on me to look up into the "Heavenly Jerusalem" whose beauty has taken a daily firmer hold upon me. *But for all that, I have not looked to the heavenly city as one does to a dream; for I have not been looking for a sort of refuge from everyday monotony and the burden of existence in some airy mirage or other.* On the contrary; to me, that mother-country of freedom, with all its royal majesty and heavenly splendor, is something to be seen at the very heart of *earthly reality,* right at the core of all the confusion and all the mischances which are, inevitably, involved in its mission to men.[79]

De Lubac's pioneering work of *ressourcement* advances a theology in which nature and grace, time and eternity compenetrate and transform human history from within. The Church is the locus of this transformation, and it is not some "airy mirage" but an "earthly reality" in "heavenly splendor." And as our eyes adjust to this splendor uncovered by de Lubac's *ressourcement,* we will begin to see the contours of a blessed countenance: the mystery of the Church bears preeminently the features of the countenance of Mary.

Having acquainted ourselves with the broad features of de Lubac's life and work, we now turn to examine de Lubac's masterpiece of Marian *ressourcement,* namely his chapter on Mary and the Church in *Méditation sur l'Église.*

---

78. Joseph Ratzinger, preface to the 1988 English edition of *Catholicism,* 11.
79. *Splendor,* 9; emphasis added.

CHAPTER 2

"L'Église et la Vierge Marie"

De Lubac's Preconciliar Marian *Ressourcement*

Méditation sur l'Église (1953) has been described as a preconciliar work of "magisterial expression" that is "inspired by the church's prophetic tradition" and through which *Lumen Gentium* came "on the horizon."[1] Early on, it garnered international acclaim with translations into Italian, German, Dutch, English, and Spanish, and, more recently, into Russian and Polish. As Archbishop of Milan, Giovanni Battista Montini, the future Pope Paul VI, distributed de Lubac's book to all the clergy of his diocese, and it was specifically the final chapter on "L'Église et la Vierge Marie" that drew Montini's exultant praise.[2] This chapter is de Lubac's principal writing on Mary, and in it he offers an approach to Mariology that is wholly situated in relationship to the

1. John McDade, "Epilogue: '*Ressourcement*' in Retrospect," in *Ressourcement: A Movement for Renewal in Twentieth-Century Catholic Theology*, edited by Gabriel Flynn and Paul Murray (Oxford: Oxford University Press, 2012), 512.

2. Georges Chantraine, "Note historique" in *Henri de Lubac. Oeuvres complètes*, 8 vols. (Paris: Cerf, 1999), 8: xxx–xxxi; Chantraine recounts the testimony of Wladimir d'Ormesson, the French Ambassador to the Holy See, of Montini's laudatory comments on de Lubac's chapter on "The Church and Our Lady." See also ASC, 75, on Paul VI's personal esteem for de Lubac, further manifested in two letters which have been duplicated in ASC, 307 [4:40], and ASC, 379–82 [9:9]; the latter is a personally signed letter sent to de Lubac to congratulate him on his eightieth birthday and to thank him for his work.

Church, a sort of "differentiated Marian ecclesiology" that synthesizes elements of the biblical, patristic, and liturgical renewals. It is quintessentially de Lubac's work of Marian *ressourcement*. Our study examines the first half of de Lubac's chapter, proceeding in three sections. The first two sections will examine de Lubac's retrieval of the tradition, first on Mary and the Church as *mother*, and second on Mary and the Church as *virgin bride*. The third section examines de Lubac's discussion of the proper theological configuration of Mary's relationship to the Church and concludes with a survey of de Lubac's many patristic sources. The latter half of de Lubac's chapter, in which he appropriates a Marian reading of the Song of Songs, constitutes a "scriptural *ressourcement*" and will be explored in the next chapter.[3]

Retrieving the Tradition on Motherhood: *La Mère des chrétiens*

De Lubac's chapter is a kaleidoscopic presentation of the Christian tradition on the topic of Mary and the Church. Two themes that consistently emerge are the dual aspects of *virginity* and *maternity* as the constitutive dimensions of their mystical identification. Both Mary and the Church are virgin mothers, and the title *Mater Ecclesia* effectively captures this key concept in de Lubac's preferred ecclesiology.[4] De Lubac maintains that Christianity is a life into which Christians are born, and "the mother who gives birth to us in it is the Church."[5] The mystery of this birthing, that is the Church's motherhood, is best illumined by the mystery of Mary's divine maternity.

As a good historian, de Lubac first reports on the illustrious voices of tradition on ecclesial motherhood—a reality he describes as "the Church as sanctifying." He notes that while the Church Fathers rarely spoke of the

---

3. The five untitled sections of the 1999 English edition of "L'Église et la Vierge Marie" actually correspond to subtitled headings in the original French edition: (1) *Le Miroir de l'Église*; (2) *La Mère des chrétiens*; (3) *La gloire de Jérusalem*; (4) *Commentaires du Cantique*; and (5) *L'Épouse parfaite*. The 1963 English edition by Deus Books (Paulist Press) contains no subdivisions, and the 1999 English edition by Ignatius Press has untitled subsections demarcated by a visual divider of three asterisks, as seen on pages 321, 338, 353, and 364. My survey of the first three sections will generally follow de Lubac's structure.

4. De Lubac explores at length the idea of the Church as mother in his book, *The Motherhood of the Church*, and in chapter 7 of *Méditation sur l'Église*, entitled "Ecclesia Mater," 236–78.

5. Preface to the German-language edition of *Les églises particulières dans l'Église universelle, suivi de la maternité de l'église* (Paris: Aubier Montaigne, 1971), as reproduced by de Lubac in ASC, 135. The presentation of these topics is inverted in the English translation so that the discussion on the motherhood of the Church precedes the discussion of universal and particular churches.

spiritual maternity of Mary vis-à-vis the Church (this idea only develops later), it was commonplace to refer to the spiritual maternity of the Church who, as mother, "brings forth daily him whom the Virgin Mary brought forth" (cf. Gal 4:26).[6] Tracing the broad historical development, de Lubac notes that the early Church saw the baptismal font as the womb through which the faithful are reborn in the Spirit, and the sacraments as the milk of sanctifying nourishment. The inscription in the baptistery of St. John Lateran, for instance, reads: "At this spring the Church our Mother bears in her virginal womb the sons whom she has conceived under the breath of God."[7] Moreover, the earliest reference to the Church as a mother is found in a famous letter, dating back to the second century, in which the Christians of Vienne and Lyons referred to the Church as "our virginal Mother."[8] This reference, says de Lubac, was made with "a clear though implicit allusion to our Lady."[9]

The first explicit allusion to the motherhood of the Church with reference to Mary is found in St. Ambrose's commentary on the second chapter of the Gospel of Luke, the same commentary in which Ambrose made the first explicit reference to Mary as *typus ecclesiae*. The bishop of Milan draws a direct connection between the motherhood of Our Lady and the motherhood of the Church, stating: "Well-espoused, but a virgin, because she is a type of the Church, who is immaculate but a bride. The virgin conceived us of the Holy Spirit; the virgin gave birth to us without pangs."[10]

After Ambrose, the theme of the Church as simultaneously mother and virgin burgeoned. It became an especially favored theme of St. Augustine,[11] who spoke of the Church as the "'holy virgin' and 'spiritual mother' who is 'wholly like unto Mary' in her act of birth."[12] He exhorts his hearers to

---

6. De Lubac gives two sources for this quotation: Berengard, *In Apoc.*, 12, 3–5; Pseudo-Augustine, *In Apoc.* (PL 100, 1152d); as quoted by de Lubac in *Splendor*, 321–22.

7. *Splendor*, 323; see also MC, 52–53, for a more complete version of the inscription on the architrave of the Lateran baptistery.

8. The letter from the Christians of Vienne and Lyons is preserved in Eusebius's *Ecclesiastical History*, bk. 5, chap. 1, no. 45 (PL 20, 240); as referenced in *Splendor*, 323.

9. *Splendor*, 323.

10. Ambrose, *In Lucam*, bk. 2, chap. 7; as quoted by de Lubac in *Splendor*, 324n49: "Bene desponsata, sed virgo, quia est Ecclesiae typus, quae est immaculata, sed nupta. Concepit nos virgo de Spiritu, parit nos virgo sine gemitu"; translation is mine.

11. See Augustine, *De Sancta virginitate*, chap. 2 (PL 40, 397); *Sermo* 138, no. 9 (PL 38, 768); *De nuptiis et concupiscentia*, bk. 2, chap. 4, no. 12; *In Joannem*, tract. 120, no. 2 (PL 35, 1953); and *In Ps. 40*, no. 10 (PL 36, 461) for some of the references to Augustine which de Lubac provides in *Splendor*, 324n50–55.

12. Augustine, *Epist.* 34, no. 3 (PL 33, 132); *De sancta virginitate*, chap. 6 (PL 40, 399); and *Sermo* 213, no. 7 (PL 38, 1064); as quoted by de Lubac in *Splendor*, 325.

honor the Church who has given them birth while remaining a virgin like Mary: "Who has given birth to you? I hear the voice of your heart: it is the Mother Church, this holy, honored Church who, like Mary, gives birth and is virgin."[13] And just as Mary becomes the mother of many through the birth of Christ, so too, the Church, in bringing forth many becomes the "mother of unity."[14] These writings of Ambrose and Augustine hold preeminence in the tradition, and their enduring significance will be evident in Vatican II's exposition on Mary.

This understanding of the Church's motherhood as rooted in Mary's divine motherhood is also found in liturgical texts. The Gelasian Sacramentary, for example, exclaims, "As Mary thrilled with joy at the birth of God, so the Church thrills with joy in the mystery of the birth of her children."[15] The Mozarabic liturgy, in particular, draws an extensive parallel between the virginal childbearing of Mary and the fruitful chastity of Mother Church.[16] In the Scholastic era, this theology of ecclesial motherhood continued to receive robust development. Isaac of Stella, for example, teaches: "Mary, sinless, gave the body its Head; the Church, in the remission of all sins, gives the Head its body. Both are thus Mother of Christ, but neither of the two bears him wholly, without the other."[17]

Moreover, allusions to the motherhood of the Church in relationship to Mary developed with reference not only to the sacrament of baptism but also to the sacraments of the Eucharist and Holy Orders. "Just as the maternal function of Mary is to give the God-Man to the world, so the maternal function of the Church, which culminates, as we have seen, *in the celebration of the Eucharist,* is to give us Christ, 'the Head, Sacrifice, and Food of the members of his mystical body.'"[18] The implications of this parallel between

---

13. Augustine, *Sermo* 192, 2; 195, 2; 213, 7 (PL 38, 1013, 1018, 1061); as quoted by de Lubac in MC, 57.

14. Augustine, *Sermo* 192, no. 2; as quoted by de Lubac in *Splendor,* 325.

15. Gelasian Sacramentary, in Mohlberg, *Missale gothicum,* 88; as quoted by de Lubac in *Splendor,* 326.

16. *Missa in vigilia paschae, Inlatio;* as quoted by de Lubac in *Splendor,* 326n63. See also de Lubac's reference to the ancient Mozarabic rite in MC, 58.

17. Isaac of Stella, *Sermo* 61 (PL 194, 1683); as quoted by de Lubac in *Splendor,* 327; de Lubac also notes how Rupert of Deutz similarly draws a close association between Mary and the Church in referring to "Mother Church" as "the Mother of Christ"; see Rupert of Deutz, *In Joannem* (PL 169, 285c).

18. *Splendor,* 329; emphasis added. De Lubac also provides a lengthy quotation from Carl Feckes's "Maria als Vorbild, Mutter und Herz der Kirche," in *Das Mysterium des h. Kirche,* 2nd ed. (Paderborn, 1935, 270–71), which begins: "As Mary bore the earthly Christ, so the church bears the Eucharistic Christ."

Mary and the Church in relationship to priesthood and the Eucharist will play out in Vatican II's sacramental ecclesiology: the hierarchical and institutional elements of the Church are subordinate to the mystery of the Church as mother.

In all of these instances, the transmission of divine life to the new Christian is seen as a mystical extension of Mary's birthing of Christ. De Lubac writes, "St. Leo the Great, having shown 'in the generation of Christ the origin of the Christian people,' goes on to show how the actual mystery of our being brought to birth by the Church is the *conclusion* of the historical birth of Christ through Mary—its continuation, as it were, under the influence of the same Spirit."[19] With this statement, de Lubac establishes a direct link between the historical birth of Christ and the birth of Christians into ecclesial communion. The latter is not only a consequence and continuation of the former but "its *conclusion*."[20] Ecclesial maternity is not merely a semblance of Mary's maternity but an actual concrete extension of it. And of great importance is the causal source of this continuity: it is not Mary but the power of the Holy Spirit. The Church thus does not owe its existence directly to Mary but to God who acts in both Mary and the Church and establishes their bond of unity.

In this light, the motherhood of Mary positively informs and illumines the Church's understanding of her own motherhood, that dimension of ecclesial existence through which the Church generates new Christians, particularly in baptism and the Eucharist. Within the order of grace, Mary's spiritual motherhood is fundamental for ecclesial motherhood; the latter "acts on the basis and by virtue of that of Mary, and that of Mary continues to act in and by that of the Church."[21] These rich theological aspects of divine and ecclesial maternity will come to a mature synthesis in Vatican II's teaching on the mission of the Church to sanctify, through its teaching authority and the sacraments, especially the Eucharist. Additionally, given the controversy that later ensued regarding Pope Paul's promulgation of Mary as Mother of the Church at the end of the Second Vatican Council (to be examined in chapter 6), de Lubac's exposition here is significant.[22]

19. *Splendor*, 337; de Lubac is quoting from St. Leo the Great's *Sermo 63*, chapter 6 (PL 54, 211c and 356b-c); emphasis added.

20. *Splendor*, 337; emphasis added.

21. Matthias Scheeben, *Dogmatik*, bk. 5, no. 1819; as quoted by de Lubac in *Splendor*, 333.

22. Cf. *Splendor*, 333.

Retrieving the Tradition on Virginity:
La gloire de Jérusalem

In tandem with the mystery of ecclesial motherhood is the tradition on the Church as the virgin bride of Christ. Whereas the Church as mother refers to the Church's mission and sanctifying ministry, this second aspect of the Church as bride refers to her status as "sanctified" and further reflects Mary as *la gloire de Jérusalem*. As with the idea of spiritual motherhood, this idea of the virgin bride is first established in Scripture with reference to the Church as the bride whom Christ cleansed "by the washing of water with the word" (Eph 5:26), and only later is the *bridal* dimension applied to Mary, with an emphasis on her bodily and spiritual virginity.

Mary's wholly sanctified state is manifest throughout the mysteries of her life, but it is most prominent at the event of the Annunciation, whence Mary's virginity took on a new dimension of fruitfulness. Her unadulterated faith enabled her to hear and receive the Word of God so completely that the Word became incarnate in her womb. De Lubac follows Aquinas in asserting that Mary spoke her consent on behalf of the entire human race, and this consent was necessary to manifest "a certain *spiritual wedlock* between the Son of God and human nature," which the Incarnation signified.[23] Mary's assent in humanity's stead thus serves as the concrete realization of the bridal dimension of the human race in relationship to God. *Bridal* humanity came into existence in the person of Mary even though it was only recognized later in time with the advent of the Church.

Our Lady's holiness contains the seed of the Church's own flourishing. Following the inspiration of Irenaeus of Lyons, de Lubac outlines the events of Mary's life in tandem with the Church's own. He asserts that Mary also spoke the words of the *Magnificat* in the name of the whole Church,[24] and her presentation of the child Jesus into the arms of Simeon was "the beginning of the Church's offering to the Father of the sacrifice for our sins."[25] She held the Church's place at the foot of the Cross: "[In] the name of the whole Church and on behalf of every generation of Christians, she contemplated that Cross which is the principle of all understanding."[26]

Yet this ontological interpenetration of Mary and the Church as "sancti-

---

23. St. Thomas Aquinas, *Summa Theologiae* III. q.30. a.1, emphasis added.
24. Cf. Irenaeus, *Adversus haereses*, bk. 3, chap. 10, no. 2; as referenced in *Splendor*, 343.
25. *Splendor*, 343.
26. *Splendor*, 344.

fied" does not end at the Cross but peaks in the Lord's resurrection. Mary's own participation in Easter glory is completed in the consummate reality of her Assumption into heaven, described as an attestation to her purity and as a harbinger of the Church's own future glory. The dogma of Mary's Assumption into heaven represents "the complete and definitive triumph of the divine action ... right up to its consequences in the bodily order" and is the "pledge and anticipation" of the Church's own triumph.[27] It is "the dawn of the new creation whose first rays filter through into the darkness of this world."[28] Mary personifies the reality of the Church as sanctified. Mary precedes the Church in the journey of faith, arriving first at this consummate glory so as to attest to the triumph of grace and to serve as the archetype of ecclesial existence. De Lubac states: "If it is true that the Church ... reconstitutes bit by bit the first paradise, then our Lady is the first cell of the organism of that restored paradise which is more glorious than the original one."[29] She is the source of unwavering hope for the Church's own journey to the eternal banquet of the Lamb.

Mary's sanctified state and her personal cooperation with grace provide a perfect model of human cooperation in the work of Redemption. However, Mary does not stand merely as a static model from a distant past. Rather, having embraced the maternal role Christ entrusted to her on Calvary, she is mother to all the faithful and remains ever-present in this capacity until the final end is achieved and all are gathered into the one body of Christ. Insofar as the maternal and bridal dimensions of Our Lady's life and mission permeate the life and mission of the Church, her Assumption establishes her as a proper icon of the Church's own final, consummate reality.

This teleological perspective highlights the depth of the ontological bond between Mary and the Church. Mary is the preeminent one, an eschatological icon of the Church, who exercises a final causality that draws the Church forward to its consummate glory. Our Lady is not only the "perfect form"[30] or formal cause of the Church, but one might employ the Aristotelian/Scholastic terminology further and say that she is also the "final cause" of the Church. It is *in her* that the Church reaches its goal and "takes part in the 'celestial liturgy of the eternal High Priest, and his permanent

---

27. *Splendor*, 345.

28. Jean Daniélou, "Le Dogme de l'Assomption," *Études* 267 (December 1950): 301–2; as quoted by de Lubac in *Splendor*, 346n168.

29. *Splendor*, 338.

30. Pseudo-Ildephonsus, *De Assumptione, sermo* 3 (PL 96, 257a; 269d); as quoted by de Lubac in *Splendor*, 342 and 320.

intercession before the Father'; in her … the 'royal priesthood' of the whole People of God is brought to a glorious consummation."[31] These dual aspects of the Church and Mary as both virgin and mother show that Mary carries within herself the whole mystery of the Church and that that mystery is personified and anticipated in her.

Ressourcement as Maximalism Reconfigured?

From these meaty sections of "L'Église et la Vierge Marie," we witness de Lubac's feasting at the lavish table of the patristic and medieval traditions. While his assembly of patristic and medieval texts on Mary and the Church is vast and can appear to be somewhat diffuse, they reflect the richness and diversity of the centuries-old tradition that he is re-sourcing. The beauty of that tradition is evident, but one might opine that the high honors accorded to Mary in de Lubac's chapter tend toward an excessive Marian maximalism. Does de Lubac's statement that "our Lady 'comprises in an eminent degree all the graces and all the perfections' of the Church"[32] betray a harmful maximalist tendency?

The answer is evidently nuanced. On the one hand, de Lubac revives the treasures of both patristic and medieval traditions on Mary without demur. Yet, what sets him apart from the Marian maximalists of his day is how he contextualizes everything that is said of Mary, situating Mary's titles and privileges squarely in relation to the Church. When he quotes Honorius of Autun (1080–1140) that "everything that is written of the Church may also be read as applying to Mary,"[33] de Lubac himself adds the reverse principle, that "what is written of our Lady can also—as to essentials—be read as applying to the Church."[34] It is not surprising, therefore, that de Lubac's chapter would provide an ideal template and inspiration for achieving an integrated Marian ecclesiology, as the Second Vatican Council would be challenged to do a decade later.

As evidenced in this survey of his retrieval of the tradition on Mary and the Church, de Lubac decisively does not propose Marian minimalism as an antidote to the reigning maximalism of the nineteenth and twentieth centuries. Rather, his *ressourcement* entails a revival of the vast riches of

---

31. *Splendor*, 347n174.

32. *Splendor*, 341; with reference to Jean-Jacques Olier, *Vie Intérieure de la très sainte Vierge, Ouvrage Recueilli des Écrits de M. Olier* (Rome: Salviucci, 1866), vol. ii, 75.

33. Honorius of Autun, as quoted in *Splendor*, 323.

34. *Splendor*, 323.

Christianity in both its doctrine and devotion to Mary within a proper *ecclesiological* context. And he does so with an astute ecumenical perspective. In the remainder of this section, we explore how de Lubac turns on its head the Protestant critique of Catholic Marian doctrine and uses it to illumine the essence of the relationship of Mary and the Church. We will also explore three central paradigms de Lubac proffers for a better understanding of that relationship: perichoresis, "*specialis*," and typology. These are the key ingredients to de Lubac's Marian *ressourcement*, and they will have a direct application to the complex ecclesiological questions discussed at and after Vatican II.

Protestant Objections

As a foil to his argument on the close association of Mary and the Church, de Lubac begins by considering the fundamental Protestant criticisms of the Catholic cult of Our Lady and uses these criticisms as a springboard for his reflections on the preeminence accorded to Mary in Catholic thought. Like the fathers at the Second Vatican Council would later be, de Lubac was cognizant of the consternation amongst Protestants regarding the traditional Catholic conception of the Blessed Virgin's role in salvation history and of their tendency to see the Marian cult as a threat to the unicity of Christ as mediator and the absolute sovereignty of God in the work of redemption. In particular, de Lubac examines the observation of Karl Barth (1886–1968), the eminent theologian of the Reformed tradition, that in Catholic doctrine, Our Lady is "the principle, prototype, and summing up of the Church."[35] Although stated as a fundamental criticism against the Catholic cult of Our Lady, Barth's comments focus and underscore the key link between Our Lady and the Church in Catholic thought: she is truly *le miroir de l'Église*. Marian dogma is, indeed, a "crucial dogma of Catholicism"[36] because, as de Lubac explains: "Catholic faith regarding Our Lady symbolically sums up the doctrine of human cooperation in Redemption and thus provides the synthesis, or matrix concept [*l'idée-mère*], as it were, of the dogma of the

---

35. Karl Barth, 157 and 160; as quoted by de Lubac in *Splendor*, 316. Although Barth was not able to be present at the Council due to illness, he did visit Rome post-festum in 1966, after which he published a report of the discussions he had with leading Catholic theologians in Rome: *Ad Limina Apostolorum* (Zürich: EVZ-Verlag, 1967); English translation, *Ad Limina Apostolorum: An Appraisal of Vatican II*, trans. Keith Crim (Richmond, VA: John Knox Press, 1968); see also Philip J. Rosato, SJ, "*Ad Limina Apostolorum* in retrospect: The Reaction of Karl Barth to Vatican II," in *Karl Barth: Centenary Essays* (Cambridge: Cambridge University Press, 1989).

36. *Splendor*, 315.

Church."[37] Our Lady exemplifies perfect human collaboration in the mystery of salvation, and this cooperation establishes an intrinsic link between Mary and the Church.

In further contemplating this link that defines the relationship of Mary and the Church, de Lubac asserts, "As long as we stop short at positing a functional analogy between the two, and a more or less exterior one at that, we have not fully grasped the reason of it."[38] In an attempt to go beyond a mere "functional analogy," de Lubac explores the *intrinsic connectedness* between Mary and the Church, identifying their commonality as found in a profusion of patristic and medieval images: both Mary and the Church are the New Eve from the side of the New Adam; both are figures of Paradise as well as of the Ark of the Covenant; both are described as the Temple of God, Jerusalem on high, the Bride arrayed for her husband, and the Woman clothed with the sun.[39] However, Mary and the Church are not entirely *identical* realities. Tradition also holds to a difference in the degree of eminence between the Virgin and the Church.

> If the Church is the Temple of God, Mary is the Sanctuary of that Temple; if the Church is that sanctuary, Mary is within it as the Ark. And if the Church herself be compared to the Ark, then Our Lady is the Propitiatory, more precious than all else, which covers it. If the Church is paradise, Our Lady is the spring from which flows the river that waters it; the river that makes glad the City of God (Psalm 46:4).[40]

For de Lubac, "There is in all this something much more than a case of parallelism or the alternating use of ambivalent symbols."[41] Seeking a deeper penetration of the mystery of Mary and the Church, de Lubac offers the following three key paradigms drawn from the full range of the modern, medieval, and patristic traditions.

---

37. *Splendor*, 316. To draw a full contrast, de Lubac quotes the words of Martin Luther, who posited salvation to be "by the grace of God alone and the sole working of the Holy Spirit, without any human action"; cf. Martin Luther, *Dictata super Psalmos*, in "Psalm 71," *Opera*, ed. Weimar, 3:468; as quoted in *Splendor*, 314.

38. *Splendor*, 316.

39. See *Splendor*, 317–20.

40. *Splendor*, 352.

41. *Splendor*, 320.

Perichoresis

The first paradigm is adopted from Matthias J. Scheeben's idea that the relationship of the Church to Our Lady is best perceived as "a sort of mystical participation or identity, which is the fruit of a certain perichoresis or mystical participation."[42] *Perichoresis* or its Latin alternative, *circumincession*, is the theological term referring to the mutual indwelling and intimate interpenetration of the three Persons of the Trinity. Yet, just as the three Divine Persons are essentially one, they simultaneously and authentically remain as three. Following Scheeben, de Lubac posits that Mary and the Church also share an analogous co-inherence such that they are distinct but inseparable realities that mutually inform one another.

One insightful example of this "mutually informing" relationship is the positive correlation between Mary's Immaculate Conception and the doctrine of papal infallibility. Writing in 1870, Scheeben noted "a fertile and striking analogy between the dogma of the Immaculate Conception, the absolute purity of the *Sedes Sapientiae*, and the dogma of the Infallibility of the Holy See, the absolute purity of the *Cathedra sapientiae*."[43] For de Lubac, Mary's pondering heart (cf. Lk 2:19) "prefigured that long train of memory and intense meditation which is the very soul of the tradition of the Church,"[44] and the Church's faith and teaching should mirror Mary's virginity.

Isaac of Stella's "universiter / specialiter / singulariter"

The second paradigm, drawn from the medieval tradition, consists of a trio of terms found in the works of Isaac of Stella (c. 1100–1170). In his sermon, *In Assumptione beatae Mariae*, Isaac assigns the terms *generaliter, specialiter, singulariter* to the realities of the Church, Mary, and the soul, respectively: "The same thing is said *universally* [or generally] of the Church, *specially* of Mary and *singularly* of the faithful soul.... In the universal sense the inheritance of the Lord is the Church; in the special sense, it is Mary; in the singular sense, it is each faithful soul."[45]

De Lubac states that to understand this set of adverbs properly, one must "go right back to Ticonius, whose fourth 'rule for the interpretation

42. *Splendor*, 336; cf. 328 as well.

43. Matthias Scheeben, *Periodische Blätter* (1870), 508–9; as quoted by de Lubac in *Splendor*, 328n72; *Cathedra sapientiae* refers to the chair of Peter as the magisterial Seat of Wisdom.

44. *Splendor*, 343–44.

45. Isaac of Stella, *In Assumptione beatae Mariae, sermo* I (PL 194, 1863a); as quoted by de Lubac in *Splendor*, 347n177.

of Scripture'—*de specie et genere*—was taken up by St. Augustine and commented upon by the whole Latin tradition."[46] According to Ticonius, Scripture often conceals "the species under the genus—for example, the whole body under a member."[47] De Lubac states, "This principle may be applied to the relation of the Church to our Lady."[48] "In the Gospel texts where she is mentioned we may see, performed *in specie,* what was to be realized later on *in genere.*"[49] What is achieved in her is to be achieved for all in the body of Christ. Our Lady is the individual member of the Church who contains, in seed, the perfection of the whole body which is the Church. Just as the genus is said to be "anticipatorily concentrated in the species,"[50] Mary contains *in specie* what is to be the consummate ecclesial reality. She is the pure concentration of what it means to be "Church."

On the basis of Mary's "special excellence,"[51] de Lubac suggests that a third term is needed in addition to "species" and "genus," which would distinguish Our Lady and give to her "her proper place of preeminence—without, however, in any way straining the bond of reciprocal inclusion witnessed to by tradition."[52] It is here that he introduces and expounds Isaac of Stella's employment of the terms *generaliter, specialiter, singulariter.* The application of the term *specialis* or *specialiter* to Mary and *singularis* or *singulariter* to the individual faithful soul establishes the needed distinction, since *singulariter* does not assign any particular excellence to its subject but only distinguishes the subject from what is said *pluraliter.* "*Singulariter*" is applicable to any faithful soul. "*Specialiter,*" on the other hand, denotes a subject who stands out in special grace and favor.[53] St. Paschasius Radbertus (c. 785–865) had

46. *Splendor,* 348, with reference to Ticonius, *Regulae* (PL 18, 33–46) and St. Augustine, *De Doctrina christiana,* bk. 3, chap. 34, nos. 47–49 (PL 34, 83–86).

47. *Splendor,* 348; Ticonius's usage of "species" and "genus" predates the contemporary usage of the terms to denote biological classification involving a taxonomy that defines "species" as a subtype of a "genus." For Ticonius, "genus" simply refers to the whole to which a part, or "species," belongs. Although de Lubac clearly means to align the term "species" with "a member" and "genus" with "the whole body," it appears that he inadvertently inverts the terms in this quotation.

48. *Splendor,* 348.

49. *Splendor,* 348, with reference to St. Paschasius Radbertus, *In Matt.,* bk. 2 (PL 120, 103d, 104c-d, 106c).

50. *Splendor,* 348; a continuation of the previous quotation.

51. *Splendor,* 349–50: "[I]f the heavenly Bridegroom celebrates in the womb of his Mother his wedding with the whole of human nature, our Lady, nonetheless for that, rejoices in a 'special glory' and 'special power' because she is and will be the 'special bride,' the object of a 'special dilection.' She is 'specially united to the Holy Spirit,' and from this 'special privilege' she, and she alone, draws a 'special excellence'"; cf. footnotes 184–89, with reference to the sequence from the *Missale Trecensis* of 1497, St. Peter Damian, Denis the Carthusian, Goefroy, and Peter Cellensis.

52. *Splendor,* 348.

53. *Splendor,* 348–49.

begun to realize this distinction in his commentary on Psalm 44, written for consecrated virgins. According to de Lubac, Paschasius exhorted these women to the ideals of their state by explaining that the titles "virgin" and "spouse"—which are applied in Scripture to the whole Church—properly referred to them as consecrated virgins in a *special* way.[54] Ever more fittingly are these titles to be applied to the Blessed Virgin, in whom "*specialis* corresponds exactly to *singularis et unica*, and *specialiter* to *singularis et superexcellenter.*"[55] Our Lady is both *singularis* and *specialis*.

De Lubac's discussion of the work of Isaac of Stella further highlights a "universalized" dimension of Mary's being. This move is significant because it opens up a framework that unites Mary with the collective identity of the Church.[56] Following the principles *de specie et genere*, Our Lady singularly represents a special excellence and unparalleled perfection. This, in turn, constitutes her as a unique embodiment of the *universalis* that, according to de Lubac, "includes all instances, and Our Lady is as much a member of the Church as each one of us."[57] "Mary may be said to be 'the universal creature'"[58] whom God has filled "to an eminent degree with the substance of which the Church is formed."[59] She is both a member of the Church and a "genuine, *universal concrete* [who] includes to an eminent degree and in a pure state the sum perfection of all the other members."[60] A very similar conception of the universal dimension of a single individual is Maurice Blondel's notion of the "concrete universal." Although he does not expound it here, de Lubac studies the topic in greater depth in his commentary on Teilhard de Chardin, *L'Éternel féminin* (1968), to be explored in chapter 4.[61] What is already evident here is the pattern that de Lubac traces: there is a development from the *singularis* (the individual reality of Our Lady) to the *specialis* (Our Lady's preeminence), and further to the *universalis* (Our Lady's

54. See *Splendor*, 349; from Paschasius Radbertus, *Expositio in Ps.* 44 (PL 120, 996b, 1001a and d, 1005a, 1053a).

55. *Splendor*, 349n183; de Lubac is referencing Rupert of Deutz, *In Cant.* (PL 168, 941d) *et alii*.

56. This framework of the unity of one and the many will have profound implications for ecclesiology.

57. *Splendor*, 351.

58. Olier, *Traité des saints ordres*, pt. 3, chap. 6; as quoted in *Splendor*, 351n197.

59. Olier, miscellaneous ms., 107; as quoted in *Splendor*, 351n199.

60. *Splendor*, 351; emphasis added.

61. Cf. Maurice Blondel, *Exigences philosophiques du christianisme* (Paris: Presses universitaires de France (P.U.F.), 1956), 185; and *L'Action: essai d'une critique de la vie et d'une science de la pratique* (Paris: P.U.F., 1893), 461; see also de Lubac, *The Eternal Feminine: A Study on the Poem by Teilhard de Chardin Followed by Teilhard and the Problems of Today* (London: William Collins, 1971), 120 and 234.

mystical identification with the Church). Moreover, Isaac of Stella's application of this threefold category to the realities of Church-soul-Mary "manages the union-through-distinction of the three subjects"[62] and underscores that, at its core, the Church-soul-Mary trio constitutes one final reality ["union"] in which Mary can be seen to be the decisive element.

Type / Antitype

The third paradigm is the patristic notion of typology to which de Lubac alludes when he says: "As far as the Christian mind is concerned, Mary is the 'ideal figure of the Church,' the 'sacrament' of her, and the 'mirror in which the whole Church is reflected.'"[63] Ideal figure. Sacrament. Mirror. These ideas represent a foundational Mariological concept found in the patristic tradition: Mary is the figure or type of the Church. Saint Ambrose (340–397 AD) was one of the first to speak explicitly of Our Lady as *typus Ecclesiae*, the one who "shows forth in herself the figure of the holy Church."[64] She "speaks and acts in the name of the Church at every moment of her existence … because she already carries the Church within her, so to speak, and contains her in her wholeness, in her own person."[65]

For de Lubac as a theologian of mystery and paradox, the relationship of a type to its antitype is never a superficial one.[66] Rather, it is characterized by an intrinsic existential link. When de Lubac describes manna as a symbol of the Eucharist and the sacrifice of the Paschal Lamb as the prefigurement of Christ's redemptive death, for instance, he says that the relationship between a type and its antitype is not based on any external resemblance. Instead, "there is between the two an 'inner continuity' and 'ontological bond' because of the same divine Will that is at work on both sides, pursuing from stage to stage one and the same Plan."[67] The same can be said of the relationship of Mary and the Church in de Lubac's thought.

----

62. *Splendor*, 347.

63. *Splendor*, 320; de Lubac combines three sources for this statement: Mary as the "ideal figure" is quoted from Dillenschneider, *Le Mystère de la corédemption mariale* (1951), 79; Mary as the "sacrament" of the Church is quoted from a thirteenth-century hymn, *Mariae praeconio*, (*Analecta humn.*, 54:391); and Mary as the "mirror" of the whole Church is quoted from Pierre Ganne, SJ, "La Vierge Marie dans la vie de l'Église," in *Dialogue sur la Vierge* (1950), 152; see footnotes 28–30, respectively.

64. Ambrose, *In Luc.* bk. 2, no. 7 (PL 15, 1555a); as quoted in *Splendor*, 320.

65. *Splendor*, 320.

66. De Lubac makes a detailed study of the terms type and antitype, mystical, *mysterium*, and *sacramentum* in chapters 2 and 3 of *Corpus Mysticum*.

67. *History and Spirit*, 462.

To say that Our Lady is a type of the Church is to go beyond proposing a mere functional analogy. It is to assert an ontological bond linking the two realities, with "the same divine Will … at work on both sides." The unity of Mary and the Church is not caused by either side of the type/antitype equation, as if Mary were the source of the Church and of all that is realized in the Church; rather, the causal source of the intrinsic relatedness of Mary and the Church is God's wisdom that so ordains this mysterious unity. The patristic conception of Our Lady as *typus ecclesiae* does not establish a causal connection but points to a real, ontological bond founded on the order of grace. This is why de Lubac, following the Church Fathers, does not write about Mary in herself but only in relation to Christ and the Church within the economy of salvation. In this way, de Lubac is able to avoid in his own writings the maximalist tendencies that want to accord the highest praises to Mary apart from the context of her interconnectedness with the Church in the divine plan of salvation.

Recapitulation

In exploring the aspects of the Church as sanctifying (mother) and as sanctified (virgin bride), de Lubac highlights the Assumption of Mary as the pledge and anticipation of the Church's own destiny. On the basis of the theological meaning of the Assumption, Our Lady exemplifies the perfect and final form of the Church's consummate state. Scheeben's theology of perichoresis explicitly places considerations of the Mary-Church configuration in the realm of mystery. Additionally, Isaac of Stella's trio of terms offered a differentiation of that mysterious unity in which Mary is *specialiter* that which is said of the Church *generaliter* and of the faithful soul *singulariter.* De Lubac's further commentary, stating that Mary might also be considered a "*universal concrete* [who] includes to an eminent degree and in a pure state the sum perfection of all the other members"[68] will have weighty application to the Council's ecclesiology on the relationship of the local (i.e., concrete) Church to the universal Church. Likewise, the third paradigm of the Church's relationship to Mary as type to antitype taps into the wealth of patristic theology and serves as a key retrieval of Vatican II. To round out our study of de Lubac's "L'Église et la Vierge Marie" with an emphasis on his attempt to recover the breadth of tradition regarding Mary and the Church, we now turn specifically to his *ressourcement* of patristic sources.

---

68. *Splendor,* 351; emphasis added.

Patristic Sources

De Lubac's dense study of Mary and the Church exhibits his erudite knowledge of the Church Fathers and medieval theologians in connection with contemporary theological developments. His references to prominent Church Fathers like Origen and Augustine alongside obscure figures such as Anastasius of Antioch and Germanus of Constantinople as well as medieval theologians and contemporary authors constitute the rich tapestry of the Christian tradition on Mary from which the Second Vatican Council will also find its inspiration and direction forward. De Lubac's chapter, which spans sixty-five pages in the English edition (Ignatius, 2000), contains a total of 324 footnotes, most of which contain multiple references. The sheer number of de Lubac's sources bespeaks the extent of his *ressourcement*. We would do well to document them in the following index (see Table 2-1).

A significant number of these sources employed in "L'Église et la Vierge Marie" will be directly referenced in both the first schema and the final draft of the Council's chapter on Mary. As a prelude to our study of the Council's Marian debates, we can note that St. Augustine and St. Ambrose—two Latin fathers who have a prominent place in de Lubac's Mariology, will appear again as exemplary figures in the Marian schemata of Vatican II. Augustine, who is referenced over ten times in the Council's original schema and five times in the final draft, appears twenty-three times in de Lubac's chapter. The key text, *de Sancta Virginitate* (PL 40, 399), is cited repeatedly in "L'Église et la Vierge Marie." Ambrose's patristic witness to Mary as a *typus Ecclesiae* in his commentary on Luke 2 (*In Lucam* II; PL 15, 1555) is also deployed in all three texts. Other mutually cited texts include Epiphanius's *Adversus haereses,* Irenaeus's *Adversus Haerses,* and John Damascene's treatise, *de Fide* and various *Homilies.* The Eastern Fathers cited by the Council—such as John Damascene, Andrew of Crete, Germanus of Constantinople, Anastasius of Antioch, and Epiphanius of Salamis—are also common sources utilized by both de Lubac and Vatican II.

In reading "L'Église et la Vierge Marie," moreover, one gets the sense of attending a banquet in which the host has prepared an impressive array of delicacies and dishes of every kind, and as with the widow of Zarephath, the flour bin is not depleted (1 Kings 17). De Lubac's "L'Église et la Vierge Marie" is a magnificent presentation of patristic, medieval, liturgical, and theological sources. With over three hundred footnotes, de Lubac provides invaluable access points into the rich texture of the Christian tradition. What

TABLE 2-1 Selected Footnotes from de Lubac's "The Church and Our Lady"

Page #	Note #	Work	Reference
315	3	**John Damascene**, *The Orthodox Faith*, bk. 3, ch. 12	PG 94, 1029C
317	12	John Damascene, *In Dormitionem*, 4, 1, no. 8	PG 96, 712
318	16	John Damascene, *In Dormitionem*, hom. 1	PG 96, 714
320	27	John Damascene, *In nativ. Mar.*, hom. 2	PG 96, 684a–b
317	11	**Ireneaus**, *Adversus haereses*, bk. 3, ch. 22, no. 4	
343	159	Irenaeus, *Adv. Haer.*, bk. 3 ch. 10, no. 2	
317	12	**Origen**, *In Cant.*, bk. 3	Baehren's edition, 193
317	12	**Augustine**, *De Gen. ad litt.*, bk. 11, ch. 25, no. 32	PL 34, 442
319	22	Augustine, *Sermo 37*	PL 38, 221–35
320	33	Augustine, *De symbolo ad cat.*, ch 1	PL 40, 661
323	44	Augustine, *Sermones*	PL 38, 1019, 1074; PL 46, 937–38
323	44	Augustine, *De sancta virginitate*, ch. 3	PL 40, 398
324	50	Augustine, *De sancta virginitate*, ch. 2	PL 40, 397
324	50	Augustine, *Sermo 138, no. 9*	PL 38, 768
324	51	Augustine, *De sancta virginitate*, ch. 2	PL 40, 397
324	52	Augustine, *De nuptiis et concupiscentia*, bk. 2, ch. 4, no. 12	PL 44, 443
324	52	Augustine, *In Joannem, tract. 120, no. 2*	PL 35, 1953
324	52	Augustine, *In Ps. 40, no. 10*	PL 36, 461
324	55	Augustine, *Sermo 191, no. 2*	PL 38, 1010
324	55	Augustine, *In Ps. 147, no. 10*	PL 37, 1920
324	55	Augustine, *Contra Julianum*, bk. 2, ch. 10, no. 37	PL 44, 700
324	55	Augustine, *In Joannem, tract. 13, no. 12*	PL 35, 1499
328	75	Augustine, *De sancta virginitate*, ch. 5	PL 40, 397
340	133	Augustine, *De sancta virginitate*, ch. 5–6	PL 40, 399
340	137	Augustine, *Sermo 191, no. 3*	PL 38, 1010
347	175	Augustine, *De sancta virginitate*, ch. 24	PL 40, 409
348	178	Augustine, *De doctrina christiana*, bk. 3, ch. 34, nos. 47–49	PL 34, 83–86
356	220	Augustine, *Sermo 46, no. 35*	PL 38, 290
356	220	Augustine, *Sermo 138, no. 9; Speculum*	PL 38, 768
356	220	Augustine, *Speculum*	PL 34, 925
379	320	Augustine, *Sermo 252, no. 11*	PL 38, 1178
317	12	**Honorius of Autun**, *In Cant.*	PL 172, 639a
346	170	Honorius of Autun, *Sigillum*, 4	PL 172, 506a

TABLE 2-1 (*continued*)

Page #	Note #	Work	Reference
352	205	Honorius of Autun, *Sigillum Beatae Mariae*	PL 174, 498a–499c
372	294	Honorius of Autun, *Expositio in Cantica*	PL 172, 494c–d
318	16	**Anastasius of Antioch**, In Annunt.	
318	16	**Paschasius Radbertus**, *Expositio in Ps. 44, 1,1*	PL 120, 1009a
324	51	Paschasius Radbertus, *In Ps. 44*	PL 120, 1101c
324	53	Paschasius Rabdertus, *De partu virginis*	PL 120, 1384b
329	78	Paschasius Radbertus, *In Matt.*	PL 120, 104c
340	134	Paschasius Radbertus, *Expositia in Matt.*, bk. 2, ch. 3	PL 120, 172–74
348	179	Paschasius Radbertus, *In Matt.*, bk. 2	PL 120, 103d, 104c–d, 106c
318	16	**Laurence of Brindisi**, *Sermo 1 in Assumptionem,* ch 10	*Opera Omnia*, 1928, 1:583
352	203	Laurence of Brindisi, *Super fundamenta ejus, sermo 4, ch 1*	
318	17	**Jerome**, *In Ezech.*, bk. 13	PL 25, 416–20
318	17	Jerome, *Epist. 48, no. 21*	PL 22, 510
339	130	Jerome, *In Jer. 1, 44; In Matt. 1, 15*	PL 26, 57a
339	130	Jerome, *Adversus Jovinianum*, bk. 1, ch. 31	PL 23, 254
341	143	Jerome, *Epist. 9, ch. 9*	PL 30, 132a–b
347	175	Jerome, *Tract. de Ps. 86*	Anedota Maredsolana, bk. 3,2, p. 104
356	220	Jerome, *Epist. 53 & 107*	PL 22, 547 and 876
358	229	Jerome, *Tract. de Ps. 86*	
364	256	Jerome, *Epist. ad Paulum et Eust.*	PL 30, 134–35
318	20	**Origen**, *In Exod.*, hom. 9, no. 3; *In Ps. 18, v. 6*	PG 12, 1243–44
331	89	Origen, *In Joannem*, bk 1, no. 6	PL 14, 12
340	137	Origen, *In Cantica*, prol. "Immaculata Ecclesia"	Baehren's ed.
347	175	Origen, *In Cantica*, bks. 1 & 3	Baehren's ed., 90 and 232
351	200	Origen, *In Cantica*, hom. 2	Baehren's ed., 51
358	229	Origen, *In Cantica comm.*	PG 13, 207c
318	20	**Andrew of Crete**, *In Nativitatem BM, sermo 4*	PG 97, 877d
318	20	Andrew of Crete, *In Dormitionem S Mariae, sermo 3*	PG 97, 1090
352	205	Andrew of Crete, *In Dormitionem, sermo 2*	PG 97, 1101
319	22	**Bede the Venerable**, *De Muliere forti libellus*	PL 91, 1039–52
319	24	Bede the Venerable, *Explanatio Apocalypsis*, bk 2	PL 93, 165–66

TABLE 2-1 (*continued*)

Page #	Note #	Work	Reference
324	55	Bede the Venerable, *In Joannem*	PL 92, 675b
328	75	Bede the Venerable, *In Lucam, I, no. 2*	PL 92, 330
329	77	Bede the Venerable, *In Apoc.*	PL 93, 165–66
341	143	Bede the Venerable, *In Cant., bk. 4*	PL 91, 1148–50
345	166	Bede the Venerable, *In Lucam, bk. 1*	PL 92, 346–47
348	178	Bede the Venerable, *In Apoc., preface*	PL 93, 131–32
373	299	Bede the Venerable, *In Apoc.*	PL 93, 206c
319	24	**Rupert of Deutz**, *In Apoc., bk 4, ch. 12*	PL 169, 1043a
321	38	Rupert of Deutz, *De Spiritu Sancto, bk. 1, ch. 8*	
330	83	Rupert of Deutz	PL 169, 170
331	89	Rupert of Deutz, *In Joannem, bk. 13*	PL 169, 789–90
338	126	Rupert of Deutz, *In Cantica, bk. 4*	PL 168, 895–97
341	140	Rupert of Deutz, *In Cantica, bk. 4*	PL 168, 899a–b
349	183	Rupert of Deutz, *In Cantica*	PL 168, 941d
351	196	Rupert of Deutz, *In Apoc., bk. 7, ch. 12*	PL 169, 1043a
352	209	Rupert of Deutz, *In Isaiam, bk.2, ch. 31*	
363	248	Rupert of Deutz, *In Mattaeum, bk. 2*	PL 168, 1348c
367	272	Rupert of Deutz	PL 169, 1550
369	283	Rupert of Deutz, *In Cantica, bk. 7*	PL 168, 962a
372	294	Rupert of Deutz, *De glorificatione Trin, bk. 6, ch. 13*	PL 169, 155
320	33	**Ambrose**, *In Luc., bk. 2, no. 7*	PL 15, 1555a
321	35	Ambrose, *De institutione virginis, ch. 14, no. 89*	PL 16, 326
323	46	Ambrose, *In Lucam, bk. 2, ch. 57*	PL 15, 1573a
324	49	Ambrose, *In Lucam, bk. 2, ch. 7*	PL 15, 1555b
324	49	Ambrose, *De virginibus, bk. 1, ch 3, no. 12*	PL 16, 192a
324	49	Ambrose, *De institutione virginis, ch. 14, vv. 88–89*	PL 16, 322c–d, cf. 344a–b
331	89	Ambrose, *In Lucam, bk. 10, no. 134; bk. 6, no. 5*	PL 15, 1838a–b, 1700c
333	93	Ambrose, *Epist. 63, no. 33*	PL 16, 1198b
340	137	Ambrose, *De virginitate, bk. 1, ch. 6, no. 31*	PL 16, 197
340	137	Ambrose, *In Lucam, bk. 2, ch. 26*	PL 15, 1562a
351	201	Ambrose, *In Lucam bk. 2, ch. 26*	PL 15, 1561d
358	229	Ambrose, *De Isaac, ch. 1, no. 2*	PL 14, 503a
358	229	Ambrose, *In Lucam bk. 8, ch. 10*	PL 15, 1768a–b
358	229	Ambrose, *De sacramentis, bk. 5, ch. 2, nos. 5–8*	

TABLE 2-1 *(continued)*

Page #	Note #	Work	Reference
264	256	Ambrose, *De inst. virginis, 87–89*	PL 16, 326–27
371	290	Ambrose, *De virginitate, ch. 4, no. 20*	PL 16, 271b
377	314	Ambrose, *De Spiritu Sancto, bk. 3, ch. 11, no. 80*	PL 16, 795a
321	37	**Ambrose Autpert,** *Sermo de lectione evangelica*	PL 89, 1302b; cf. 1304d
343	160	Ambrose Autpert, *In Purif.*	PL 89, 1294–1304
345	166	Ambrose Autpert	PL 89, 1301
323	44	**Leo the Great,** *Sermo 21, ch. 1*	PL 54, 191b
323	46	Leo the Great, *Sermo 24, ch. 3*	PL 54, 206a
323	46	Leo the Great, *Sermo 63, ch.6*	356b–c
337	122	Leo the Great, *Sermo 26, ch. 2*	PL 54, 213b
337	123	Leo the Great, *Sermo 63, ch. 6*	PL 54, 356b–c
323	47	**Epiphanius of Salamis,** *Expositio fidei*	PG 42, 776a–b, 781 c–d
330	84	Epiphanius of Salamis, *Haeres. 78, ch. 18*	PG 42, 728–29
356	220	Epiphanius of Salamis, *Expositio fidei*	PG 42, 776–85, 809, 821
327	67	**Isaac of Stella,** *Sermo 61*	PL 194, 1683
327	67	Isaac of Stella, *Sermones 27 & 45*	cols. 1778–79; 1841
337	124	Isaac of Stella, *In Assumptione BM, sermo 1*	PL 194, 1863a
375	308	Isaac of Stella, *In Assumptione BM, sermo 1*	PL 194, 1865c, 1866a
330	84	**Peter Chrysologus,** *Sermo 117*	PL 52, 521b
331	89	**Gerhoh of Reichersberg,** *Liber de gloria, ch. 10*	PL 194, 1105c
342	148	Gerhoh of Reichersberg, *Liber de gloria, ch. 10*	PL 194, 1105b
351	196	Gerhoh of Reichersberg, *Liber de gloria*	PL 194, 1105d
359	231	Gerhoh of Reichersberg, *Liber de gloria*	PL 194, 1105b
369	280	Gerhoh of Reichersberg, *Liber de gloria, ch. 10*	PL 194, 1105b
337	121	**Cyril of Alexandria,** *Hom. Div., 4, in fine*	PG 77, 992
341	141	Cyril of Alexandria, *Hom. Div., 4*	PG 77, 996
358	229	Cyril of Alexandria, *Fragmenta in Cantica*	PG 69, 1284c
340	134	**Germanus of Constantinople,** *In Praesentione Deiparae, hom. 1*	PG 98, 297
370	286	**Godefridus of Admont**	PL 174, 972

will be explored further in chapter 5 is the significant increase in patristic sources between the first schema and the final text of Vatican II's *De Beata Maria Virgine*. Moreover, the continuity between de Lubac's preconciliar writing and the patristic sources deployed at the Council point to the likelihood that the Council fathers indubitably drew from the same wellspring of inspiration as our *ressourcement* theologian.

"L'Église et la Vierge Marie" is both similar to and different from the writings of de Lubac's contemporaries who also sought to return to the sources of early Marian thought. With the authors of Marian *ressourcement* on the eve of the Council, de Lubac shares the aim of resurrecting the rich sources of Scripture and Tradition on Mary. Unlike his contemporaries, however, de Lubac's chapter on Mary and the Church is not intended to be a scholarly analysis. As he explains in the introduction to the book, the chapters of *Méditation sur l'Église* were collected from various conferences for priests from 1946–1949. He states plainly that "the reader should not expect it to be 'scientific.' Still less should it be treated as a pocket treatise on the Church."[69] This context explains why de Lubac sometimes employs his sources uncritically.

De Lubac's tone in "L'Église et la Vierge Marie" contrasts with what one finds in the writings of other *ressourcement* theologians, such as Yves Congar. Christopher Ruddy has shown that "Congar's Mariology unfolds largely in the clash between two theological approaches: an isolated maximalism and an economic-soteriological integration."[70] This clash gave Congar's works on Mary a sustained polemical tone and tenor. Reflecting in his diary on his experience in the Council's Preparatory Theological Commission in 1961, Congar describes his "need to fight, in the name of the Gospel and of the apostolic faith, against a development, a Mediterranean and Irish proliferation, of a Mariology which does not come from Revelation, but is backed up by pontifical texts."[71] The same reactionary and polemical tone is not to be found in de Lubac's chapter or elsewhere in his other writings on Our Lady and the Church.

De Lubac does caution against "certain possible exaggerations"[72] on the

---

69. *Splendor*, 9.

70. Christopher Ruddy, "A Very Considerable Place in the Mystery of Christ and the Church? Yves Congar on Mary," in *Mary on the Eve of the Second Vatican Council*, ed. John Cavadini and Danielle Peters (Notre Dame, IN: University of Notre Dame Press, 2017), 115.

71. Yves Congar, *My Journal of the Council*, trans. Mary J. Ronayne and Mary C. Boulding (Collegeville, MN: Liturgical, 2012), 54.

72. *Splendor*, 334.

superiority of Mary to the Church, but his tone is sober and markedly positive. He judiciously avoids false exaggerations of Mary's status without falling into a pusillanimous hesitancy to acknowledge her due honor as the Christian tradition has professed it. Moreover, de Lubac is true to the methodology he describes in the introductory remarks to *Méditation sur l'Église*; his goal is to provide "the reader a direct line on the essential texts of Tradition; for my ambition is simply to be its echo—that is all. I simply want to share with others the recurrent thrill that comes from recognizing that impressive and undivided voice in all its modulations and all its harmonics."[73]

De Lubac's work of *ressourcement* will come to full flowering at the Council. His advocacy of the idea of Mary as Mother of the Church, his theological sensitivity to the significance of Mary's perpetual virginity (which was challenged on the eve of the Council), and his ecumenical sensitivity, especially on the topic of Mary's mediation, constitute a few of the seeds of continuity between de Lubac's chapter and the Council's teaching on Mary and the Church. Moreover, de Lubac anticipated the synthesis that the Council worked so hard to define, a synthesis achieved by way of an even-handed *ressourcement,* retrieving the robust tradition within its proper context and without falling into a deconstructive minimalism. Written ten years before the start of the Vatican II Council, this dense, final chapter of *Méditation sur l'Église* represents a theological gem of the Christian understanding of the multifaceted relationship between Mary and the Church. Its sober steadiness in reporting the sources of the Christian tradition serves as a perennial paradigm of *ressourcement* and integration.

73. *Splendor,* 9.

CHAPTER 3

Patristic and Medieval Exegesis

A Scriptural *Ressourcement*

In the previous chapter, we examined de Lubac's retrieval of the maternal and virginal dimensions of Mary and the Church as found in the patrimony of the Church Fathers and medieval theologians. This chapter completes our study of "L'Église et la Vierge Marie" with what may be called de Lubac's "scriptural *ressourcement*." When it comes to the direct Scriptural foundations of Mariology, however, de Lubac does not expound the typical texts which one might expect to find in a systematic treatment of Mariology. Some attention is given, for example, to Luke's account of the Annunciation and Visitation as well as to the book of Revelation, but these passages do not constitute de Lubac's key Scriptural focus. Rather, the Scriptural text to which de Lubac devotes the entire latter half of his chapter on "L'Église et la Vierge Marie" is a book of the Old Testament: the Song of Songs.

In view of de Lubac's interest in spiritual exegesis, as manifested by his voluminous publications on the topic, the Song of Songs—a book filled with nuptial imagery and figurative meaning—is a likely choice for his Marian *ressourcement* because it lends itself to his fundamental orientation to mystery, the essential context for all of de Lubac's theology.[1] As one scholar has

---

1. In his memoirs, de Lubac reveals the centrality of mystery and mysticism for his work,

noted, "De Lubac's mysticism is a discovery of spiritual meaning in historical realities.... a mysticism of the incarnate rather than an escape to something otherworldly or disembodied."[2] This insight into de Lubac's orientation to mystery and an "incarnate" or historically-embedded mysticism helps us understand de Lubac's concentration on the Song of Songs. The epithalamic tradition enshrined in the text illumines the mystery of both Mary and the Church as virgin bride.

In this chapter, we explore de Lubac's predilection for the spiritual sense of Scripture and how it leads him to the culminating Marian meaning of the Song of Songs. His reading of the Song draws especially from the medieval exegete, Rupert of Deutz, in whose commentary de Lubac finds the themes of bridal love, mystical union, and anagogical fulfillment. These are the golden threads in the tapestry of Christian mysticism, and they all converge in "Marian exegesis" as an interpretative key to the close relationship of Mary and the Church. In an effort to contextualize de Lubac's Scriptural *ressourcement*,[3] we first consider the enduring value of the spiritual interpretation of Scripture in relation to the emergence of the Catholic biblical movement.

Spiritual Exegesis

De Lubac's Predilection for the Spiritual Sense

On the feastday of St. Jerome in 1943, Pope Pius XII issued a major encyclical which became the Magna Carta of biblical studies. With its approval of modern critical methods, *Divino Afflante Spiritu* represented a quantum leap for Catholic biblical scholarship in its affirmation of a recovery of the literal sense of Scripture through textual criticism. Even as the encyclical did not deny the value of spiritual exegesis, the underlying tension between the two methods is evident, and this tension continued until the Second Vatican Council affirmed both approaches.[4]

Around the same time as the landmark 1943 encyclical, de Lubac was

stating that "the idea for my book on Mysticism has been my inspiration in everything; I form my judgments on the basis of it, it provides me with a means to classify my ideas in proportion to it"; ASC, 113.

2. Susan Wood, *Spiritual Exegesis and the Church in the Theology of Henri de Lubac* (Grand Rapids, MI: Eerdmans, 1998), 211.

3. *Histoire et esprit: l'Intelligence de l'Écriture d'après Origène* (1950) and the multivolume *Exégèse médiévale: les quatres sens de l'ećriture* (1959, 1961, 1963, 1964) are unparalleled contributions to theology and exegesis.

4. *Dei Verbum*, no. 12.

also engaged in scholarship on exegetical topics, but specifically on spiritual rather than critical exegesis. In 1942, he launched the series *Sources chrétiennes* with Jean Daniélou, devoting the premier issue to Gregory of Nyssa's spiritual interpretation of the book of Exodus, *La Vie de Moïse*. De Lubac's own study of Origen's spiritual interpretation of Scripture, *Histoire et esprit,* came into print in 1950 and the multivolume *Exégèse médiévale* in the subsequent years of Vatican II. De Lubac recognized the need for rigorous historical-critical exegesis, often expressing his "deep sympathy with the immense work of research going on today."[5] Yet his own scholarship maintained an unwavering concentration on the spiritual sense. What value did he see in it?

For de Lubac, spiritual exegesis was a movement of genius and creativity "in accordance with ... a very pure conception of the Christian life."[6] He argues that it "constitutes one of the most remarkable phenomena of the early Church,"[7] and because it grew out of the direct religious experience of the early Christians who interpreted their newly found way of life by reflecting on the Old Covenant and expounding its fulfillment in the New, it propagated the message of Christianity with great potency. De Lubac was convinced of the close association of the spiritual sense and the spiritual life, stating in an essay on mysticism that "the mystical or spiritual understanding of Scripture and the mystical or spiritual life are, in the end, one and the same. Christian mysticism is that understanding pushed to its most fruitful phase by its four traditional dimensions—history, 'allegory' or doctrine, ethics or 'tropology,' and anagogy—each of which is absorbed by the following one."[8] For de Lubac, the pulse of the Christian life is embodied in the spiritual senses and comes to perfection in anagogical or eschatological fullness in Christ. The entire dynamic is Christocentric.

The Spiritual Sense of Nuptial Love

The attention that de Lubac accorded to the Song in his discussion of Mary and the Church is best understood in light of the Song's unique content. Also called the Canticle of Canticles or the Song of Solomon, the Song of

5. Henri de Lubac, *Paradoxes of Faith* (San Francisco: Ignatius Press, 1948), 7, and "A Theologian Speaks," 32. See also de Lubac's defense of both spiritual and scientific exegesis in ASC, 311–14 [5:2].

6. Johann A. Möhler, *L'Unité dans l'Église,* appendix 7, French trans. in *Unam Sanctam* (1938), 260–61, as quoted in *History and Spirit,* 429.

7. *Medieval Exegesis,* 1:xix.

8. "Mysticism and Mystery," 58.

Songs is essentially a love poem focused on the courtship and consummation of the love of the bride and bridegroom, complete with vivid descriptions of their passionate longing for one another.[9]

The Song's language of sensual desire has been the cause of some debate, specifically over the appropriateness of its inclusion in the Hebrew Scriptures and its further adoption into the Christian canon.[10] However, the ancient writers of both the Jewish and Christian traditions have come to concur that the text should not be read merely for its literal sense (i.e., carnal expressions of passion) but for its spiritual sense, revealing the intensity of divine love.[11] In *Méditation sur l'Église,* de Lubac refers to the commentary of Rabbi Akiva (d. AD 135), who defended the canonicity of the Song with this statement: "God forbid that anyone refute the authority of the Song! ... [F]or all the ages are not worth the day on which the Song of Songs was given to Israel; for all the Writings are holy, but the Song of Songs is the Holy of Holies."[12] In other words, "the Song of Songs was admitted to and retained in the Jewish canon of the Scriptures because the Jews saw it as a symbolic expression of the love between Israel and Israel's God."[13]

Origen of Alexandria, one of the first Christian commentators on the Song of Songs,[14] also warned: "For anyone who does not know how to listen

9. Cf. Marvin Pope's *Song of Songs: A New Translation with Introduction and Commentary,* Anchor Bible (Garden City, NY: Doubleday, 1977), an excellent, comprehensive work. See also J. Paul Tanner's helpful overview of "The History of Interpretation of the Song of Songs," *Bibliotheca Sacra* 154 (1997): 23–46. In addition to his extensive commentary, Roland Murphy's *The Song of Songs: A Commentary on the Book of the Canticles or the Song of Songs* (Minneapolis: Fortress Press, 1990), 203–20, provides a chronological bibliography of works on the Song of Songs. For a theological commentary, see Paul Griffiths, *The Song of Songs* in the Brazos Theological Commentary series (Grand Rapids, MI: Brazos Press, 2011).

10. Cf. James A. Fischer, *Song of Songs,* Collegeville Bible Commentary (Collegeville, MN: Liturgical Press, 1986); Fischer describes the qualms regarding the inclusion of the Song in the list of sacred writings, stating: "The problem with the Song of Songs is to find some honest reason why it should be in the Bible. Unlike most other books of the Old Testament, it has nothing to do with the sacred history, the law, the covenant, or the prophets. In fact, it does not even mention God" (789).

11. According to R. Murphy, there is general scholarly consensus that although the Song's canonicity in the Jewish tradition cannot be exactly determined, it is probable that the book had already entered the Jewish canon by AD 100, as direct reference to the Song is found in the Mishnah (*Song of Songs: A Commentary,* 6).

12. Cf. *Splendor,* 355; de Lubac provides part of this quotation but does not provide a reference; the full quotation can be found in Herbert Danby, trans., *The Mishnah* (London: Oxford University, 1933), 782; see also Pope, *Song of Songs: New Translation,* 19.

13. *Splendor,* 354.

14. Origen, *Homiliae in Canticum canticorum* and *Commentarium in Canticum canticorum* in *Origenes Werke,* ed. W. A. Baehrens, vol. 8 (GCS 33; Leipzig: J.C. Hinrichs, 1925), 20–241; English translation: *Origen: The Song of Songs. Commentary and Homilies,* Ancient Christian Writers Series 26, trans. R. P. Lawson (London: Longman/Green, 1957).

to the language of erotic desire with chaste ears and a pure mind will pervert what he hears and be turned from the inner self to the outward, from the spirit to the flesh; and he will foster carnal desires within himself, and it will appear to be the case that he is roused and encouraged to carnal lust by the Scriptures."[15] According to Origen, the Song is intended only for those who have attained real spiritual maturity because only they are capable of grasping the spiritual meaning of the Song's depiction of love's desire for union.

De Lubac notes that the divine, nuptial mysticism that constitutes the central meaning of the Song of Songs is "a scriptural theme that goes back to the prophet Hosea, is to be found in the books of Isaiah, Jeremiah, and Ezekiel, and is worked out in the Forty-Fourth Psalm."[16] Paul's letters also manifest evidence of an awareness and appreciation of the nuptial dimension of the Song and of the aptness of its application to the Church.[17] In the Epistle to the Ephesians, Paul describes the Church as a bride "glorious ..., not having spot or wrinkle" (Eph 5:27), and to the Corinthians, he writes of God's divine jealousy (2 Cor 11:2). Even within this longstanding motif of nuptial love in Scripture, the Song of Song stands out for de Lubac with its singular figure of the bride who represents not only Israel but also the Church, every individual soul, and the blessed Virgin Mary. No other instance of nuptial imagery in Scripture has enjoyed a Marian interpretation as the Song of Songs. De Lubac's theological *ressourcement* of the spiritual sense of Scripture highlights Marian exegesis as the peak development of the exegetical tradition on the Song, throwing into grand relief the terminus and telos of the entire dynamic of spiritual development, leading us "into a deeper penetration into the plan of God."[18] We next survey the stages of this development.

Patristic Exegesis: A Precursor to Marian Exegesis

Patristic exegesis focused on the spiritual meaning of Scripture, expounding the Christological and ecclesiological readings of the Song. This spiritual sense was an essential precursor to the Marian exegesis that would follow in later centuries. Initially, the "deeper penetration into the plan of God" (as quoted above) consisted primarily in the transposition of the Song as a

15. Origen, *In Canticum Canticorum*; the translation provided here is taken from Richard Alfred Norris, ed., *The Song of Songs: Interpreted by Early Christian and Medieval Commentators* (Grand Rapids, MI: Eerdmans, 2003), 2.

16. *Splendor*, 354.

17. Cf. *Splendor*, 356–57.

18. *Splendor*, 355.

symbolic expression of God's love for Israel to an expression of Christ's love for the Church, a kind of ecclesial, nuptial mysticism. The Church Fathers otherwise did not expound the Marian dimension of the Song beyond associating a few isolated verses with Mary.

It was Hippolytus of Rome (c. 170–236 AD) who first applied the Song to the union of Christ and his Church and thus also provided the first Christian commentaries with "what was to be their unchanged foundation throughout all the centuries."[19] The ecclesiological interpretation of the Song that Hippolytus expounded set an important exegetical precedent, and the reception of the Song into the Christian canon in the patristic era suggests an awareness that "within the framework of the history of salvation, the Church, after the Incarnation of the Word, carried on the role of Israel."[20] The Song thus represented, for Hippolytus and the Christian exegetes after him, a point of continuity and distinction between Israel and Christianity. It is a transition from "history" to "allegory" as a consequence of the "great real *transitio*, the great and unique and decisive 'passing over' from the Old Testament to the New."[21] Spiritual exegesis of the Song thus underscores the continuity and distinction between the Old Testament and the New Testament, as propounded by de Lubac in *Exégèse médiévale*.[22]

In addition to this profound transition, some "scattered traces" of a seminal Marian exegesis began to appear in the early Church, in the writings of Epiphanius, Andrew of Crete, Theodore the Studite, George of Nicomedia, and Ephrem.[23] In the Christian West, Jerome and Ambrose associated Mary's perpetual virginity with Song 4:12: "A garden enclosed, my sister, my bride, a garden enclosed, a fountain sealed." In *Adversus Jovinianum*, Jerome explained the verse in this way: "In being closed and sealed, it is like the Mother of the Lord, Mother and Virgin. Hence too in the Saviour's new sepulcher which was hewn in the hardest (purest) rock, no one else was laid before or after. And yet this perpetual Virgin is Mother of many virgins."[24]

---

19. *Splendor*, 355–56; cf. Hippolytus of Rome, *Fragmenta in Canticum canticorum* (PG 10, 627–30). According to Murphy (*Song of Songs: A Commentary*, 14–15), there are only extant fragments of Hippolytus's commentary, covering Song 1:1–3:8, originally written in Greek and preserved in various languages.

20. *Splendor*, 355.

21. *Splendor*, 357.

22. See "Unity of the Two Testaments," in *Medieval Exegesis*, 1:225–68.

23. Cf. *Splendor*, 364.

24. Jerome, *Adversus Jovinianum* 1.31 (PL 23, 254), as quoted in Rachel Fulton, "'*Quae est ista quae ascendit sicut aurora consurgens?*': The Song of Songs as the *Historia* for the Office of the Assumption," *Mediaeval Studies* 60 (1998): 55. In *Splendor*, 364n256, de Lubac provides reference

De Lubac further notes that Origen's mystical exegesis expresses a kind of coalescence of the Church and the soul, the respective subjects of allegorical and tropological exegesis. He says that the espousal of both the Church and the soul to Christ "constitute, not two keys that can be used alternatively, but one—'*idem est.*'"[25] Furthermore, the fact that "the dominant interpretations of earlier periods tended to be absorbed, rather than discarded, by later interpretations"[26] allowed for an ever-deepening interpretation of the figure of the bride. It is within this "organic exegesis"[27] established by the Church Fathers that a Marian exegesis develops in the medieval era. In championing the spiritual meaning of the sacred texts, patristic exegesis served as an important precursor to the robust Marian exegesis that emerged in the Middle Ages.

Medieval Exegesis: An Anagogical Emphasis

The commentary tradition which laid emphasis on the allegorical and tropological senses continued to proliferate in the monastic exegesis of the Middle Ages.[28] Until then, with but a few exceptions, the early commentaries rarely applied the Song to Mary.[29] Beginning with the writings of Carolingian Abbot of Picardy, Paschasius Radbertus (785–865), though, one finds a new and ample application of the Song to Mary. In his exposition *De Assumptione Beatae Mariae Virginis* (also known as *Cogitis me*), Paschasius employs the Song extensively in his exposition on the Assumption of Mary, and his work is considered by scholars to be his greatest contribution to Song exegesis.

The subtle shift of emphasis away from identifying the bride as both *ecclesia* and *anima* to identifying her as the individual figure of Mary was motivated, in large part, by developments in the liturgical tradition of the Latin West. As the liturgy evolved, so too did the the exegetical tradition, and these developments gave rise to a specifically Marian exegesis—something

---

to St. Jerome, *Epist. Ad Paulum et Eust.* (PL 30, 134–35), and St. Ambrose, *De inst. virginis*, 87–89 (PL 16, 326–27).

25. *Splendor*, 360.

26. E. Ann Matter, *The Voice of My Beloved: The Song of Songs in Western Medieval Christianity* (Philadelphia: University of Pennsylvania Press, 1990), 201.

27. *Splendor*, 360.

28. See *Medieval Exegesis*, 2:143–53.

29. See Ann W. Astell, *The Song of Songs in the Middle Ages* (Ithaca, NY: Cornell University Press, 1990), 42–72. According to Astell, early exegetes—namely Ambrose, Jerome, Justus von Urgel, Bede, two Carolingian writers (Paul the Deacon and Paschasius Radbertus), and Peter Damian—laid the groundwork for a Marian interpretation of the *Canticum*.

of an exegetical novelty.[30] In the Carolingian era, the addition of the feasts of the Assumption and the Nativity of the Virgin to the Frankish calendars occasioned the incorporation of passages from the Song of Songs into the Office. For example, Song 6:9, "Who is she who ascends like the rising dawn, beautiful as the moon, chosen as the sun, terrible as the ordered ranks of the army?" became the antiphon for the feast of the Assumption.[31] This adaptation of the Song for liturgical purposes opened the way for further developments in the commentary tradition.[32]

Considering that the medieval commentators of Scripture were monks and canons whose lives revolved around the liturgy, it was only natural that liturgical developments employing the Song of Songs would give rise to more formal exegeses of the texts. Exegetical insights derived from the monks' *lectio divina* were imported into their theological treatises.[33] Then, once certain verses of the Song of Songs were introduced into the liturgy for the Marian feasts of the Assumption and Nativity, identifying the bride as Mary, the medieval exegetes began to see the *entire* Song as an apt expression of the mystical union of love between God and Mary.

Although de Lubac does not comment in detail on these liturgical developments, he does note that the writings of Paschasius Radbertus show how commonplace this Marian interpretation had become by the ninth century.[34] In the twelfth century, a systematized Marian exegesis formally took shape, beginning with Honorious of Autun (1080–1140) and taking its most comprehensive form in the writings of Rupert of Deutz (c. 1075–1129).

---

30. See Rachel Fulton, "Mimetic Devotion, Marian Exegesis, and the Historical Sense of the Song of Songs," *Viator* 27, no. 1 (1996): 85–116; Matter, *Voice of My Beloved*, 151–77; and Astell, *Song of Songs in the Middle Ages*, 42–72, for in-depth studies of this historical development.

31. Here we witness how the antiphon is adapted for the liturgy: the Vulgate text uses the word *progreditur*, or "to go forth"; but the liturgical text employs a different word altogether, *ascedit*, to draw the connection of Song 6:9 to the Assumption of Mary.

32. Fulton, "Mimetic Devotion, Marian Exegesis," 90; see also Brian Daley, "The *Nouvelle Théologie* and the Patristic Revival," *International Journal of Systematic Theology* 7, no. 4 (2005): 364.

33. Cf. Fulton, "Mimetic Devotion, Marian Exegesis," 86; Fulton contests the thesis that the Marian reading of the Song developed directly from Scriptural exegesis and argues instead for its liturgical provenance: "The Marian reading depended not upon the antecedent allegorical and tropological readings of the Song, but on the use of the Song in the liturgies for the Assumption and the Nativity of the Virgin . . . liturgical use had no patristic precedent." While Fulton has a point that the liturgical use of the Song does not have a patristic precedence, I am inclined to assert that that liturgical use developed in continuity with the patristic exegesis that preceded it, since, as noted above, these liturgical developments flourished in the monastic context and its practice of *lectio divina* and spiritual exegesis.

34. Cf. *Splendor*, 365, with reference to Paschasius Radbertus, *In Matthaeum*, bk. 2, proemium (PL 120, 106). See also the sermons of Ambrose Autpert (eighth century) and Peter Damian (eleventh century).

Rupert of Deutz, De incarnatione Domini

When de Lubac speaks of the "fruitful spontaneity" of monastic exegesis that preserved and expounded the doctrine of the spiritual sense inherited from the Fathers, he highlights Rupert's contribution and refers to him as the Benedictine who "stands like a giant at the threshold of the twelfth century."[35] For de Lubac, Rupert is a "most perfect witness of the traditional monastic theology"[36] and "an eminently traditional author"[37] who "has so profoundly assimilated it [the patristic method] that he proceeds with ease as though still being one of the ancients. Instead of slavishly copying their interpretations, he freely participates in their spirit."[38]

In *Histoire et esprit*, de Lubac attributes to Rupert "some true strokes of inspiration: such as the application to the Virgin Mary ... of texts already understood of the Church and of each soul."[39] In *Exégèse médiévale*, he describes Rupert's creative genius as "the liberty of a great mind ... a free but deep reflection upon the most central themes of the most traditional thought."[40] The evidence de Lubac provides of this "free but deep reflection" is, again, Rupert's exegesis of the Song of Songs, a contribution considered to be "the first coherent commentary that celebrates the marriage of Christ and the Church in their principle, in the mystery of the incarnation of the Word."[41]

This commentary, entitled *De incarnatione Domini* (c. 1125/1126), seeks out the Marian meaning of each verse of the Song.[42] It was a bold innovation at the time, and John van Engen, Rupert's biographer, explains that the Benedictine exegete justified his work "on the grounds that just as all Scripture tends toward Christ the Word, so also all prophecy converges upon Mary, the bearer of that Word."[43] Although it departed from the tradition that preceded him, Rupert's Marian interpretation carefully situated itself in

35. *Medieval Exegesis*, 3:163.

36. *Medieval Exegesis*, 3:173.

37. *Medieval Exegesis*, 3:172.

38. *Medieval Exegesis*, 3:170.

39. *History and Spirit*, 480–81.

40. *Medieval Exegesis*, 3:171.

41. *Medieval Exegesis*, 3:171.

42. Rupert of Deutz, *De incarnatione Domini* (PL 168, 837–962); see also *Corpus Christianorum Continuatio Medievalis* (CCCM) 26, ed. Rhaban Haacke (Turnhout: Brepols, 1974); the title "*De incarnatione Domini*" is found in *Bibliothèque Royale* cod. 10608 (c.13), a manuscript now in Brussels; Rupert also wrote on the Gospels of John and Matthew, the Apocalypse, the twelve minor prophets, the Pentateuch, and the former Prophets.

43. John van Engen, *Rupert of Deutz* (Berkeley: University of California Press, 1983), 294.

the context of the mystery of the Incarnation, maintaining a Christocentric framework for interpreting the figure of the Bride as Mary.

This Christocentrism is crucial because it validates the focus on Mary as essentially a focus on the Lord; Mary always leads to her Son. Moreover, de Lubac's statement describing Rupert's commentary as one that "celebrates the marriage of Christ and the Church *in their principle*, in the mystery of the incarnation of the Word"[44] draws a critical connection between the nuptial relationship of Christ and the Church as his bride and the nuptial relationship of the Word and human nature. The latter relationship—namely, that of the Word and human nature in the mystery of the Incarnation—is the essential principle of all nuptial mysticism, particularly the nuptial mysticism relating to Mary in Rupert's exegesis.

The Marian sense of the Song unites the historical and spiritual senses. Historical interpretation is evident in Rupert's focus on the events of Mary's life. A further level of mystical interpretation is found in the bride's expressed sentiments of love and longing, which are interpreted as words from Mary's own contemplative heart.[45] The opening verses of the Song provide a concrete example: "Let him kiss me with the kisses of his mouth" (Sg 1:2). Following Rupert, de Lubac explains this verse, saying that a Marian interpretation of the Song intends "to celebrate the first union of the Word with human nature in the womb of our Lady."[46] This "first union" is signified by "the kisses of his mouth," and the Incarnation is both that "first kiss of the Word" and His "pledge of the final union."[47]

De Lubac also cites other medieval writers such as Philip of Harvengt who "has no hesitation about seeing in the Song 'a whole allegory of the Virgin,'"[48] and Guerricus of Tournai who advocated an application of the Song to the Assumption of Our Lady.[49] Quoting Gerhoh of Reichersberg, another medieval writer, de Lubac asserts: "In point of fact it is impossible not to consider Mary as being the beloved Bride par excellence of the Bridegroom: '*inter omnes sponsas prae omnibus fuit ac permanet ornata.*'"[50] Marian

---

44. *Medieval Exegesis*, 3:171; emphasis added.

45. Cf. Fulton, "Mimetic Devotion, Marian Exegesis," 87.

46. *Splendor*, 366.

47. *Splendor*, 366.

48. *Splendor*, 368; de Lubac does not provide a reference to Philip of Harvengt's work. Other medieval exegetes who produced Marian commentaries, although de Lubac does not mention them in his own text, include Honorius Augustodunensis, Alan of Lille, William of Newburgh, and Alexander Neckham; see Norris, *Song of Songs Interpreted*.

49. *Splendor*, 368, with reference to Guerricus (PL 185, 190d).

50. *Splendor*, 369, with internal quotation from Gerhoh of Reichersberg, *Liber de gloria*, ch. 10 (PL 94, 1105b).

exegesis is "the privileged explanation, last in order of time and discovery but logically first."[51] It is the mature fruit of a long harvest of the spiritual meaning of Scripture.

Marian Exegesis as the Privileged Explanation

A Marian interpretation of the Song of Songs has tremendous import for de Lubac's Marian ecclesiology in that it underscores key themes of his thought: mystery as the essential context for understanding the Church and mystical union as the eschatological reality of all Christian/ecclesial existence, all the while providing the Church with a concrete personal identity in Mary. To substantiate de Lubac's statement that Marian exegesis is "logically first" as "the privileged explanation" of the Song, we will examine, first, the preeminence of its subject, the Virgin Mary, who *specialiter* exemplifies the nuptial mysticism of the Song; and second, the conceptual priority of anagogy in Marian exegesis—what might also be called a "Marian eschatology."

The Preeminence of Mary, *Specialiter*

Earlier in "L'Église et la Vierge Marie," de Lubac had given an account of a trio of terms provided by Isaac of Stella (c. 1100–1170), who described a threefold association of the Church-soul-Mary in his sermon on the Assumption of Mary, saying: "The same thing is said *universally* [or generally] of the Church, *specially* of Mary and *singularly* of the faithful soul."[52] In applying "*specialiter*" to Mary, Isaac succeeded in highlighting her preeminence while also maintaining her close association to both the Church and its members. According to de Lubac, Isaac's trio of terms is "one of the finest among [the] dogmatic compositions" in tradition because it exemplifies how Mary might be said to be the "universal creature" whom God has filled "to an eminent degree with the substance of which the Church is formed."[53] Moreover, the preeminence of the unique graces bestowed on her does not separate Mary from the Church, but, rather, reveals the essential *Marian form* of the Church and of every Christian soul.

The Church Fathers bore witness to this "Marian" reality, and the medieval writers made it explicit. With references to Origen and to Ambrose,

---

51. *Splendor,* 369.

52. Isaac of Stella, *Sermon 61,* on the Assumption (PL 194, 1863a), as quoted by de Lubac in *Splendor,* 347n177; emphasis added.

53. *Splendor,* 347, 351.

de Lubac says, "[God's] word is born in each one of the faithful, as in the Church as a whole; but this is *in the likeness of his birth in the soul of our Lady,* and in addition, if faith is to bear its fruit, there must be in each of us the soul of our Lady, who magnified the Lord, and the spirit of our Lady, who rejoiced in God."[54] De Lubac also quotes the words of Godefridus of Admont (d. AD 1165) who echoes Isaac's emphasis on Mary's preeminence, saying:

> All the mysteries of this book [the Song of Songs] fit perfectly either the universal Church, or each faithful soul in the bosom of the Church, conveying in a spiritual manner (thanks to the mystical sense) the mutual love of the Bridegroom and the Bride, [yet] they nevertheless seem to fit more "specially" the Blessed Virgin Mary, who, above all souls, was singularly full of a "special" dilection and deserved above all to be "specially" loved by the Bridegroom.[55]

Building on these patristic and medieval writers, de Lubac highlights the unity of the Christian mystery, mutually shared by the Church, the Christian soul, and Mary: "The Christian mystery is one: it is the same thing in our Lady, in the Church, and in each individual soul."[56] He also says that "the mystery of the Church is the continuation of the mystery of our Lady rather than the prefigured replica of it; the same mystery deepens and unfolds."[57] This assertion of continuity suggests a mutual co-inherence of Mary and the Church in all its members: "In the sacrament of these nuptials 'the Virgin Mary becomes the Church and every faithful soul,' or again the Church and all faithful souls *'become the Virgin Mary'* by virtue of 'integrity of will and purity of faith.'"[58] According to de Lubac, a "firm hold" on this ideal transformation is provided by Rupert, who envisions "the great scattered body of the Church as unified and drawn together as to its center or its peak in the unrivaled soul of Mary, the uniquely beloved."[59] In identifying Our Lady as "the unrivaled soul" who is "uniquely beloved," de Lubac underscores that Mary is *"specialis"* in relation to the Church and to Christian souls: she is "the first-beloved ... [in whom] all saintly souls, and

---

54. *Splendor,* 351, emphasis added, with reference to Origen, *In Cant.,* hom. 2, and Ambrose, *In Lucam,* bk. 2, chap. 26.

55. Godefridus of Admont (PL 174, 972), as quoted in *Splendor,* 370.

56. *Splendor,* 371, as previously quoted.

57. *Splendor,* 371.

58. *Splendor,* 372; emphasis added.

59. *Splendor,* 372, with reference to Rupert of Deutz, *De glorificatione Trinitatis,* bk. 6, ch. 13.

primarily the Church, whose 'form' she is, are loved also."[60] The mystery of Mary and the Church involves the mystery of their unity, a unity in difference rooted in Our Lady's eminent status among the faithful and in the exemplary nature of her bridal love.

It may also be noted that de Lubac was well-acquainted with the exegetical tradition of the Song of Songs from an early stage. Although his discussion of the topic is only found in *Méditation sur l'Église* (1953), there is evidence that de Lubac had already been drawn to this familiar theme in his earliest major work, *Catholicisme* (1938). In the appendix of *Catholicisme*, de Lubac included an extract from Isaac of Stella's sermon,[61] and in a footnote in chapter 6 on the interpretation of Scripture, he wrote: "Had it been possible to lengthen an already overlong chapter, I should have liked to show how, according to tradition, in addition to the Church and the soul, which are everywhere present in Scripture, and more especially in the Canticle, there is a third 'person,' Mary, who is the bond of their unity."[62] It seems that de Lubac achieved his desire in writing the chapter *"L'Église et la Vierge Marie"* in *Méditation sur l'Église* fifteen years later when he indeed expounded the perichoretic relationship of the Church, the soul, and Mary in which, with regard to the Church and the individual soul, Mary is "the bond of their unity." This connection, moreover, underscores the continuity of de Lubac's thought on the relationship of Mary and the Church and the hidden significance of these key writings.

The Priority of Anagogy: A Marian Eschatology

Another important element of de Lubac's Scriptural *ressourcement* is the anagogical perspective that explicitly links Mary to the eschatological glory promised to the Church. The unique contribution of what I am calling a "Marian eschatology" is established on the principle of the priority of anagogy over allegory and tropology. Whereas the allegorical sense is related to the historical coming of Christ in the Incarnation and the tropological sense is related to the coming of Christ to each individual soul, the anagogical sense relates to the final coming of Christ at the eschaton, the finality of salvation history. As the first two advents are oriented to the third, anagogy carries the dynamic of spiritual interpretation to completion. In this

---

60. *Splendor*, 371, with reference to Jean de Saussure, "Méditation sur la Vierge" (1950); Paul Claudel, *L'Épée et le miroir*, 42, 73; and St. Ambrose, *De virginitate*, ch. 4, no. 20.

61. Isaac of Stella, *Sermon 61* (PL 194, 1863, 1865); extract 37 in *Catholicism*, 420–21.

62. *Catholicism*, 215n208.

way, the anagogical sense takes precedence over the allegorical and tropological senses, and this priority is also realized in the preeminence of Mary
specialiter.[63]

It is not merely coincidental that Marian exegesis of the Song of Songs
developed within the liturgical context of the feast of her Assumption, a feast
which celebrates eschatological completeness. Mary's assumption into heav-
en establishes her preeminence in an anagogical sense. She has completed
her earthly journey and is the first of the human race to arrive at the consummation of God's promises. And insofar as the same end is promised to
the Church, the doctrine of the Assumption highlights for all Christians the
anticipated reality of their own destiny in Christ, announced and prefigured
in Mary's glory. Hence, reading the Song of Songs in a Marian light does not
detract from its ecclesiological and moral senses but intensifies them with
ultimate meaning. Marian exegesis of the Song illumines the Church's own
eschatological glory.

A focus on the anagogical sense in light of Mary's assumption into heav-
en renders Marian exegesis first amongst other interpretations, not only
because Our Lady was the *first* to arrive at that final heavenly destination
promised to all the faithful (an antecedence in the *material* sense of the doctrine of the Assumption), but also because the theology of the Assumption
gives Scripture its comprehensive *spiritual* sense. The anagogical focus of
Marian exegesis subsumes the literal, allegorical, and tropological senses in
a culminating interpretation, one that assumes priority over other interpretations. It conveys an ultimate meaning and thus holds a conceptual priority,
as "logically first," in the hierarchy of meaning.

As the final phase in the discovery of the spiritual meaning of Scripture,
the anagogical sense is the culmination of all that precedes it. It "realizes the
perfection both of allegory and of tropology, achieving their synthesis. It is
neither 'objective' like the first, nor 'subjective' like the second. Above and
beyond this division, it realizes their unity. It integrates the whole and final
meaning."[64] The allegorical and tropological senses are brought to completion when "they unite in anagogy."[65] In other words, for de Lubac, the whole
rhythm of exegesis is eschatological, and anagogy "conveys us to the final

---

63. De Lubac notes that Origen, Gregory of Nyssa, Didymus, and Jerome all identified anagogy as one of the spiritual senses, and that the term became more specialized in the writings of John
Cassian; see *Medieval Exegesis*, 2:180.

64. *Medieval Exegesis*, 2:187.

65. "On an Old Distich: The Doctrine of the 'Fourfold Sense' in Scripture," in *Theological
Fragments* (San Francisco: Ignatius Press, 1989), 118.

synthesis; it is the last phase of the unique rhythm."[66] The historical, allegorical, and tropological senses of Scripture are *perfected* in the anagogical sense. In Marian exegesis, the anagogical sense takes on a concrete and personal quality.

It is significant that, following his exposition of the preeminent quality (*specialiter*) of Mary, de Lubac proceeds to describe her as "the unique case, the genuine *universal concrete*, which includes to an eminent degree and in a pure state the sum of perfection of all the other members."[67] This reference to Our Lady as a "universal concrete" is a key component in the Mariology de Lubac received from Pierre Teilhard de Chardin, which will be discussed in the next chapter. For now, it can be noted that de Lubac associates this *special* quality of Mary as "universal concrete" with the spiritual senses of Scripture. He states: "Allegory, which refers to the Church, tropology, which concerns the soul, and anagogy, which looks above, all converge at a peak that soars above them all in order to describe this unique marvel."[68] And by "this unique marvel" de Lubac is referring to the marvel of the Word of God, incarnate and born of Mary, who is born also in the Church and in each one of the faithful.

It thus appears that de Lubac is making a rich multilayered association between the (Teilhardian) conception of Mary as a universal concrete, the three figurative senses of Scripture, and the threefold reality of Church-soul-Mary. Although he does not state directly that the anagogical sense refers to Mary, the correlation is implied. It can be deduced that anagogy, here described as the sense that "looks above," fittingly looks to Mary in whom God has gathered "all the excellence in the spiritual universe, which is the Church."[69] She alone has completed her earthly journey and arrived at the final eschatological end by way of her Assumption into heaven and her coronation as Queen of Heaven.[70] The Church and the soul, both closely associated with Mary, are thus swept into the rhythm and orientation of her eschatological glory. In other words, Mary is the personification of Christian hope; looking to Our Lady, the faithful discover their own end and find grounds for confidence in the fulfillment of God's promises as He has done for the Blessed Virgin.

Assumed into heaven, Mary unequivocally exemplifies the anagogical

---

66. "On an Old Distich," 118.
67. *Splendor*, 351; emphasis added.
68. *Splendor*, 351–52, with reference to St. Bonaventure, *De nativitate B.V.M., sermo* 5.
69. *Splendor*, 352, with reference to St. Laurence of Brindisi, *Super fundamenta ejus, sermo* 4, ch. 1.
70. Cf. *Splendor*, 346.

sense, and thus, as another commentator says, Marian exegesis convincingly "incorporates the entire tradition of the Song of Songs commentary throughout the Latin Middle Ages, absorbing every level of understanding which it had inherited."[71] In view of the preeminence of its subject and the priority of the anagogical sense, it can thus be recognized that a Marian exegesis of the Song of Songs is indeed first among its privileged explanations. It takes us to "the very center of the mystery prefigured by the revelation made to Israel and enshrined in the Song,"[72] and because "the mystical or spiritual understanding of Scripture and the mystical or spiritual life are, in the end, one and the same,"[73] one might further deduce that the Christian life in its fullest manifestation is Marian.

Revelation and the Bride of Salvation History

In the anagogical sense, de Lubac discovers a "wonderful parallelism" between the bridal imagery of the Song of Songs and the book of Revelation, a parallel that bespeaks the unity of Scripture and acts as a kind of capstone for de Lubac's Mariology. Revelation 21 describes the new Jerusalem as a "holy city ... descending out of heaven from God, prepared *as a bride adorned for her husband.*"[74] De Lubac notes that both brides speak to their beloved, and it is with regard to their respective dialogues that "the whole of revelation and the whole story of salvation are summed up in one and the same song of love."[75] De Lubac writes: "Together with her [Mary] the whole Church hears the call of the Bridegroom in the Song: 'Come from Libanus, come' (Sg 4:8) and with her replies, 'Come, my beloved, let us go forth' (Sg 7:11)." Furthermore, he associates this reply with the words of the bride in Revelation, saying that it is "the cry that she [the Church] still utters across the centuries toward the consummation, as the last pages of the Bible tell us: 'Come, Lord Jesus!' (Rev 22:17)."[76]

For Rupert, the kiss of the bride in Song 1:2 intimated Mary's own reply, her "fiat," which brought to concrete realization the "kiss" of the Incarnation. Her response continues to reverberate throughout time in the "fiat" of all believers, until the fulfillment of that divine "pledge of the final union" wherein the Church partakes in the wedding banquet of the Lamb (see Rev 21 and 22).

71. Matter, *Voice of My Beloved,* 169.
72. *Splendor,* 366.
73. "Mysticism and Mystery," 58, as previously quoted.
74. Revelation 21:2; emphasis added.
75. See *Splendor,* 373.
76. *Splendor,* 373.

The parallel dialogues of love in the Song of Songs and in the book of Revelation thus sums up the mystery of Redemption, and, as de Lubac says, are the "prelude to the song of eternity"; they are the song of Mary.[77]

De Lubac's exposition, drawing out the connection between the bride of the Song and the bride of Revelation and associating them both with Mary, can be expanded to encompass the first bride who was given to Adam in the garden of Eden. Although de Lubac does not make this connection explicitly, it is founded in the Christian tradition and consonant with everything de Lubac has said.[78] In so doing, we draw out the fullest meaning of the symbol of the bride in the economy of salvation: "The woman who stands *at the end* of the history of creation and salvation, corresponds evidently to the one about whom it is said *in the first pages* of the Bible that she 'is going to crush the head of the serpent.'"[79] Altogether, there are three key images of the bride—from the book of Genesis, the Song of Songs, and Revelation— and each is associated with Mary.

In this way, the analysis can be extended further such that the three images of the bride provide a unifying framework for the story of salvation as it is recorded in Scripture. The symbol of the bride that appears in both the first and in the final book of the Bible suggests a deeper significance, namely that the symbolism provides markers or bookends to salvation history. In sum, the fallen bride of Genesis traverses the pages of Scripture until she comes to that complete union of love, prefigured in the Song and consummated in Revelation where, cleansed and sanctified (see Eph 5:26), she enters, at last, into the wedding banquet of the Lamb. Analogously, God's creative Word in Genesis becomes incarnate in the womb of the Virgin Mary and is born into the hearts of humankind so that all might be gathered into that one Bride of Christ who will give her word of assent, "Come, Lord Jesus!" (Rev 22:17). Marian exegesis, which sees in Mary the culminating figure of the bride, allows these connections to emerge with clarity, underscoring the coherence of Scripture and the unity of its message.

De Lubac identifies the "focal point" of the analogy between Mary and the Church when he says: "The whole of her [Mary's] maternal role as far as we are concerned consists in her leading us to him [Christ]. That is Mary; and so also is the Church our Mother—the perfect worshipper; there lies

---

77. *Splendor*, 373.

78. Cf. Irenaeus, *Adversus haereses* 3.22 and 5.19, wherein Irenaeus expounds the typology of Mary as the New Eve.

79. James Gavigan, *et al.*, eds., *The Navarre Bible: The Book of Revelation: Texts and Commentaries* (Dublin: Four Courts Press, 1992), 27, emphasis added.

the focal point of the analogy between them, for there is the same spirit at work in both."[80] It might thus be said that the spiritual motherhood of Mary and the Church, "the focal point of the analogy between them," serves one singular end of leading human beings into loving union with Christ. It is this end that de Lubac helps us to see in his exposition on the Marian meaning of the Song of Songs.

An Appraisal

A Survey of Recent Literature

De Lubac's concentration on a Marian reading of the Song of Songs is significant because such attention to the Marian dimension of the Song in contemporary exegesis is rare. For example, J. Paul Tanner's commentary on the Song in the *Bibliotheca Sacra* series gives to Marian exegesis just five sentences in his twenty-three page essay.[81] James Fischer's work in the Collegeville Bible Commentary also makes only a passing reference to the application of various passages of the Song to the Virgin Mary on her feasts, but does not provide any further discussion.[82] It seems that, with a few exceptions, the majority of contemporary exegetes favor more literal and critical interpretations of the Song as a collection of love poems celebrating human love and the goodness of conjugal union. Roland Murphy, for example, employs form criticism and asserts that "the Canticle is not to be applied in a literal sense to Mary in such fashion as to refer individual words to her" because to do so would be "to disregard the parabolic nature of the poem."[83] Murphy excludes a Marian reading altogether.

A more nuanced perspective is found in Paul Griffiths's commentary, which frequently alludes to the close parallel between the Church and Mary and makes copious references to Marian allusions within the Canticle. Griffiths acknowledges the inherent difficulties of such exegesis, but he notes nonetheless that it "remains true that the Marian thread is woven deeply

---

80. *Splendor*, 377. De Lubac's statement might be read as a hint of what has been called a "doxological ecclesiology"; see Christopher Ruddy's article "'In my end is my beginning': *Lumen Gentium* and the Priority of Doxology," *Irish Theological Quarterly* 79, no. 2 (2014): 144–64, in which the author considers the doxological dimension of the Church according to *Lumen Gentium*.

81. Tanner, "History of Interpretation," 28–29.

82. Fischer, *Song of Songs*, 789.

83. Roland Murphy, "The Canticle of Canticles and the Virgin Mary," *Carmelus* 1 (1954): 26–27. Murphy's essay in *Carmelus* takes issue with Alfonso Rivera's defense of a Marian reading of the Song, arguing that Mary's intimate relationship to both Christ and the Church, a relationship which is the basis for Marian exegesis, "is not a necessary part of the literal sense of the Canticle."

into the fabric of Christian interpretation of the Song."[84] Perhaps the most positive attention that has been given to Marian exegesis of the Song has come from Mariological circles and scholarship in medieval studies. Mariologist Alfonso Rivera argues for an interpretation that applies the Song to the Virgin Mary, basing his position both on the Semitic notion of a corporate personality binding the individual subject to the collective and on the marital theme as it has been applied to Israel throughout the Old Testament.[85] Additionally, the historical studies of E. Ann Matter, Ann W. Astell, and Rachel Fulton, cited throughout this chapter, present notable scholarship on the topic of Marian exegesis.

This brief survey of perspectives shows that the development of Marian exegesis has been explored and assessed in many different lights. Bearing in mind this diversity of perspectives on the topic of Marian exegesis, it appears that de Lubac has something unique to offer that is carefully considered and valuable. De Lubac laments the loss of spiritual exegesis, but he does not simply strive to reinstate the whole apparatus of patristic and medieval exegesis. Rather, using that very methodology, he identifies some enduring gains from that Tradition. Marian exegesis of the Song of Songs can be counted among the gems uncovered in de Lubac's *ressourcement* and the mining of spiritual exegesis.

De Lubac's Assessment and Contribution

De Lubac espouses a nuanced and astute perception of the value of the spiritual interpretation of Scripture as well as of Marian exegesis, in particular. His historical survey of the development of Scriptural interpretation through the centuries exhibits a keen awareness of the complexities of historical development and the waxing and waning of certain biblical traditions. He notes that patristic exegesis yielded an abundant harvest,[86] and monastic exegesis continued the tradition it received from the Church Fathers "with a truly fruitful spontaneity"[87] until the rise of thirteenth century Scholasticism, in which "reason awoke from its symbolical dream" and brought about

---

84. Griffiths, *The Song of Songs*, xli.

85. Alfonso Rivera, "Sentido mariologica del Cantar de los Cantares," *Ephemerides Mariologicae* 1 (1951): 437–68, and 2 (1952): 25–42.

86. Cf. *History and Spirit*, 481: "Once past the age of intense ferment where it [the spiritual interpretation of Scripture] had been formed, mystical exegesis had furnished a weapon to apologists; the Doctors had drawn from it a unified vision of the divine Economy; the monks had borrowed from it a method for *lectio divina*."

87. *History and Spirit*, 480.

a pursuit of new methods and approaches to theology.[88] Exegesis became very scientific and methodical. The "onslaught of Protestantism" and the consequent Catholic counterreform yielded a polemical use of Scripture that maintained its insufficiency in an effort to underscore the necessity of tradition.[89] Consequently, "the spiritual interpretation of the sacred texts … was almost completely abandoned."[90] Exegesis was increasingly rational and specialized in the modern era, developing into a "positive science" that disregarded the Bible's mystical dimension.[91] De Lubac reprehends the "myopia" of an otherwise "good enough historian" who considers allegory to be "only 'intellectual pastimes,' 'ingenious ornaments,' uninteresting 'mystiquerie [that] cannot be enjoyed by judicious people.'"[92] He is adamant that it was not spiritual exegesis per se that hindered the modern development of critical interpretation. Rather, "it was false science; it was bad literalism, 'taking everything literally, through wanting to follow the literal sense alone.'"[93]

De Lubac makes an important distinction, arguing that the "positive science" of the Bible is not the *entire* science of sacred Scripture. Moreover, he says that scientific exegetes, whose function as specialists "has become in recent centuries very necessary and very important," should know that "their very specialization marks out their limits; that their 'science' is not, consequently, the whole science of Scripture."[94] There must be room for the spiritual sense to emerge if the Word of God is truly to be grasped.

On the other hand, de Lubac is just as critical of the "narrow-minded 'figurists' [who] believe themselves obliged to take literally certain expressions of the Fathers and want to find mysteries beneath every word of the Bible." His assessment is trenchant: "Just as a vanquished religion, scorned by the emperor, ends by depreciating itself and being the source of its own caricature, what survived of the old exegesis seemed to be striving to authorize such judgments." "The last adherents of allegorism never ceased to exaggerate its faults. They grasped its inner spirit no better than its detractors."[95]

88. *History and Spirit,* 482.

89. *History and Spirit,* 482–83.

90. *History and Spirit,* 483.

91. Cf. *History and Spirit,* 483–84.

92. *History and Spirit,* 484, with reference to Richard Simon, though de Lubac does not provide a citation.

93. *History and Spirit,* 430.

94. *History and Spirit,* 483n171; de Lubac asserts that these scientific exegetes are not obliged, as specialists, to give the complete science of the Bible; "they must not even harbor the ambition to do so," but rather, be cognizant of the inherent limitations which their specialization poses.

95. *History and Spirit,* 486.

Though de Lubac upholds the ongoing relevance of patristic interpretation, he does not advocate for a slavish imitation of the Church Fathers. He reminds his reader that "spiritual exegesis has long since accomplished an essential part of its task" of articulating the Christian mystery and building up the Church. It has continuing value due to its "connaturality with Scripture,"[96] bringing the believer into contact with that "sacred element that belongs to the treasure of the faith."[97] The patristic witness to this faith can neither be discarded nor replaced, but rather, it is to be emulated and cultivated. De Lubac continues poignantly: "The Fathers are the witnesses of a springtime, of an adolescence—and that is a privilege that cannot be taken from them. But we must manage, in return, to represent maturity."[98]

De Lubac sketches the contours of this state of "maturity," stating that a revived spiritual exegesis would "remain ... purely Christological"; "it will strive always to be sensitive to that 'marvelous depth' of the divine words ... to the Mystery signified in the history."[99] Moreover, the modern "historical sense" would be united to that profound "sense of history" that spiritual exegesis was apt to bring out, "giving history its proper value."[100] Only then might one come to "know better the eternal youth of the old text" and be able to deploy anew the symbolic function of understanding and produce "new fruits in the unforeseeable freedom of the Spirit."[101]

Spiritual exegesis broadens the horizons of revelation. It substantiates the patristic perspective on the interrelatedness of Mary and the Church, enabling the faithful to see in the figure of Eve a New Eve whose perfect bridal consent informs the Church's own assent. In particular, the anagogical sense situates Mary as a concrete and personal icon of the heavenly Jerusalem. In her, we contemplate the Church in eschatological glory, presented to Christ as a "bride adorned for her husband" (Rev 21:2). Marian exegesis enables this intimate vision of flawless love and discloses the nuptial mystery at the heart of de Lubac's Marian *ressourcement*.

96. *History and Spirit*, 490.

97. *History and Spirit*, 491.

98. *History and Spirit*, 491.

99. *History and Spirit*, 491–92.

100. *History and Spirit*, 492, and *Medieval Exegesis*, 2:72.

101. *History and Spirit*, 493, with reference to A.-M. Dubarle, *Revue des sciences philosophiques et théologiques* (1949), 180.

CHAPTER 4

Contemporary Building Blocks of de Lubac's Marian Thought

Having examined de Lubac's patristic and Scriptural *ressourcement* in the previous chapters, we have witnessed how the theologian's erudition provided him with a wellspring of inspiration. In this chapter, we proceed to assess how he pursued this inspiration and engaged the sources anew, especially in conversation with two of his contemporaries: Pierre Teilhard de Chardin and Jules Monchanin, through whose influence de Lubac's ideas on Mary took shape. The works of these two like-minded thinkers constitute the contemporary building blocks to de Lubac's Marian synthesis.

In his early groundbreaking work, *Catholicisme*, de Lubac names Pierre Teilhard de Chardin and Jules Monchanin (along with Yves de Montcheuil[1]) his principal *"inspirateurs immédiats."*[2] The duo is also mentioned in de Lubac's postconciliar commentary, *Paradoxe et Mystère de l'Église.*

1. Fr. Yves de Montcheuil, who was arrested and executed by the Gestapo in the Second World War, does not figure much in de Lubac's writings on Mary and the Church. De Lubac pays tribute to Montcheuil in *Trois Jésuites nous parlent: Yves de Montcheuil 1899–1944, Charles Nicolet 1897–1961, Jean Zupan 1899–1968* (Paris: P. Lethielleux, 1980); English translation: *Three Jesuits Speak: Yves De Montcheuil 1899–1944, Charles Nicolet 1897–1961, Jean Zupan 1899–1968,* trans. K. D. Whitehead (San Francisco: Ignatius Press, 1987).

2. *Catholicisme, Foi Vivante* series 13 (1965), 15.

Alongside Hans Urs von Balthasar and Paul Claudel, de Lubac considered Teilhard and Monchanin to be thinkers "deeply impregnated with the Catholic spirit" and whose Marian thought exemplifies the Council's teaching.[3] In *The Motherhood of the Church*, de Lubac mentions these same four figures as authors who have "taken up again [the theme of the virginal maternity of the Church] in our own times, sometimes expressed with rare success and great depth of thought."[4] And in yet another work, *L'Éternel féminin*, he again refers to the same quartet of key contributors to an understanding of Mary's close association with the Church.[5] In continuity with de Lubac's *ressourcement* of patristic and medieval sources, this close association is founded on mystery and characterized as a mystical identification.

This mystical identification is encountered in Teilhard's writings in the concept of the "concrete universal"—one of the most fundamental aspects of de Lubac's Mariology. The "concrete universal" is a notion that refers to a universal reality, one which first exists as a concrete, personal reality.[6] This idea has a potent application to the relationship of Mary and the Church which de Lubac will expound in accord with the tradition. As a concrete universal, Mary's concrete historicity can be applied to the Church universally.

Correspondingly, a Trinitarian mysticism with Marian dimensions is witnessed in the life and legacy of Jules Monchanin. The attention and admiration that de Lubac accords to Monchanin underscores a unique affinity between the two and reveals the profound extent of Monchanin's influence on de Lubac. In Monchanin's poem to the "Virgin of the Indies," quoted by de Lubac in his commentary on the Mariology of *Lumen Gentium*, one

3. CPM, 62.

4. MC, 56–57.

5. *L'Éternel féminin, étude sur un texte du Père Teilhard de Chardin. Suivi de Teilhard et notre temps* (Paris: Aubier-Montaigne, 1968), English translation: *The Eternal Feminine: A Study on the Poem by Teilhard de Chardin followed by Teilhard and the Problems of Today*, trans. René Hague (London: William Collins, 1971), hereafter cited EF, with a quotation from Claudel's *L'Épée et le Miroir* (1939): "[T]his grand concept [of the perichoresis between Mary and the Church] has been obscured, so that in our own days it can be found only in a very few writers.... Claudel shares with Teilhard the responsibility for this renaissance. 'This woman,' he writes, 'who is the Church.' Monchanin finds matter for contemplation in that same concept.... Hans Urs von Balthasar developed it more profoundly, and made it current in theological circles, so that it was soon to receive official approval in Vatican II's Constitution *Lumen Gentium*" (EF, 29–30).

6. See EF, 118–22. De Lubac asserts that Teilhard's usage of the expression "concrete universal" is completely different from that of Hegel. Instead, it has the same fundamental meaning with which Blondel uses the term when he says: "True unity ... to which Christianity leads us, 'consists' in the presence in us and in all things of one and the same real mediation, of *a concrete universal* which, without being involved in the imperfections of creatures and their finite mode of being, is nevertheless, itself and complete, in all things" (M. Blondel, *Exigences philosophiques du christianism* [Paris: P.U.F., 1956], 185).

recognizes distinct allusions to common themes: the Song of Songs, the mystical unity of Mary and the Church, and a virginal love that bears fruit in cosmic motherhood—themes in continuity with de Lubac's presentation in *Méditation sur l'Église*. After surveying what Teilhard and Monchanin have to offer on the topic of Mary and the Church, the latter part of the chapter explores the implications of their Mariology for de Lubac's writings on mystery and Buddhism, showing how deeply Mariology pervades these aspects of his oeuvre.

Teilhard de Chardin

Pierre Teilhard de Chardin (1881–1955) was a fellow Jesuit and a mystic-scientist with whom de Lubac shared a special intellectual connection.[7] Around the time of the Council, de Lubac had also been commissioned by the Society of Jesus to elucidate his confrere's work and to bring his own testimony to bear about Teilhard's orthodoxy because of his close knowledge of his thought.[8] Multiple publications resulted from this work.[9] The particular one that pertains to Mariology is de Lubac's book-length commentary on Teilhard's eponymous poem from 1918, *L'Éternel féminin*.[10] De Lubac notes in his memoirs that writing this commentary gave him the "opportunity to bring out some fundamental aspects of Teilhardian thought that were

7. Twenty-three letters from Teilhard to de Lubac, written between 1930 and 1949, bear witness to their correspondence; *Lettres intimes à Auguste Valensin, Bruno de Solages, Henri de Lubac, André Ravier, 1919–1955*, ed. Henri de Lubac (Paris: Aubier-Montaigne, 1972).

8. Cf. ASC, 324 [6:7]. In a letter to the Vicar General on 5 May 1961, de Lubac writes, "In the present case, it happens too that I am one of the very rare men who have a good knowledge of both the life and writings of Father Teilhard. That creates an obligation of conscience in me. Some adversaries of the Christian faith, ... have decided to adopt it [Teilhard's work] themselves by means of transforming it, through a clever exploitation, into a weapon of war against the Church."

9. Henri de Lubac, *La pensée religieuse du Père Pierre Teilhard de Chardin* (Paris: Aubier-Montaigne, 1962), English translation: *The Religion of Teilhard de Chardin*, trans. René Hague (New York: Desclee, 1967); *La prière du Père Teilhard de Chardin* (Paris: A. Fayard, 1964), English translations: *The Faith of Teilhard de Chardin*, trans. René Hague (London: Burns & Oates, 1965), and *Teilhard de Chardin: The Man and His Meaning*, trans. René Hague (New York: Hawthorn Books, 1965); *Blondel et Teilhard de Chardin: correspondance, commentée par Henri de Lubac* (Paris: Beauchesne, 1965), English translation: *Correspondence*, trans. William Whitman (New York: Harper and Harper, 1967); *Teilhard, missionnaire et apologiste* (Toulouse: Éditions Prière et Vie, 1966), English translation: *Teilhard Explained*, trans. Anthony Buono (New York: Paulist Press, 1988); *L'Éternel féminin* (EF, 1968); *Teilhard posthume: réflexions et souvenirs* (Paris: Fayard, 1977).

10. Teilhard's poem can be found in the collected works, *Écrits du temps de la guerre*; English translation: "The Eternal Feminine," in *Writings in the Time of War*, trans. René Hague (New York: Harper & Row, 1968), 191–202. References to Teilhard's poem hereafter will be cited as Teilhard, EF in WTW, and should not be confused with de Lubac's commentary, cited as EF.

generally misunderstood or distorted."[11] Surprisingly, Teilhard's reflections on the Blessed Virgin and the place of the feminine in the evolution of the cosmos have otherwise neither gained much attention nor undergone much development.[12] De Lubac's extended commentary is therefore highly noteworthy, as it reveals the notion of the "concrete universal" and the significance of Mary's virginity to be two constitutive components of Mariology that de Lubac adopts from Teilhard.

The Eternal Feminine

At the outbreak of World War I, Teilhard, already an ordained priest, joined the French Army as a stretcher-bearer. His four and a half years in service constituted a period of exceptional intellectual and spiritual activity. Teilhard would be seen in the trenches, jotting down his thoughts and bringing to formulation his vision of an all-embracing unity within the universe. These essays, first published in 1965, are pervaded by his reflections on virginity and the feminine. "*L'Éternel féminin*," in particular, was Teilhard's lyrical expression of the convergence of these themes in the veiled Virgin—the Blessed Virgin Mary.

In 1968, fifty years after Teilhard's composition of "*L'Éternel féminin*," de Lubac completed an extensive study of the poem in which he examined Teilhard's letters and journals to trace the development of his inspiration and provide an in-depth commentary on the poem. He notes that Teilhard had been contemplating the feminine ideal as early as 1916, as evidenced in his May 1916 journal entry: "What attracts me in this subject [of the feminine] is the conjunction of a completely certain revealed fact (the excellence of virginity) with a human instinct (the sexual and maternal instinct)."[13] Teilhard intuitively perceived femininity to be more than mere biological sex. It represented a vital human instinct that is, in the words of de Lubac, "eminently endowed with the power to develop itself, to enrich itself with countless ever more spiritualized refinements, and to direct itself to a great variety of objects, and particularly to God."[14] Teilhard's poem explores his

---

11. ASC, 108.

12. Beyond de Lubac's commentary, the only other book-length studies devoted to the theme of the feminine in Teilhard's thought include André Devaux's *Teilhard and Womanhood* (Paulist, 1968) and Catherine R. O'Connor's *Woman and the Cosmos: The Feminine in the Thought of Pierre Teilhard de Chardin* (Englewood Cliffs, NJ: Prentice-Hall, 1974).

13. EF, 10.

14. EF, 10.

thoughts on chaste (spiritual) love and its power to unite not only human persons, but all things in the cosmos, drawing them to a culmination in the eternal Feminine.

The poem is dedicated to Beatrice, Dante's muse in both the last book of the *Divine Comedy* and in real life. Like Beatrice, Teilhard's eternal Feminine represented "the beauty running through the world ... the ideal held up before the world to make it ascend,"[15] and the embodiment of a beloved feminine figure who was his own spiritual guide through life. On 2 September 1916, Teilhard wrote in his diary, "The true, pure Feminine is pre-eminently a luminous and chaste Energy, compact of courage, ideality and goodness = the Blessed Virgin Mary."[16] It was this understanding that uniquely informed his evolutionary theory that both matter and spirit, nature and the supernatural, belong to one trajectory of evolution, and that the "spiritualization of the flesh" will take place through the "glory and bliss of chastity"[17] epitomized in Mary. At the climax of the poem, the veil of the virgin is swept aside and she identifies herself as Mary and the Church: "I am the Church, the bride of Christ. I am Mary the Virgin, mother of all humankind."[18]

The Dynamic of Chastity and Personalism

Chastity and personalism are two unique currents in Teilhard's evolutionary theory, and they are directly informed by his understanding and devotion to the Immaculate Virgin Mary. In *La Prière du Père Teilhard de Chardin* (1965), de Lubac explains that Teilhard conceived of the mystery of Mary as "first and foremost a mystery of purity"[19]—a mystery that is the key to the universalization of "the chaste essence of the Feminine." Purity is not only about sexual abstinence, but is fundamentally about the proper disposition of the soul. It is "the rectitude and the impulse introduced into our lives by the love of God sought in and above everything."[20] It is the single-hearted, unadulterated love that seeks God before all other goods. Purity is the virtue that "concentrates God in us and in those who are subject to our influence." According to Teilhard, "In our Lady, all modes of lower, disordered activity disappear in this single, luminous function of attracting and receiving

15. Teilhard, EF in WTW, 192.
16. EF, 11; the symbol is as found in Teilhard's notebooks.
17. Teilhard, EF in WTW, 199.
18. Teilhard, EF in WTW, 200–201.
19. de Lubac, *Teilhard de Chardin: The Man and His Meaning*, 63.
20. *The Divine Milieu* (New York: Harper & Row, 1960), 133.

God and allowing him to pass through her."[21] The Blessed Virgin becomes, in Teilhard's view, the essential vehicle for evolutionary progress, for the intensity of her chaste love draws the cosmos forward toward its evolutionary peak. In this way, the eternal Feminine embodies the *natural* fullness of the world upon which the *supernatural* fullness of Christ is founded.

Before exploring further the dynamic of personalism in Teilhard's "*L'Éternel féminin,*" let us take inventory of Teilhard's influence on de Lubac on this topic, the first traces of which are intimated in *Catholicisme*. Although there are few direct references to Teilhard in that text, (the index of the French edition lists six in addition to a lengthy excerpt from Teilhard on "Christianity and Personalism" included in the appendix[22]), Teilhard's ideas can be found in abundance. One might, for example, recognize the figure of Teilhard in de Lubac's comments on the progress made by the sciences. In a statement about the achievements of man appropriate to the science of each time period (in contrast to revelation that transcends time), de Lubac writes, "Neither the biblical writers nor the Fathers nor the medieval theologians could have known, obviously, about the Neanderthal man or *Sinanthropus*, nor could they have had precise knowledge about the Chinese."[23] Although he does not name Teilhard here, the mention of *Sinanthropus* and the Chinese are undeniably made with reference to Teilhard himself, who participated in the associated archeological discoveries.

To one who studies the works of the two Jesuits in relation to one another, the affinity between them is undeniable. The key to their deep theological affinity is an emphasis on *personalism*. In a chapter titled "Person and Society" in *Catholicisme,* de Lubac explores the inner paradox of the mystery of man and his drive toward unity: "For we find that the higher a living thing rises in the scale of being the more internal unity does it acquire."[24] This statement notably reflects Teilhard's conception of the law of complexity-consciousness: the positive correlation between complexity and consciousness is such that the more developed a being is, the higher its level of spiritual (non-material) activity. The essence of this law of complexity-consciousness is succinctly conveyed in the title of Flannery O'Connor's collection of short stories, *Everything That Rises Must Converge,* a title derived

---

21. *The Making of a Mind, Letters from a Soldier-Priest 1914–1919,* trans. René Hague (New York: Harper & Row, 1965), 246–47; as quoted by de Lubac in *Teilhard: The Man and His Meaning,* 63.

22. *Catholicism,* Appendix no. 50, 437–38; taken from Teilhard de Chardin, "La Crise présente: Réflexions d'un naturaliste," in *Études* (20 October 1937), 164.

23. *Catholicism,* 352.

24. *Catholicism,* 328.

from Teilhard's idea that the entire cosmos is progressively evolving toward the "Omega Christ."[25] De Lubac's subsequent discussion of the successive levels of complexity in different types of beings corresponds to Teilhard's theory on the "spiritualization of the cosmos."[26] This spiritualization happens through the *personal* dimension of existence. De Lubac asserts that "spiritual union takes place only through what is most personal in us,"[27] and he quotes Teilhard directly to argue that unity is attained in the strongest concentration of personality: "The Whole … is 'not the antipodes, but the pole of Personality.'"[28]

The paradoxical reality of the personal (or individual) and the universal marked Teilhard's vision of a "personalistic universe" in which "the most incommunicable and therefore the most precious quality of each being is that which makes him one with all the rest. It is consequently by coinciding with all the rest that we shall find the centre of ourselves."[29] For Teilhard, universality is "the prerogative of the strongest personality,"[30] meaning that universality is constituted by what is most personal. The eternal Feminine is not a mythical expression of cosmic beauty. Rather, she is universal because she is personal—a real concentration of personality. She embodies, in person, the cosmic force of chaste love and is the culmination of all beauty. Chaste and pure love is the driving force of evolutionary ascent, and absolute personalism, achieved in the Cosmic Christ, is its end.

It must be acknowledged that Teilhard's Marian thought, historically predating the *ressourcement* of Vatican II, reflects a preconciliar Marian theology. It lacks a historical context, being derived from Teilhard's own spirituality as a mystic and a scientist. One finds a strong accent on purity and femininity interwoven with his evolutionary outlook.[31] The eternal Feminine is the figure of the created fullness of the natural world, and her personal self-identification as both the Church and Mary posits a mysterious

---

25. See *The Phenomenon of Man* (New York: Harper, 1959), 300ff. See also Flannery O'Connor, *Everything That Rises Must Converge* (New York: Farrar, Straus, and Giroux, 1965).

26. See Teilhard de Chardin, "Creative Union" (1917), in *Writings in the Time of War*, xii, 159 E; 205 F.

27. *Catholicism*, 345.

28. *Catholicism*, 330, with reference to Teilhard de Chardin, "La Crise présente," 164.

29. "Sketch of a Personalistic Universe" (1936), in *Human Energy*, trans. J. M. Cohen (New York: Harcourt, 1969), 65; also referenced in endnote 43 of EF, 118.

30. EF, 118, as previously quoted; with reference to Teilhard's "Esquisse d'un Univers personnel"; English translation: "Sketch of a Personalistic Universe" (1936), cited previously.

31. The critique of essentialism has especially been levelled at Teilhard's *Eternal Feminine*. See Wolfgang Smith's *Teilhardism and the New Religion* (Rockford, IL: Tan Books, 1988) for a critical appraisal from a traditional Catholic perspective.

configuration of the union of the personal and universal, an idea of which de Lubac says "is one of the fundamental themes of Teilhard's thought."[32] This is "where we meet the boldness of Teilhard's Mariology"[33] and where we find Teilhard's fundamental contribution to de Lubac's own Marian thinking: the Virgin Mary is the eternal Feminine because she, being absolutely free of sin, is the pure concentration of created personhood. She is a concrete universal, and the feminine mystique is singularly enclosed and perfected within her.

"*L'Éternel féminin*" highlights Teilhard's vision of how all the energy of the cosmos and all of its powers of attraction come to a focus in Mary's purity.

> The Lord had conceived me in his wisdom, and I had won his heart.
> Without the lure of my purity, think you, would God ever have come down, as flesh, to dwell in his creation?
> Only love has the power to move being.[34]

It is Mary's immaculate love that draws God toward humanity and to the point of perfect and personal concentration in her womb. The peak significance of Mary's graced perfection of purity is manifested at the Annunciation wherein the Word is enfleshed in her. Teilhard sums up his meditation on this mystery with the title: "Annunciation: Mystery of the Feminine," and according to de Lubac, it was "the *mystery* he saw enclosed in the *Virgin* and receiving its fullest significance from her,"[35] not vice versa. De Lubac also states that it is of "prime importance" to see that for Teilhard, if we "speak of symbol, we shall not be saying that in this context the Virgin Mary is the fully realized symbol of the universal Feminine, but rather that this universal Feminine must be understood, in its pure essence, as the Virgin Mary."[36]

In Teilhard's mystical conception, Our Lady exemplifies the virtue of chastity as the powerful medium between matter and spirit, a channel of what he calls the "spiritual force of matter."[37] Mary's purity is thus exemplary for the entire created order; she is "the perfect model of what the creature should be before the face of God."[38] In this light, the universalization of Our Lady

---

32. EF, 118.

33. EF, 122.

34. Teilhard, EF in WTW, 200.

35. EF, 119; emphasis added to highlight the ordering.

36. EF, 119.

37. See chapter 3 of Teilhard's *Hymn of the Universe* (New York: Harper & Row, 1961), which bears this title and which depicts material creation as the necessary precondition for the coming of the spirit.

38. EF, 126.

means that the entire created order must also take up the "chaste essence of the Feminine," which is concretized in Mary. All creatures stand as feminine before God, and the "natural fullness of the world"[39] consists in the spiritualization of the cosmos in the chaste essence of Mary.[40]

The Mystical Identification of Mary and the Church

De Lubac states in his commentary that the relationship of Mary and the Church is "an association so close as to amount to a mystical identification."[41] As he did previously in *Méditation sur l'Église*, de Lubac, in *L'Éternel féminin*, again describes this mystical identification with the Trinitarian term "perichoresis." He writes, "There is a 'perichoresis' (alternation) between the two, and if Mary, in giving birth to the *One*, is thereby mother of the Multitude, so the Church, in giving birth to a Multitude, is thereby in her turn mother of the *Oneness*."[42] A maternal dimension thus unites Mary and the Church, and their offspring is twofold: Mary gives birth to Christ, the One; the Church gives birth to the Multitude, namely Christians. Additionally, de Lubac's statement reveals that in giving birth to Christ, Mary is, by extension, also mother of "the Multitude," and in giving birth to that "Multitude," the Church consequently becomes mother of "the *Oneness*," namely, the unity of the Multitude. "Since there is but one Christ, they [Mary and the Church] are in some way identical in their maternal function."[43]

In the final premise, birth of the Oneness—a unity that might be thought of as the consummate body of Christ the Omega Point—hinges upon the first premise, the birthing of Christ himself by Mary. In other words, the final unity of the body of Christ is still in progress. It is a becoming that commenced with Mary's *fiat* and is now in the process of attaining its consummation through the perichoresis of the Church and Mary as a concrete universal. The eternal Feminine is the symbol of this interpenetration.

The mysterious union of Mary and the Church is founded on the "glory and bliss of chastity" of the eternal Feminine, a perfect purity that allows the

---

39. Teilhard to Blondel; as quoted by de Lubac in EF, 84.

40. EF, 103.

41. EF, 28.

42. EF, 29; emphasis added; de Lubac refers to Bérengard, *In Apocalypsin*, 12, 3–5, and Augustine, *Sermon* 192. He gives credit to Matthias Scheeben for the original application of the term "perichoresis" to Mary and the Church in endnote 6 and notes that such an application of the term can only be found in a very few writers, namely Paul Claudel, Jules Monchanin, Gertrud von le Fort, Edith Stein, and Hans Urs von Balthasar.

43. EF, 29.

final blossoming of the cosmos in union with its Creator.[44] Teilhard's poem comes to a second climax with these words:

> Lying between God and the earth, as a zone of mutual attraction, I draw them both together in a passionate union.
> —until the meeting takes place in me, in which the generation and plenitude of Christ are consummated throughout the centuries.
> I am the Church, the bride of Christ.
> I am Mary the Virgin, mother of all humankind.[45]

The eternal Feminine is the "meeting place" of God and humanity, and the passionate union that she serves to bring about endures to the consummation of time: "I draw them both [God and the earth] together in a passionate union.—[*sic*] until the meeting takes place in me, in which the generation and plenitude of Christ are consummated throughout the centuries."[46] Only then is the veil swept aside and the Virgin identifies herself: "I am the Church, the bride of Christ. / I am Mary the Virgin, mother of all humankind."[47]

This self-identification as both the Church and Mary is indicative of an intimate relationship between the two. Teilhard asserts their unity while also maintaining their distinction with the idea of "the generation and plenitude of Christ." These words convey, respectively, the corporeal *generation* of the Word Incarnate, born of Mary, and the mystical *plenitude* of the body of Christ, born of the Church. The Virgin's fecundity reflects the fact that she draws forth the incarnation of the Word not only in her womb but also in the Church in which the "mystical plentitude" of Christ is achieved.[48]

The perfect virginity of Our Lady has become the meeting place of God with creation and is universalized in and through the Church. One might even say that it is not possible to take on a universalized Marian disposition in isolation, but that, because Mary is the concrete universal, the natural fullness of creation converges in her. One can therefore only take on a Marian

44. Teilhard, EF in WTW, 199.
45. Teilhard, EF in WTW, 200–201.
46. Teilhard, EF in WTW, 200.
47. Teilhard, EF in WTW, 200–201.
48. Cf. EF, 29. As we have repeatedly seen, this intersection of the maternal functions of Mary and the Church finds its provenance in Tradition; it was expounded by the Fathers of the Church and by the theologians of the medieval West as one of the major characteristics of the Catholic faith.

disposition in communion with others, with the cosmos, and, particularly, with the Church. This living communion in Mary *is* the Church.

The idea of Mary as a concrete universal is comparable to that medieval paradigm offered by Isaac of Stella and expounded by de Lubac in *Méditation sur l'Église*. As previously seen, Isaac described the relationships of the Church, Mary, and the individual soul in the trio of terms: *generalis, specialis,* and *singularis*: "The same thing is said universally of the Church, specially of Mary and singularly of the faithful soul.... In the universal sense the inheritance of the Lord is the church; in the special sense, it is Mary; in the singular [individual] sense, it is each faithful soul."[49] De Lubac considers Isaac's sermon one "of the finest among dogmatic compositions"[50] found in the Christian tradition. When Teilhard refers to Our Lady as *Virgo Singularis*, as de Lubac himself does,[51] he is underscoring her unique identity (*specialiter*) as the perfection of creaturely existence. What is found in the Church *generaliter* and in the soul *singulariter* is exemplified in Mary *specialiter*. Furthermore, it is precisely this unparalleled personal excellence that constitutes Mary as a personal universal—a unique embodiment of the *universalis*. Isaac of Stella's threefold relationship and Teilhard's conception of the concrete universal (or synonymously, personal universal) both embody a structure of "unity-in-distinction." In Isaac of Stella's conception, that which is found in common between the Church, the soul, and Mary constitutes a *unity*, and that unity retains a *distinction* of subjects, with reference to the aspect by which the unity is considered (i.e., whether generally, singularly, or specially). Similarly, in Teilhard's notion of the personal universal, the "personal" dimension allows uniqueness and individuality to be preserved while also serving as a "universal" foundation or focal point of unity. The fundamental paradox here is that the personal is not abolished by the universal; rather, the universal is derived from that which is *most* personal. This notion of unity-in-distinction will enable the identification of a Marian dimension in the relationship of the universal Church to particular churches, to be explored in a later chapter.

49. Isaac of Stella, *In Assumptione beatae Mariae, sermo* I (PL 194, 1863–65), as quoted in *Splendor*, 347–48n177.

50. *Splendor*, 347.

51. De Lubac refers to Mary as *Virgo Singularis* in both *Méditation sur l'Église*, 350, and EF, 122n64.

Jules Monchanin

Perhaps one of the most significant and influential friendships in de Lubac's lifetime was that which he shared with Jules Monchanin (1895–1957), a fellow Frenchman and Catholic priest, whose life was devoted to Hindu-Christian dialogue.[52] Born near Lyon in 1895 and ordained to the priesthood in 1922, Monchanin was known by his contemporaries to be an outstanding priest and eminent scholar on Far Eastern religions. His Benedictine companion, Henri Le Saux, with whom he founded a Christian hermitage in India called *ashram Saccidānanda* (ashram of the Holy Trinity),[53] describes Monchanin as "one of the most brilliant intellects among the French clergy, a remarkable conversationalist, at home on every subject, a brilliant lecturer and a theologian who opened before his hearers marvelous and ever new horizons."[54] Close in age, Monchanin and de Lubac first met some time in February or March of 1930 when de Lubac assumed his teaching position at the *Institut Catholique de Lyon*, where Monchanin was an established scholar and lecturer. This was the beginning of a life-long friendship. De Lubac writes in his memoirs: "I would have to speak at length about him [Monchanin], for my meeting with him and the friendship that followed were so decisive for me."[55] Under Monchanin's influence, de Lubac embarked on the study of Buddhism, an area that captivated his attention in the decades both before and after the Council, resulting in three books and numerous articles.[56] In 1967, on the tenth anniversary of Monchanin's death, de Lubac published a biography to honor his friend. The work, titled *Images de l'Abbé Monchanin,* was meant to be an "expression of my admiration and gratitude for this extraordinary man, this genial priest, who was both a mystic and a

---

52. The most authoritative studies of Jules Monchanin's life and legacy to date include: Henri de Lubac's *Images de l'Abbé Monchanin* (Paris: Éditions Montaigne, 1967); Jules Monchanin, *In Quest of the Absolute: The Life and Work of Jules Monchanin,* trans. J. G. Weber (Kalamazoo, MI: Cistercian Publications, 1977); and Sten Rodhe, *Jules Monchanin, Pioneer in Hindu-Christian Dialogue* (Delhi: Indian Society for Promoting Christian Knowledge, 1993). The biographical details presented here are taken from these works. For a broader survey of works on Jules Monchanin, see the survey provided by Rodhe in chapter 10 of *Jules Monchanin, Pioneer in Hindu-Christian Dialogue:* "The Legacy," 62–69.

53. See Weber, introduction to Monchanin, *In Quest of the Absolute,* 5.

54. Henri le Saux, as quoted in Harry Oldmeadow, *Journeys East: 20th Century Western Encounters with Eastern Religious Traditions* (Bloomington, IN: World Wisdom, 2004), 221.

55. ASC, 113.

56. *Aspects du bouddhisme* (1951); *La Rencontre du bouddhisme et de l'Occident* (1952) and *Aspects du bouddhisme: Amida,* vol. 2 (1955); additionally, five essays are published in *Théologies d'occasion* (Desclée de Brouwer, 1984).

saint."[57] Comprised of ten chapters that present in chronological order the details of Monchanin's life and the development of his thought, the work introduces him in this way: "Images of a man who found himself inexorably driven far from images, pilgrim of 'the way beyond signs,' enraptured in the desert by an 'implacable calling,' attracted by the One who is at the secret heart of everything only because he is beyond everything."[58] Jacques Prévotat comments: "These two spiritual men immediately understood one another; in the diversity of their gifts, they secretly burned with a single flame."[59] This flame might be identified as the mystical life of prayer, a life in the Spirit, which sealed their friendship and characterized every aspect of their life's work.

In view of the intimate friendship between Monchanin and de Lubac and the influence of the former on the latter, we first consider the affinity of thought between Monchanin and Teilhard in addition to the Monchanin's Trinitarian mysticism. These points provide the context for examining Monchanin's Marian thought, as found in his meditation on "the Virgin of the Indies," which de Lubac quotes in *Paradoxe et mystère de l'Église*.

Evolution and Trinitarian Mysticism

Besides employing the same language and ideas that were idiosyncratically Teilhard's own, the intuition that evolution was above all a process of spiritualization linked Monchanin closely to Teilhard. As one author has noted, Monchanin "anticipated many of the ideas of ecumenism and of the new theology which came to light in the Second Vatican Council, and [that] *he was one of the first to appreciate the work of Teilhard de Chardin*."[60] For example, his writings on the "noosphere" as the "coming of man"[61] echo Teilhard's own use of the term and his idea of the law of complexity-consciousness mentioned above.[62] Additionally, Monchanin's assertion that "man arises

57. ASC, 114; de Lubac actually expresses his dissatisfaction with how his book only gave a "faint expression" of his great admiration.

58. De Lubac, *Images de l'Abbé Monchanin*, 9: "Images d'un homme qui se trouvait inexorablement chassé loin des images, pèlerin de 'la voie hors des signes,' ravi au désert par un 'implacable appel,' attiré par Celui qui n'est au Coeur secret de tout que parce qu'Il est au-delà de tout"; unless otherwise noted, translation is mine.

59. Jacques Prévotat, *Jules Monchanin (1895–1957) as Seen from the East and West: A Collection of Colloquium Essays from 1995* (Delhi: Saccidananda Ashram/Indian Society for Promoting Christian Knowledge (ISPCK), 2001), 59.

60. Bede Griffiths, preface to Monchanin, *In Quest of the Absolute*, 3; emphasis added.

61. Monchanin, *In Quest of the Absolute*, 142.

62. See Teilhard's *Phenomenon of Man*, 1961; "Hominization: Introduction to a Scientific Study of the Human Phenomenon" (1923), in *The Vision of the Past* (London: Collins, 1968), 51–79.

from life as life arises from matter"[63] resonates with Teilhard's theory of the spiritual potency of matter. Monchanin adopts Teilhard's ideas and terminology to describe the trajectory of evolution, and he defines the realm of the "Omega Christ" as "the christosphere," meaning that the evolutionary process is brought to perfection in the Omega Christ, through whom "the eternal is received into the temporal." Through Christ and in Christ, "[t]he time of the noosphere, of the biosphere, of the cosmos is eternalized."[64]

These evident resonances between Monchanin and Teilhard were not lost on de Lubac, who brings out a further dimension of Monchanin's thought, namely Trinitarian mysticism, or a "theological mysticism ... [which] is essentially a Trinitarian synthesis."[65] As a missionary to India, Monchanin's singular goal was to allow the visible form of Christianity to emerge from within the native culture in a truly Indian way which was nonetheless Trinitarian at its core.[66] He approached the missionary endeavor with great fervor for the Christian faith and in a spirit of inculturation. "My life has no other meaning than praising and contemplating this total and unique mystery [of the Trinity]. India does not yet know the Trinity.... Who will reveal it? I sense that I am called more than ever."[67]

Monchanin's rich Trinitarian spirituality informed his views on the Church and on Mary. With a clear understanding of the Christian life as a mystical participation in the life of the Trinity, Monchanin was adamant that this participation is never an individualistic reality but a communal one; it is the essence of the Church and Mary. Monchanin writes: "The time of the Church is that of *reception* because it is the intemporal rhythm of God, the Trinitarian circumincession *received* in the becoming, which has become the Christic and pneumatic rhythm of deification."[68] This idea resonates with de Lubac's own view of Christianity's place in the world: ecclesial existence—an existence in time—is characterized by a paradoxical reception of eternity. One finds that this perfect reception is possible and has been realized in the mystery of the Incarnation of the Word in Mary's womb. Mary's receptivity is the prototypical "rhythm of deification." In Mary, "the eternal

<hr>

63. Monchanin, *In Quest of the Absolute*, 140.

64. Monchanin, 144.

65. De Lubac, *Images de l'Abbé Monchanin*, 19: "Mystique théologique ... est essentiellement une synthèse trinitaire"; translation is mine.

66. See Monchanin's discussion of the threefold task of Christianizing non-western civilizations in "Christianization of Oriental Cultures," in *In Quest of the Absolute*, 125–26.

67. Monchanin, 30.

68. Monchanin, 144; emphasis added.

is received into the temporal."[69] The Trinity-in-Mary is a prototype of the Trinity-in-Church.

It might also be said that Monchanin's focus on the mystery of the Trinity brings the Teilhardian concept of the Omega Christ to a culminating synthesis in the Trinity. For Teilhard, the evolution of the cosmos from primitive matter through new layers of consciousness in the noosphere comes to a final apex in the Omega Christ. For Monchanin, this finality is explicitly situated in a Trinitarian context in which "The christosphere, the end of the noosphere, … is its own finality."[70] Given the Mariological dimension of cosmic finality as a disposition of receptivity in Teilhard's conception of the role of the eternal Feminine, Monchanin's assertion precludes any pantheistic misinterpretation of Teilhard's thought and indicates that his Trinitarian perspectives bear Mariological significance as well.

"La Vierge aux Indes"

The Trinitarian dimensions of Monchanin's Marian thought are found in his brief but bold reflections on "the Virgin of the Indies,"[71] a poetic reflection in which he pursues the possible affinities between Christianity and Indian religion. He introduces Mary into his articulation of Christianity as one whose role is central and whose veneration is in accord with Indian religiosity: for Monchanin, the Indian worship of goddesses as the faces of Advaita is positively disposed to an experience of the cosmic grandeur of the Virgin Mother.[72]

It is thought-provoking that de Lubac quotes Monchanin's "Virgin of the Indies" extensively in his discussion of the Council's treatment of the topic of Mary and the Church in *Paradoxe et Mystère de l'Église*, describing it as an important witness to the tradition of the mystical analogy between Mary and the Church, which the Council endorsed. The poem draws an astonishing parallel between the motherhood of Mary and the Fatherhood of God.[73] Monchanin had written that "her [Mary's] childbearing is comparable

---

69. Monchanin, 144, as previously quoted.

70. Monchanin, 144.

71. Monchanin's meditation can be found in "La Vierge aux Indes," *Dieu Vivant: Perspectives religieuses et philosophiques* 3 (1945), 47–48; it is quoted by de Lubac in CPM, 65–66.

72. Monchanin, "La Vierge aux Indes," 48.

73. Monchanin's insight must be qualified with the understanding that God the Father alone is father in the absolute sense, because His fatherhood refers to Him alone as the principal and source of all being.

rather to the generation of the Word by the Father than to the childbearing of other women: *prius concepit mente.*"[74] Like Augustine and the Church Fathers, Monchanin prioritized Mary's conception of Jesus first *in her mind and heart* before conceiving him in her womb.[75] Next, he makes another rather bold assertion that in conceiving the Word Incarnate through the power of the Holy Spirit, Mary, in a sense, bears forth the two manifestations of the Father (the Word and the Spirit).[76] This is a subtle but certain allusion to Monchanin's statement, previously quoted, that "the time of the Church is … the intemporal rhythm of God, the Trinitarian circumincession *received* in the becoming, which has become the Christic and pneumatic rhythm of deification."[77] De Lubac appropriates Monchanin's idea that Mary has received the Trinitarian circumincession so perfectly that she embodies the "Christic and pneumatic rhythm" of deification, and that her graced participation in the life of God thus "revives contemplation of the Trinity."[78] Being "full of grace," she "appeal[s] to the Father whose paternity she temporarily shares in, to the Son whom she brings forth to *kenosis* and to growth, and to the Spirit that, of her superabundance, she communicates to creation."[79]

It is, moreover, Mary's perfect virginal love that makes her the perfect creature, "receptive to God, fecund for and of God."[80] Monchanin draws a direct link between virginity and the unicity of virginal love in Our Lady. Because Mary embodies the culmination of perfect love, "everything virginal in the world before her announced her, and all virginity after her will be integrated in her."[81] She is essential to God's plan of salvation because she is the one who "summons the Church to the secret of the Father." She is, says Monchanin, "a cosmic mother, in fact, universal mediatrix, … the reflection of the Principle, of the Mediator, and of the Spirit." Monchanin's astounding assertion risks misinterpretation, but what he ultimately means is clear: Mary is the "prototype of the Church and its achievement."[82]

---

74. Monchanin, "La Vierge aux Indes," 47; as quoted by de Lubac, CPM, 65.

75. See St. Augustine, Sermons 196, 1; 245, 4; and 215, 1 (PL 38, 1074).

76. Monchanin, "La Vierge aux Indes," 47–48; as quoted by de Lubac, CPM, 65: "[S]he who bears Christ and the Spirit, the Spirit who is her gift, whose fullness she possesses and whose spouse she is, and the Christ to whom she continues to give birth, these two manifestations of the Father: she summons the Church to the secret of the Father."

77. Monchanin, *In Quest of the Absolute,* 144, as previously quoted; emphasis added.

78. Monchanin, "La Vierge aux Indes," 48; as quoted in CPM, 65.

79. Monchanin, "La Vierge aux Indes," 48; as quoted in CPM, 65–66.

80. Monchanin, "La Vierge aux Indes," 47; as quoted in CPM, 65.

81. Monchanin, "La Vierge aux Indes," 47; as quoted in CPM, 65.

82. Monchanin, "La Vierge aux Indes," 48; as quoted in CPM, 65.

A further point to notice is that Monchanin makes a brief allusion to the Song of Songs in his poem about the Virgin of the Indies, saying:

> India, the worshiper of goddesses, of virgins—observable faces of the Advaita—will feel/experience the human and cosmic grandeur of the Virgin-Mother. Evoked by the Canticle under the contrary images of turtledove and war—"vox turturis" (Sg 2:12), "terribilis ut castrorum Acies ordinata" (Sg 6:4)—, sweet and terrifying, she, woman and mother, reveals the God whom she bears, who puts to death and gives life "mortificat et vivificat" (1 Samuel 2:6–8).[83]

This brief allusion is significant because it resonates with de Lubac's own Mariology which sees in Mary the culmination of all created goods.

To complete this sketch of the contours of his Marian thought, attention must also be paid to what Monchanin says elsewhere of the Song of Songs. In *In Quest of the Absolute*, Monchanin describes the "burning yet chaste" passion of the lovers in the Song with their "stratagems" of love: "The stratagems of love, alternating scenes and rhythms, presence, absence, flight, return, the hind and the fawn.... There is only one *love*, substantial sign and substance. These stratagems: his stratagems. He invites Israel—the Church and myself—and (like the Lover from the Beloved) is hidden from Israel, from the Church and from me."[84] Monchanin employs the Song to describe the divine initiative of love. In expressing how the Lover is hidden from the Beloved, he names the beloved, Israel, who, in turn, is identified with "the Church and myself." In other words, Israel, the Church, and the individual soul are all identified with the beloved bride in the Song of Songs. One notices the conformity of this articulation with Isaac of Stella's medieval paradigm, which de Lubac highlights in his own writings. Furthermore, in connection to the "Virgin of the Indies" wherein Monchanin posited a link between Mary and the Trinity and stated that the Virgin is "evoked by the Song,"[85] one might

---

83. Monchanin, "La Vierge aux Indes," 48. Although de Lubac quotes almost the entirety of "La Vierge aux Indes" in *Paradoxe et Mystère de l'Église*, he omits this specific section perhaps because of its allusions to India and to Hinduism, which do not directly pertain to his commentary on *Lumen Gentium*. The passage reads in the original: "L'Inde adoratrice des déesses, des vierges—faces phénoménales de l'Advaita—sentira la grandeur humaine et cosmique de la Vierge-Mère. Evoquée par le Cantique sous les images contraires de la tourterelle et de la guerre—'vox turturis,' 'terribilis ut castrorum acies ordinata ...'—, suave et effroyable, elle manifeste, femme et mère, le Dieu qu'elle porte, qui tue et qui vivifie: 'mortificat et vivificat'"; dashes are as found in the original; translation is mine.

84. Monchanin, "The Song of Songs," in *In Quest of the Absolute*, 171–72.

85. This statement is found in the omitted portion of "La Vierge aux Indes"; see *Dieu Vivant* 3 (1945): 48.

thus posit, with de Lubac, that Monchanin's writings presuppose that the Virgin is analogous to Israel, the Church, and the individual soul, and that this analogy is constituted by an analogous receptivity to the Trinitarian mystery.

Monchanin's notion that Our Lady has *received* the Trinitarian circumincession so perfectly that she embodies the Christic and pneumatic rhythm of deification is innovative and pushes forward the Christian tradition significantly. In the Middle Ages, Mary's coronation was oft-depicted as a Trinitarian event. "La Vierge aux Indes" elucidates the significance of Mary's exaltation further. The blessed Virgin is crowned Queen of heaven and earth, not only for her own glory, but essentially so that all Christians might also partake in the life of the Trinity through a process of deification in the likeness of Mary as *Theotókos*. We too are called to participate in the Christic and pneumatic rhythm of deification.

"Mystique et Mystère"

Two decades after Monchanin's seminal essay, de Lubac published an article on the status of spirituality as a theological discipline, and he identifies Teilhard and Monchanin as among those who have "prepared the way" for the next stage of the "confrontation that must take place" between the history of religions and spiritual theology.[86] Moreover, in his critique of a statement from Frithjof Schuon, a representative of gnostic esotericism who says that there is only a "universal reality of which the Virgin herself is the expression,"[87] de Lubac avers that, contrary to Shuon's belief, Christian mysticism is firmly grounded in the *concrete* reality of the Virgin: "It is the unique reality, to which he [the Christian mystic] adheres by faith, that is the bearer of a universal fruit."[88] De Lubac is clear: Mary is not simply the "expression" of some *universal* reality. Rather, she is a *concrete* being who has received fully the mystery of God in her life and has born "universal fruit."

86. Henri de Lubac, "Mysticism and Mystery," in *Theological Fragments* (San Francisco: Ignatius Press, 1989), 37–38; hereafter cited "MM." An initial, shorter version of MM appeared as a preface to a collection entitled *La mystique et les mystiques*, ed. André Ravier (Paris: Desclée de Brouwer, 1965). Considering the significance of de Lubac's MM, it is surprising that there are very few sustained theological reflections on this work. Two exceptions are Bryan Hollon, "Mysticism and Mystical Theology," in *T&T Clark Companion to Henri de Lubac*, ed. Jordan Hillebert (London: Bloomsbury, 2017): 307–25, and Andrew Prevot, "Henri de Lubac (1896–1991) and Contemporary Mystical Theology," in *A Companion to Jesuit Mysticism*, ed. Robert A. Maryks (Leiden: Brill, 2017), 279–309.

87. Frithjof Schuon, *De l'unité transcendante* (Paris: Gallimard, 1948), 36, 86; as quoted in MM, 67.

88. MM, 67.

De Lubac notes that Schuon's assertion "is the inverse of the notion of a concrete universal, applied to Christ and the Virgin Mary by a Blondel, a Teilhard de Chardin, or a Balthasar."[89] This notion of the "concrete universal" is essential for grasping de Lubac's thought. For him, the concrete or particular reality is prior and more fundamental than the universal, and "concrete universal" refers to that which first exists as a concrete reality and which is subsequently universalized.[90] Moreover, it is significant that de Lubac specifically invokes Blondel, Teilhard de Chardin, and Balthasar on this point of the historical character of Christian mysticism. De Lubac is essentially reasserting, on their authority, the concrete historical nature of Christian mysticism, while anchoring this concreteness firmly in the Blessed Virgin.

De Lubac's opposition to Schuon's idea maintains that the Virgin Mary is not simply an expression of some mystical "universal reality." She is, rather, a real historical being in whom the mysteries of faith come to fruition with universal significance. Moreover, she does not cease being individual in being universal. On the contrary, the reality of Mary's individuality becomes all the more important as she is universalized for the sake of others. The mystical reality found in Mary can be imitated precisely because she is wholly personal and individual, because she is a concrete—or personal—universal.

De Lubac caps off his argument for the concrete interiorization of the Christian mysteries within time and history with a quotation from *Lumen Gentium* and the words of Maurice Blondel, a figure of great influence in de Lubac's early formation. Blondel underscores the goal of Christian existence as a mysticism by which one enters into "the divine relationship, *divinae consortes naturae*" through "reproducing in ourselves the divine mystery par excellence, that is, by begetting the Son and breathing the Spirit."[91] Blondel proceeds to identify the Christian mystic as "essentially *Theotókos*" and thus links the Christian to Our Lady who alone is *the Theotókos*. In her likeness, the act of "begetting the Son and breathing the Spirit" becomes the means by which the mystery of divine maternity is reproduced within each Christian soul.

89. MM, 67n112; translation revised to reflect the French original: "C'est l'inverse de la notion d'universel concret."

90. "Concrete universal" and "universal concrete" can be used interchangeably. For an excellent analysis of this concept as applied to Mary, see Paul McPartlan, "Mary for Teilhard and de Lubac," paper delivered to the Oxford branch of the Ecumenical Society of the Blessed Virgin Mary (Wallington, Surrey: Ecumenical Society of the Blessed Virgin Mary, 8 November 1987).

91. Maurice Blondel, in a letter to A. J. Wehrlé dated 13 February 1908; as quoted in MM, 66. This point, that the goal of Christian existence and mysticism is the birth and growth of the Savior in the heart of human persons, is another expression of the idea of ecclesial motherhood.

What is even more intriguing is that this reference to the eternal processions of the Word and Spirit from God the Father, made in relationship to Mary, echoes a very similar connection found in Monchanin's conception of the Virgin of the Indies, where the Trinitarian dimension of Our Lady's divine maternity was also expounded: "[Mary's] childbearing is comparable rather to the generation of the Word by the Father than to the childbearing of other women: *prius concepit mente.*"[92] Elsewhere, Monchanin also stated that "the time of the Church is ... the intemporal rhythm of God, the Trinitarian circumincession *received* in the becoming, which has become the Christic and pneumatic rhythm of deification."[93] Taken together, these ideas illumine the analogous Trinitarian dynamism at the heart of divine maternity. Monchanin's statement on Mary's childbearing, quoted by de Lubac in *Paradoxe et Mystère de l'Église,* coincides perfectly with Blondel's statement, quoted by de Lubac in "Mystique et Mystère." Together, these statements reveal some of the formative influences and fundamental building blocks of de Lubac's insight into the mystical analogy of Mary and the Church. Mary is the model and archetype for every member of the Church in whose soul the "eternal birth"[94] of God is to take place, mysteriously reproducing "the divine mystery par excellence, that is, by begetting the Son and breathing the Spirit ... [and becoming] essentially *Theotókos.*"[95] In identifying Mary as a concrete universal, de Lubac follows Teilhard and Blondel in enlarging to cosmic proportions the role of Mary in salvation history, all the while preserving her historical reality with his emphasis on the concrete.

Amida Buddhism

Insofar as the notion of a concrete universal encapsulates the dual dimensions of the one and the many, the historical and the transcendent, it potentially informs de Lubac's theology of history as well. On this point, de Lubac's writings on Amida Buddhism are significant and must be examined in connection with his notion of the concrete universal. In *Aspects du bouddhisme* (1951), which was written at approximately the same time *Méditation sur l'Église* came into print, de Lubac makes a striking comparison between

92. Monchanin, "La Vierge aux Indes," as quoted in CPM, 65.
93. Monchanin, *In Quest of the Absolute,* 144; emphases added.
94. MM, 67, with reference to Meister Eckhart and John Tauler.
95. MM, 66.

Mary and a Buddha figure, Avalokitesvara. Such references give Mary a place in de Lubac's work in comparative religions, and they intimate the extent to which de Lubac's Mariology informed all aspects of his work. Conversely, de Lubac's critique of Amida Buddhism further accentuates the significance of his conception of Mary as a concrete universal.

Amida, Avalokita, and Mary

Amida Buddhism is a specific variant of Mahāyāna Buddhism, also known as Japanese Pure Land Buddhism. "Pure Land" refers to the "Sukhavati" or Western Paradise, the final place of awakening into a spatial conceptualization of birth to a place of light: i.e., enlightenment. Amida is the celestial Buddha who presides over the heavenly Paradise. Long ago in a previous life, Amida had made a vow to devote himself to the illumination of all: "If, when I attain Buddhahood, the sentient beings of the ten quarters [i.e., all sentient beings] should not be born [in the Pure Land], may I not attain the supreme enlightenment."[96] With this, Amida predicated salvation on the enlightenment of all sentient beings, and his primordial vow became the anchor of hope for a universal rebirth into Paradise.

Amida Buddha's greatest disciple was bodhisattva Avalokitesvara, also known as Kuan-yin in China and as Kannon in Japan.[97] Renowned for his compassion and intercession, Avalokitesvara is often invoked in dire situations by his devotees. The cult to Avalokitesvara supplanted that of Manjusri who came before him, and Avalokitesvara's own cult will eventually be surpassed by Maitreya, the projected final incarnation of the Buddha on earth. Until then, Avalokitesvara continues interceding for the final birth of all sentient beings.

De Lubac provides excerpts from *Lotus of the True Law*, which chronicles Avalokitesvara's merits, noting that the twenty-fourth chapter is completely devoted to singing the praises of him who is an "ocean of compassion" and "whose face looks to every side." One passage reads like a litany of conditional clauses and entreaties: "If man were cast headlong into a pit full of fire by a wicked being, . . . [i]f he is surrounded by a band of enemies armed with their swords, . . . [i]f he is chained by iron or wooden links, . . . [i]f he is surrounded by ferocious beasts," each followed by a declarative that the man "has only

---

96. *Collected Works of Shinran*, 1:493, as quoted in David Grumett and Thomas Plant, "De Lubac, Pure Land Buddhism, and Roman Catholicism," *Journal of Religion* 92, no. 1 (2012): 81n98.

97. Grumett and Plant, 72–73.

to remember Avalokita!"[98] Another passage extols him thus: "O thou whose eyes are beautiful, full of kindness, compassion and purity, thou whose face is so lovable. O thou who are spotless, … Remember, remember Avalokita, this pure Being! In the times of misery and death, he is the protector, the refuge, the sanctuary."[99] De Lubac comments that in all of these prayers and hymns to Avalokita, "the Christian reader perceives … an accent which, notwithstanding the difference in spiritual climate, recalls to him in some degree the tone of a St. Bernard extolling the Virgin Mary."[100]

The Chinese variant of Avalokita is Kuan-cheu-tin, or simply Kuan-yin, "who perceives the tones [of the world]." Kuan-yin is often depicted with feminine traits, and "from these traits comes the comparison that has been made between him and the Virgin Mary, a comparison that can be based on still stronger resemblances."[101] De Lubac notes that depictions of Kuan-yin "sometimes … by herself, sometimes carrying a small child" were of astonishing "resemblance to our 'madonnas.'"[102] Then, in his discussions of Kannon of the Kondo of Joryuji, Japan's equivalent of Kuan-yin, de Lubac again associates her solemn beauty with the Catholic Madonna: "[Kannon's] beautiful face, hieratic, calm and noble, with half-open eyes, fine proportions, superb folds which, in a single stream, hang down at the sides, invincibly bring to mind the wonderful figures of the Romanesque portal of the cathedral of Chartres."[103] He further recounts how the image of the Virgin Mary, placed in the "Temple to the Flower of the Saints" at Shinking by the first Jesuit missionaries to China, was warmly embraced by the natives. Similarly in Japan during a period of persecution, the Christians of Nagasaki were able to evade their persecutors and anchor their faith in prayer to the Virgin Mary while standing before a statue of Kannon: "the faithful had transformed him into an image of the Queen of Mercy."[104] De Lubac points out another striking parallel between the traditional Marian hymn, Salve Regina and a cantata in honor of Kuan-yin: "Hail, O Bodhisattva Kuan-yin, great,

98. "Avalokita" is a variation of the name "Avalokitesvara."

99. *Lotus of the True Law*, as quoted in "Faith and Piety in Amidism" (1971) in *Theological Fragments*, 359.

100. Henri de Lubac, *Aspects du bouddhisme* in Oeuvres complètes, 21 (Paris: Cerf, 2012), 284. The English translation quoted here is from *History of Pure Land Buddhism*, trans. Amita Bhaka in *Buddha Dhyana Dana Review* 12, no. 6 (2002), pages not numbered, accessed online at http://www.bdcu.org.au/bddronline/bddr12no6/bddr12no6.html.

101. "Faith and Piety" in *Theological Fragments*, 360.

102. *Aspects du bouddhisme* in Oeuvres complètes, 21:297. Note that increasingly overtime, the figure of Kuan-yin was depicted as a female figure.

103. *Aspects du bouddhisme* in Oeuvres complètes, 21:301.

104. "Faith and Piety" in *Theological Fragments*, 360.

full of grace and mercy, in the paradise of sovereign happiness."[105] Both are tender figures to whom the imperiled seek refuge and recourse.

In all of these considerations, de Lubac insists that we must go "beyond the aesthetic analogies" to probe whether "these images conceived by Buddhist Asia could be endowed with something analogous to the 'mysterious reflected image in which everyone acknowledges the presence of the Virgin?'"[106] Although de Lubac leaves this provocative question unanswered, it is clear by the discussion he has provided that this unique alignment between Mary and the Avalokitesvara informs his own work on Buddhism. The attention de Lubac pays to this connection is but another indicator of the importance of the Virgin to different aspects of his thought. Let us turn next to de Lubac's analysis of Buddhism wherein the relevance of his adoption of Teilhard and Blondel's notion of the concrete universal is ever more pronounced.

Enlightenment as the Negation of Person

"Amida," a name which means "light," was given to Dharmakara when he achieved illumination and became Amida Buddha—no longer a human form but a form of infinite light. Reflecting on the state of illumination, de Lubac comments that "when Amida takes on vaster proportions, becomes a supernatural being and seems to begin to take on a divine dignity, it is to inaugurate the process at the completion of which he *vanishes like a phantom.* In the cosmic or supracosmic principle that receives him, his *personality is not sublimated but abolished.*"[107] This means that there are no substantial beings in the Pure Land because, in the state of illumination, an individual's identity is not sublimated but abolished.

At the core of Buddhism is the belief that individual personhood is a principal form of suffering ("dukkha") from which one must seek liberation through detachment and negation of self. The nature of salvation in Amida Buddhism consequently involves a movement of *universalization* that negates the individual person as person. Even the teaching on *maitri,* or compassion and mercy, is intentionally emptied of its "personal" content. In *Aspects du bouddhisme,* de Lubac contrasts *maitri* with the Christian

---

105. End of chapter 5, *Pure Land Buddhism.*

106. *Aspects du bouddhisme* in Oeuvres complètes, 21:301; the internal quotation is from André Mahause, "To restore man and remind him of his greatness in a whisper," in *Problems of Contemporary Art* (1953), 45n97.

107. "Faith and Piety" in *Theological Fragments,* 368; emphases added.

understanding of charity as involving a gift of *self* to another being. *Maitri,* in de Lubac's estimation, is a "love without affection." The ultimate salvific unity that the bodhisattva seek "is only achieved through impersonality."[108] This is diametrically opposed to the Christian viewpoint in which there can be "no unitive charity, no reciprocity" if there are no persons, "no beings to give themselves to each other."[109]

This dynamic in which the concrete individual is subsumed by the universal constituted the crux of de Lubac's critique of Frithjof Schuon in "Mystique et Mystère." Moreover, the "boldness of Teilhard's Mariology"—namely, his notion of Mary as a concrete universal—is diametrically opposed to Buddhism's idea of salvation as the achievement of "impersonality." In Teilhard's Christian system, Our Lady is the highest representation of created personhood and the climactic terminus of nature's evolution through time in a process of Christogenesis. God's inbreaking in Christ is bestowed upon creation at its personal zenith in Mary. Teilhard's configuration of Our Lady, precisely as a concrete universal and the eternal feminine figure, precludes any pantheistic interpretation that might posit an evolutionary flow in which nature itself evolves into Christ. Rather, nature must be brought to this virgin peak of pure creatureliness in Mary, the most personal and hence, most universal, of all creatures.

Cyclic Time and the Denial of History

De Lubac also critiques the notion of time in Buddhist teaching. For de Lubac, history must always be grounded in eschatology as its consummation. Buddhism's concept of time, on the other hand, renounces historicity. Birth into the Pure Land is not the culmination of time but the end of the cycle of rebirth. Time, in this sense, is not linear but cyclic: "In Buddhism, we are no longer dealing with a series of irreversible events but with a cycle.... And, if there must be a Buddha in the future, it is just as there had to be one in the past, because everything repeats itself indefinitely."[110] In this conception, says de Lubac, there is no sense of history or cosmic finality.

In contrast, time in the Christian sense involves a linear succession of events from creation to consummation. Historicity is oriented to finality; time is rooted in eschatology. Within this framework, Mary stands as the concrete, personal figure of the new heavens and new earth that one finds

---

108. *Aspects du bouddhisme,* 60.
109. *Aspects du bouddhisme,* 60.
110. Henri de Lubac, "Buddhist Messianism?" (1969), in *Theological Fragments,* 373.

in Christian eschatology. As seen in the previous chapter, she embodies the anagogical sense of Scripture and is the Bride evoked in both the Song of Songs and the book of Revelation. She is an icon of the eschatological fullness of time.

Insofar as history and historicity are important to de Lubac's theology, time is of the essence—in the existential sense. De Lubac's study of Teilhard's eternal Feminine was not a study of a historical myth, but the historicity of the Church and of Mary. Moreover, his espousal of Teilhard's notion of the concrete universal paradoxically holds together both the concrete (individual and historical realities) and the universal (understood as "the prerogative of the strongest personality"[111]). "The Virgin, existing in her own individuality ... is universalized in the principle."[112] These conceptions stand in stark contrast to Amida Buddhism's universalization apart from concrete time and personal individuation.

While de Lubac has much to say about the tenets of Buddhism that do not directly pertain to his understanding of Mary and the Church, the abundant references he makes to Mary in the cited passages manifest how his own Marian thought guided his assessment of Buddhism. It is evident that de Lubac's Mariology sharpened his analyses of Eastern religions. His understanding of Mary as the eternal Feminine upholds a conviction regarding the essence of history and cosmic finality, in contrast to the Buddhist belief of samsara, the cycle of death and rebirth. His grasp of the consequences of Buddhism's negation of individual personhood further informed his theological conviction that eschatological fullness is founded on a *person*—the person of Christ who as Lord of human *history*, bestows himself upon creation, in and through the person of Mary, the eternal feminine and apogee of creation.

Conclusion

The substance of Teilhard's and Monchanin's Mariological thought reflects and retrieves to varying degrees the patristic concept of the close relationship of Mary and the Church. Teilhard's testimony was given in his poem, *L'Éternel féminin*, in which the veiled Virgin is a cosmic figure who reveals her identity as a concrete universal: "the Church, the bride ... [and] Mary

111. EF, 118, as previously quoted.
112. EF, 119.

the Virgin."[113] Similarly, Monchanin's meditation on "The Virgin of the Indies" makes a radical association between Mary's maternity and the Trinitarian processions, positing that Mary's motherhood is more akin to the Fatherhood of God than to human birthing. There is a certain congruity in these distinct articulations of Mariology, and it is recognized by de Lubac himself, who points out that Monchanin "enlarges this theme [of the maternity of Mary in relation to the Church], in the manner of Père Teilhard, almost into a kind of cosmic maternity."[114]

Mary and the Church, each virgin and mother, share in a mystically identical maternal function for the salvation of the world. Christian mysticism, as a birthing of Christ in the soul of the faithful, is patterned after his birthing from Mary, such that "he whom the Virgin bore is born again every day by the Church."[115] De Lubac was able to maintain this idea, not only on the basis of tradition but ever more through the witness of his theological interlocutors. In this way, while in conversation with his contemporaries and with contemporary concerns in mind, de Lubac gave expression to a Marian theology deeply rooted in the tradition. His capacity for *aggiornamento* is evident. The *ressourcement* theologian is not an antiquarian unconcerned with current affairs or the life of the Church and the world he inhabits. Rather, de Lubac was keenly attuned to the pulse of the ecclesial mother and to that heartbeat of the cosmos vivified in the mystery of Mary.

What emerges from our study of de Lubac's preconciliar thought is a vast synthetic vision of patristic and medieval *ressourcement,* in which de Lubac masterfully weaves the golden threads of both Scripture and tradition on Mary. His retrieval of a Marian exegesis on the Song of Songs (chapter 3), coupled with his exposition on Teilhard's eternal Feminine (chapter 4), effectively highlight the figure of Mary as the perfect bride. De Lubac's writings on the dynamics of Monchanin's Trinitarian mysticism and the notable affinity between Marian devotion and the Buddhist cult to Avalokitesvara (chapter 4) highlight the figure of Mary as a tender mother who gives life and nurtures her children. Additionally, de Lubac's recapitulation of Isaac of Stella's trio of terms (chapter 2) and Teilhard's conception of the concrete universal (chapter 4) enable him to fortify the inherent unity of Mary and the Church without compromising their proper distinction. All that is said of Mary can be said of the Church and vice-versa.

113. Teilhard, EF in WTW, 200–201.
114. CPM, 65.
115. Bérengaud, *In Apocalypsin* 12, 3–5; as quoted in EF, 29–30.

These principles of de Lubac's Marian *ressourcement,* gleaned throughout these chapters, have a direct application to contemporary ecclesiological questions. One contentious topic at the Second Vatican Council was the question of whether to integrate the treatise on Mary with the treatise on the Church. This simple question carried weighty implications for the work of ecumenism. The Council's placement of the Marian treatise—ultimately integrating Mariology *within* the mystery of the Church—will endow the Church with an understanding of itself and its institutional elements within the context of spiritual maternal and nuptial mystery.

What actually happened at Vatican II regarding Mary and the Church? How is de Lubac's Marian *ressourcement* reflected in the Council's Marian ecclesiology? Let us now turn to the Marian debates of the Council.

PART II

Conciliar and Postconciliar Developments

CHAPTER 5

A Conciliar Mariology

The Marian movement of the twentieth century had reached its zenith by the time Pope John XXIII announced his intention to call an ecumenical council on 25 January 1959. The Council itself opened on a Marian commemoration: 11 October 1962, the feast of the Maternity of Mary. In his opening speech, *Gaudet Mater Ecclesia,* Pope John XXIII set a tone of hopeful anticipation for a new Pentecost upon the Church and commended the Council's work to the protection of Mary, *Theotókos.* When the third session ended on 21 November 1964—another Marian feastday, the feast of the Presentation of Mary in the Temple—Pope Paul VI solemnly declared Mary "Mother of the Church."

Ironically, the palpable Marian context in which sessions of the Council both opened and closed did not penetrate beyond the Council itself. The Council's contentious debates and its objectively balanced Marian Ecclesiology has remained siloed in postconciliar theology. The paucity of literature on the Mariology of Vatican II contrasts starkly and surprisingly to the plethora of literature on the Second Vatican Council overall.[1] And while

---

1. Recent historical studies of Vatican II, amongst many, include Alberto Melloni, *Vatican II: The Complete History* (New York: Paulist Press, 2015); Giuseppe Alberigo and Joseph A. Komonchak, eds., *History of Vatican II,* 5 vols. (Maryknoll, NY: Orbis, 1995–2006); and a counterperspective by Agostino Marchetto, *The Second Vatican Ecumenical Council: A Counterpoint for the*

commentaries on the Marian chapter of *Lumen Gentium* can be found, there are relatively few sustained studies analyzing the proceedings which produced that Marian-ecclesial synthesis.[2] What actually happened at Vatican II regarding Mary? Why was the Council so divided on the placement of the Marian schema? We now turn to the evolution of the schema, "The Blessed Virgin Mary, Mother of God in the Mystery of Christ and the Church,"[3] highlighting in broad strokes the conciliar proceedings so as to acquaint the reader with the main figures and discussions that took place.

The Conciliar Debate on Mary

Questions about Mary and Marian doctrine were present from the very beginning. Between May 1959 and November 1960, the Antepreparatory Commission, presided by Cardinal Domenico Tardini, sent letters to the Curia, bishops, superior generals of religious orders, and Catholic Universities throughout the world to solicit topics that the Council should treat.[4] Of the

---

History of the Council (Scranton, PA: University of Scranton Press, 2010). See also multiple essays by Jared Wicks in *Catholic Historical Review* (1996–); particularly pertinent is "Recent Scholarship on Vatican Council II," *Catholic Historical Review* 105, no. 3 (2019): 531–58, which presents an archive-based account of the itinerary of the developments and final formulation of the Council's Marian teaching.

2. For the most comprehensive study of chapter 8 of *Lumen Gentium*, see Giuseppe M. Besutti, "*Lo Schema Mariano al Concilio Vaticano II* (Rome: Marianum/Desclée, 1966) and Cesare Antonelli, *Il dibattito su Maria nel Concilio Vaticano II. Percorso redazionale sulla base di nuovi documenti di archivio*, Bibliotheca Berica 14 (Padova: Edizioni Messagero di Sant' Antonio, 2009). See also Bessuti, "Note di Cronaca sul Concilio Vaticano II e lo Schema de B. Maria Virgine," *Marianum 26* (1964): 1–42, and Roberto de Mattei, *Il Concilio Vaticano II: Una storia mai scritta* (Torino: Lindau, 2010). For studies in English, see volume 37 of *Marian Studies* (1986); Jorge Medina Estevez, "The Blessed Virgin," in *Vatican II: An Interfaith Appraisal*, ed. John Miller (Notre Dame, IN: University of Notre Dame Press, 1966); and Alberic Stacpoole, "Mary's Place in *Lumen Gentium*, Vatican II's Constitution on the Church," in *Mary and the Churches* (Collegeville, MN: Liturgical Press, 1990). For commentaries by certain Council participants, see Gérard Philips, *L'Église et son Mystère au IIe Concile du Vatican: Histoire, texte et commentaire de la constitution Lumen Gentium* (Paris: Desclée de Brouwer, 1967); René Laurentin, *La Vierge au concile* (Paris: Éditions du Seuil, 1965) and "La Vierge Marie au Concile," *Revue des Sciences Philosophiques et Théologiques* 47 (1964): 32–46; and Otto Semmelroth, "The Role of the Blessed Virgin Mary, Mother of God, in the Mystery of Christ and the Church," trans. Richard Strachan, in *Commentary on the Documents of Vatican II*, vol. 1, ed. Herbert Vorgrimler (New York: Herder & Herder, 1967): 285–96.

3. The official proceedings of the Council (i.e., the acts of the congregations and the public sessions, the written and oral interventions, the different drafts of schemata, the proposed emendations, and the approbation of the documents) can be found in *Acta Synodalia Sacrosancti Concilii Oecumenici Vaticani Secundi,* hereafter cited as *Acta.* See also Floyd Anderson, ed., *Council Daybook. Vatican II.* 2 vols. (Washington, DC: National Catholic Welfare Conference, 1965).

4. These materials from 1959 to 1962 are published as *Acta et Documenta Concilio Oecumenico Vaticano II apparando.* Series I, in 14 volumes, contains the official proposals submitted in

2000 episcopal *vota* that were returned to the Vatican, around six hundred responses asked the Council to speak on the Blessed Virgin Mary. There were twenty requests for the Council to address Mary's queenship; fifty each on spiritual maternity and on coredemption; and approximately three hundred asked for a new definition on Mary as *mediatrix omnium gratiarum*. In the subsequent period from November 1960 to July 1962, ten Preparatory Commissions and three Secretariats were established to review the *vota* and draft the schemata to be discussed at the Council.[5] Seventy-five documents were produced altogether, some of which were cancelled or merged after the Central Commission reviewed them. *De Beata Maria Virgine Matre Dei et Matre Hominum* was one of the seven schemas sent to the Central Commission by the Theological Commission, with anticipation that it would be discussed in the Council's first session.[6]

De Lubac had been appointed as a consultor to the Preparatory Theological Commission, but his influence in the preparation of schemas was severely limited by the suspicion of the old-guard who were apathetic toward ecclesial reform and renewal.[7] These were generally members of the Roman Curia who also headed the Commissions, and the drafts they had prepared largely parroted modern encyclicals and theological manuals, neglecting Pope John's vision of *aggiornamento* and the underlying currents of *ressourcement* altogether.[8] As we will see, the first session of the Council consequently ended without any schemata being approved, a failure that was actually seen as a "great, surprising, and genuinely positive result" because it demonstrated the bishops' "strong reaction against the mentality behind the preparatory work."[9] This reaction has been described as "a bomb in the nave

---

preparation for the Council. Series II, in 13 volumes, records the work of the Central Preparatory Commission.

5. A list of the twenty original schemata is found in *Acta* I/1, 90–95.

6. For the Marian schema, *De Beata Maria Virgine Matre Dei et Matre Hominum* (1962), see *Acta* I/4, 92–97; for the *Praenotanda* and notes appended to the schema, see *Acta* I/4, 98–121. For an account of the development of the text, see Joseph A. Komonchak, "The Struggle for the Council during the Preparation of Vatican II (1960–1962)," in Alberigo and Komonchak, *History of Vatican II*, 1:257–60.

7. Cf. Riches, "Henri de Lubac and the Second Vatican Council," 129, and *Notebooks*, 1:93 and 1:77, in which de Lubac describes the Theological Commission as "a small academic system, ultra-intellectualist without any great intellectuality ... [into which] the Gospel is forced to fit" (20 September 1961 entry).

8. *De Fontibus Revelationis*, for example, was hotly debated from 14 to 20 November 1962 and ultimately rejected by the Holy Father, who decided that the schema needed to be revised by a new Joint Commission.

9. Joseph Ratzinger, as quoted by Ralph M. Wiltgen, SVD., *The Rhine Flows into the Tiber* (New York: 1967), 59.

of Saint Peter's: everyone had expected a council without incident, and now history had begun!"[10]

As for the schema on Mary, the original text of *De Beata Maria Virgine Matre Dei et Matre Hominum* underwent dramatic change. Early on, Msgr. Carlo Colombo of Milan, theological *peritus* of Cardinal Montini (later Pope Paul VI) and a member of the Theological Commission, suggested that the Marian treatise be located within the treatise on the Church in order to present Mary as the exemplary member of the Church. However, the main drafter, Carlo Balić (1899–1977), a Croatian Franciscan friar and the president of the *Pontificia Accademia Mariana Internazionale,* was of a different mindset, and the text he prepared focused on Mary's eminent role in the hypostatic order according to the eternal predestining decree of God. It associated Mary principally with the work of her Son and secondarily with the Church and salvation history. This was the lynchpin of the Marian movement in the early twentieth century, a Marian theology that focused on Mary's divine privileges as stemming from her union with Christ in the work of redemption. This singular and intimate union was also the basis for promoting the titles of Mary as Co-Redemptrix and Mediatrix of all graces.

Balić's draft met with some resistance. René Laurentin (1918–2017), a *ressourcement* Mariologist also serving on the Theological Commission, felt that the schema needed to be more biblically based. This idea was welcomed by Gerard Philips of Louvain (1899–1972) and Yves Congar, who both argued that a stronger biblical grounding would serve the Catholic witness to Protestants.[11]

The original text by Balić was presented to the Preparatory Commission on 5 March 1962, whence he proposed that the text be made into a distinct dogmatic constitution.[12] As no strong objections were raised here, Balić continued to revise and expand the text, enlarging the section on Mary's mediation. By April, the draft was completed and sent to Cardinal Alfred Ottaviani, President of the Theological Commission.[13]

A "little known drama" played out after Cardinal Ottaviani sent Balić's

10. Marce Grelot, *Il rinnovamento biblico nelventesimo secolo: memorie di un protagonist* (Cinisello Balsama: San Paolo, 1996), 172, as quoted in Riches, "Henri de Lubac and the Second Vatican Council," 130.

11. Congar's diary of the Council gives a glimpse of the work of the Commission, with details which are not recorded in the minutes of their session meetings. Cf. *My Journal of the Council,* trans. Mary J. Ronayne, OP, and Mary C. Boudling, OP (Collegeville, MN: Liturgical Press, 2012), 52–55.

12. See *Notebooks,* 1:102, 5 March 1962 entry.

13. Wicks, "Recent Scholarship," 550.

final draft, renamed *Constitutio de BVM—De Maria Matre Dei et Matre Hominum,* to Pope John XXIII for his initial approval before sending it to the Commission. On 25 April, Msgr. Felici, Secretary of the Central Preparatory Commission, revealed that the Holy Father initially did not want a separate constitution on Mary, but, as Cesare Antonelli reports, Cardinal Ottaviani and his secretary, Sebastian Tromp, succeeded in persuading him otherwise.[14] From there, the draft was sent to the Central Preparatory Commission in June and distributed to the fathers on 23 November 1962, printed in the same fascicle with the schema *De Ecclesia,* though as separate schemata. As early as mid-October, however, Gerard Philips, the theological *peritus* to the Belgian bishops and consultor of the Preparatory Theological Commission, had already begun working on an alternative draft, at the request of Cardinal Suenens.[15] This draft offered an integrated view with a chapter on the Virgin Mary serving as an epilogue or crowning finish to *De Ecclesia.*[16]

De Lubac's journal entry on 26 November 1962 describes a study meeting he attended at the biblical institute with other *periti* and Council fathers such as "Congar, Labourdette, Laurentin, etc., and several French bishops, including Bishop Pourchet." The purpose of the meeting was to study the Marian schema. The group was critical of the draft's prevailing "devotional ultramontanism" and its emphasis on the "maternal rights" of Mary. They also discussed the alternative draft composed by G. Philips, which was found favorable.[17]

In the final week of the first session, Cardinal Ottaviani recommended that the Council bring to a swift approval the six-page schema on the Blessed Virgin rather than begin its deliberation on the longer thirty-six-page treatise on the Church. The board of Council presidents, however, opposed the idea, opting instead to begin discussion on *De Ecclesia,* so as to gather proposals for revising it, as was already being done for the schema *De Fontibus.* Leaving the Marian text for a later date was also a nod to its ecumenical significance, for the Council's Mariology demanded careful attention, not hasty approval.[18] On

---

14. Antonelli, *Il dibattito su Maria,* 181–82.

15. Cf. Cesare Antonelli, "Le role de Mgr. Gérard Philips dans la redaction du chapitre VIII de 'Lumen gentium,'" *Marianum* 55 (1993): 17–97. Philips had the collaboration of several trusted theologians such as Congar, Colombo, Rahner, Ratzinger, Semmelroth, and McGrath, but the work was kept a secret from the Preparatory Theological Commission.

16. *Notebooks,* 1:383, 26 November 1962 entry.

17. *Notebooks,* 1:383, 26 November 1962 entry.

18. Cf. Eduardo Hontiveros, "The Blessed Virgin Mary in the Second Vatican Council," in *Ecumenism and Vatican II,* ed. Pedro S. De Achutegui, SJ (Manila: Loyola School of Theology, 1972).

the question of the placement of the treatise, Cardinal Suenens and Cardinal Montini expressed their desire for the schema on Our Lady to be incorporated into the schema on the Church with particular consideration of Mary's role as Mother of the Church.[19]

In the intersession prior to the opening of the second session, over one hundred written observations of the schema, *de Beata,* were submitted by individual bishops as well as bishops' conferences, some very lengthy and detailed.[20] The German-speaking and Scandinavian bishops were critical of the text. The Spanish bishops voiced a desire for a stronger presentation of Mary's mediatory role as Co-Redemptrix. The English and Scottish bishops wanted a distinct constitution, while the Polish bishops—represented by Bishop Karol Wojtyła of Kraków—advocated making the Marian treatise the second chapter of the schema on the Church. The Doctrinal Commission continued its work, opting to adopt and work from Philip's alternative draft that was developed into five chapters.

When the second session opened in 1963, the fathers voted to accept the revised text as the base text. In the days that followed, the Council heard many interventions. Cardinal Frings spoke on behalf of the German and Scandinavian bishops, asking for a clear definition of the relationship between the Blessed Virgin and the Church.[21] Cardinal Benjamín de Arriba y Castro of Tarragona, speaking on behalf of fifty-six Spanish bishops, was the single most outspoken voice advocating a separate Marian treatise. He spoke of the danger of Mary becoming a mere passive figure representing the Church as an elder daughter rather than as Mother of the Church by her vivifying influence.[22] On the other side, Cardinal Silva Henríquez, Cardinal Garrone, Archbishop Elchinger, and Bishop Medez Arceo were amongst the voices advocating integration. Cardinal Silva Henríquez conveyed a real theological concern in his intervention:

> We greatly desire that Marian doctrine itself be inserted into the schema *De Ecclesia.* For in our countries of Latin America piety toward and veneration of the most holy Mother of God often enough take on forms that do not have enough of a connection with the mystery of Christ and his Church. We think it is of great importance and

---

19. *Acta* I/4, 226 and 292.

20. Cf. "Animadversiones scripto exhibitae quoad schema de beata Maria Virgine," in *Acta* II/3, 306–38, 677–857.

21. *Acta* II/1, 343–46; see also Anderson, *Council Daybook,* 151.

22. Cf. Stacpoole, "Mary's Place in *Lumen Gentium,*" 87.

general interest, from both the ecumenical and pastoral viewpoints, that Marian doctrine does not appear as a sort of independent theological overgrowth, but takes its place in the whole complex of the message of salvation. Both the doctrinal exposé on the Church and that on the Blessed Virgin will gain in richness.[23]

Moreover, the Marian schema that reappeared for discussion in the second session bore a new title: *De beata Maria Virgine Matre Ecclesiae*.[24] The title *Mater Ecclesiae* reflected what became known as the "Christotypical" approach and was associated with Marian maximalists such as Balić and Gabriele Maria Roschini (1900–1977), a Servite priest and the first president of the Marianum Faculty in Rome.[25] Their focus was on the unique, individual graces imparted to Mary as the Mother of God, above and beyond her association to the Church, to whom she stood apart from as its mother. The bishops who promoted this Christotypical view desired that the Council present its Mariology in a separate schema that would esteem Our Lady's divine privileges and her preeminent role in salvation history. They especially advocated honoring Mary with the titles of Mediatrix and Co-Redemptrix.[26] On the other hand, the bishops who tended toward what was called the "ecclesiotypical" approach wanted to emphasize Mary's role, not above the Church but within it, and they advocated incorporating the Council's treatment of Mary within the schema on the Church. Their primary concern was that a separate treatise on Mary might contribute to polemics with Protestantism. Alberto Melloni notes that both the ecclesiotypical and Christotypical views were "equally valid, equally scriptural and equally traditional expressions of an authentic Catholic attitude to Mary."[27] The difference between them was more a difference of emphasis than of doctrine.[28]

On 23 October 1963, Cardinal Döpfner of Munich announced that the

23. Intervention by Cardinal Silva Henríquez; see *Acta* II/Appendix 2, no. 10.

24. *Acta* II/3, 299; see also Semmelroth, "The Role of the Blessed Virgin Mary," 286; and Jan Grootaers, "The Drama Continues between the Acts: The 'Second Preparation' and its Opponents," in Alberigo and Komonchak, *History of Vatican II*, 2:480.

25. Roschini was considered one of the greatest manualist Mariologists of the century, with voluminous publications and an entire *Dizionario di Mariologia* (Rome: Studium, 1960).

26. Cf. Hontiveros, "The Blessed Virgin Mary," 100; Stacpoole, "Mary's Place in *Lumen Gentium*," 88.

27. Alberto Melloni, "The Beginning of the Second Period: The Great Debate on the Church," in Alberigo and Komonchak, *History of Vatican II*, 3:97.

28. The terms "Christotypical" and "ecclesiotypical" are adopted from Archbishop Maurice Roy who employed them when he officially presented the Marian chapter to the Council on 16 September 1964: "The Christotypical and Ecclesiotypical interpretations in no way exclude but rather complement one another"; cf. "Patrum orationes. Relatio introductiva super Cap. VIII,"

Council's moderators had decided to hold a debate between representatives of the two positions to inform the assembly on the issues, after which the fathers would be asked to indicate their preference by voting on the matter. Cardinal König and Cardinal Santos each addressed the assembly at the fifty-fifth general congregation on 24 October 1963.[29] Cardinal Santos of Manila presented the Christotypical view. He gave attention to the special honor due to Mary and the concerns that an incorporation of the treatment on Mary into the schema on the Church "would give rise to an incomplete explanation or, worse, to one that would be dangerously prolix when compared to the section on the Trinity."[30] Although Santos did not deny the connection between Mary and the Church, he could not envision how the schema on Mary could possibly be inserted into the schema on the Church without diminishing Mary's pre-eminence. Moreover, an incorporated schema would require a radical revision of the Constitution on the Church itself.

On the other side, Cardinal König of Vienna represented the ecclesiotypical view that contended that the Council's treatment of Mary belonged within the Constitution on the Church. Theologically, explained König, such incorporation would prevent an excessively institutional conception of the Church. Pastorally, it would aid in the purification of Marian devotion, focusing on the essentials and doing away with the superfluous. Ecumenically, moreover, it would open avenues for the Church's dialogue with both the Oriental and Protestant traditions. An incorporated schema thus would not necessarily take away from the veneration of the Virgin or diminish her pre-eminence, while a separate schema would risk suggesting that the Council wanted to promote new Marian dogmas, something that was neither part of the Conciliar agenda nor favorable to the ecumenically minded.

In the subsequent days before the actual voting, the controversy escalated. The addresses of both Cardinal Santos and Cardinal König were reprinted and distributed along with additional booklets and pamphlets promoting the respective positions. E. Honiveros reports that conferences were held and leaflets were distributed "at the basilica door, even found on the Council

---

16 September 1964, in *Acta* III/1, 436; this translation is from Charles Newmann, "Mary and the Church: *Lumen Gentium*, Arts. 60–65," *Marian Studies* 37 (1986): 101.

29. These two speeches are found in *Relationes circa schema constitutionis dogmaticae de beata Maria Virgine, Matre Ecclesiae* (Typis Polyglottis Vaticanis, 1963), 1–12; *Acta* II/3, 338–45; see also Laurentin, *La Vierge au Concile*, 13–18; Anderson, *Council Daybook*, 1:212–22; and Melloni, "The Beginning," 95–98. For a summary of the speeches, see Frederick M. Jelly, "The Theological Context of and Introduction to chapter 8 of *Lumen Gentium*," *Marian Studies* 37 (1986): 50–59.

30. Melloni, "The Beginning," 95.

seats."[31] J. Grootaers states, "No part of the constitution on the Church gave rise to as many commentaries or elicited such a flood of publications as what the Council said about the Virgin Mary."[32]

A special indicative vote took place on 29 October 1963 with a procedure that required only a straight majority.[33] The bishops were asked to respond to the question, "Would it please the fathers for the schema on the Blessed Virgin Mary, Mother of the Church, to be integrated into the schema *De Ecclesia*?" Of the 2,188 votes, the results were 1,114 *placet* votes and 1,074 *non placet* votes.[34] A mere forty votes separated the two parties; had only twenty of the 2,188 votes changed, the outcome might have been entirely different.[35] The results revealed a lack of the sort of unanimity expected to characterize the Council's decisions, and it was evident that moral consensus had to be found before a new proposal would be accepted. Hence, a special commission was created with the explicit task of revising the text on Our Lady, taking into consideration the concerns of both the Christotypical and ecclesiotypical approaches. The commission consisted of both Cardinal Santos and Cardinal König, along with Bishop Doumith of Lebanon, Bishop Theas of Lourdes, Father Carlo Balić, and Msgr. Gérard Philips who was the assistant secretary of the Doctrinal Commission.[36] The bulk of the work went to the latter two. Philips was the principal author and Balić the principal redactor of the harmonizing *textus emendatus*, entitled "The Blessed Virgin Mary, God-Bearer, in the Mystery of Christ and of the Church." After protracted debates on the question of Mary's mediation and multiple emendations, the Theological Commission gave its approval on 6 June 1964. The text was then sent to Pope Paul VI who approved for it to be printed next to the *textus prior* and distributed to all the bishops.[37]

At the Council's third session, Archbishop Roy of Quebec introduced the Marian schema, reminding the fathers that the decision for an integrated

31. Hontiveros, "The Blessed Virgin Mary," 104.

32. Grootaers, "The Drama Continues," 481.

33. See Stacpoole, "Mary's Place in *Lumen Gentium*," 88.

34. *Acta* II/3, 627; see also Jelly, "Theological Context and Introduction," 60.

35. An interesting but little-known backstory is provided by T. William Coyle, "American Influence on Conciliar Decision Regarding BVM Schema," *Marian Studies* 37 (1986): 266–69. Coyle makes a convincing case for crediting the US bishops for turning the tide on this vote. More on this in the next chapter.

36. See *Schema Constitutionis De Ecclesia* (Typis Polyglottis Vaticanis, 1964), 218.

37. The textual evolution of the drafts by the subcommission is traced in Charles Newmann, "Textual Evolution of Chapter VIII of Lumen Gentium," *Marian Studies* 37, no. 17 (1986): 212–28 and in Wicks, "Recent Scholarship on Vatican II," 547–58.

treatise aimed to convey the truth that "the Blessed Virgin is intrinsically connected with the mystery of the Church."[38] The schema had been revised to present this intrinsic connection without seeking to settle the controversy between the Christotypical and ecclesiotypical tendencies. Archbishop Roy went on to explain the three main parts of the document. The first part considers Our Lady's place in salvation history, as illuminated by Scripture and Tradition. The second part examines explicitly the relationship of Mary and the Church, and the third deals with Marian devotion.[39]

Thirty-three oral interventions followed Archbishop Roy's speech in the next three days, 16–18 September. Most significant of these were the addresses of Cardinal Suenens and Cardinal Frings. Considered a man inclined to the progressive wing at the Council, Cardinal Suenens surprised many when he warned everyone against the danger of minimizing Mary's importance. He made his "valuable and independent contribution"[40] in emphasizing the reality of Mary's spiritual maternity and its intrinsic link with the Church's identity and mission, essentially and substantively fleshing out Mary's role in the Church today.[41] Cardinal Frings's address was conciliatory. He encouraged the fathers to accept the proposed text, even if it did not fulfill all of their expectations. He argued that it offered a good summary of Catholic teaching on the Blessed Virgin and that further elaboration could be left to the work of theologians.[42]

The titles Mediatrix and *Mater Ecclesiae*, which had been contentious topics from the beginning, were at the crux of the debate. Proponents of the title Mediatrix (i.e., Archbishop Pietro Parente, an officer of the Congregation of the Holy Office and Commission member; Bishop Frane Franić of Yugoslavia; and Cardinal Michael Brown, OP) appealed to its widespread acceptance and appearance in modern papal teaching. Those opposing the promulgation of the title (i.e., Cardinal Liénart, Cardinal J. Spellman, Bishop Hélder Câmara, and *periti*: G. Philips, R. Laurentin, and Karl Rahner) expressed concern over the potential ecumenical ramifications of its use.

It is said that Pope John XXIII—then Cardinal Roncalli—had expressed "considerable hesitation" regarding Pope Pius XII's institution of the feast of the Queenship of Mary in 1954. His reservations came out of ecumenical

38. *Acta* III/1, 435–38.

39. Cf. Jelly, "Theological Context and Introduction," 63–64.

40. Stacpoole, "Mary's Place in *Lumen Gentium*," 90.

41. See Joseph Komonchak, "Toward an Ecclesiology of Communion," in Alberigo and Komonchak, *History of Vatican II*, 4:55.

42. Cf. Wiltgen, *The Rhine Flows into the Tiber*, 157.

concern, fearing "serious harm to the apostolic efforts being undertaken to restore the unity of the Holy Catholic Church in the world."[43] Likewise in 1965, the idea of conferring on Mary the title of Mediatrix was deemed inopportune and counterproductive to ecumenical aims. One of the most outspoken voices was Karl Rahner who expounded the "unimaginable harm [that] would result from an ecumenical point of view, in relation to both Orientals and Protestants."[44] The bishops of the Fulda conference had concurred with this assessment early on and had suggested that the Council remain silent on the Marian title rather than create a new obstacle to ecumenical union. At the end of the day, the Commission retained the title in its text, taking up Bishop Ancel of Lyons's suggestion to place it on the same footing as other Marian titles.[45] This proved to be a judicious compromise that allowed "Mediatrix" to be retained while effectively diminishing any prominence which might be associated with it.

Regarding *Mater Ecclesiae*—a title which Laurentin had earlier opposed on the grounds that it was unfounded in the early Church, appearing only in the twelfth century[46]—the Doctrinal Commission had decided against employing the title directly in the text of the Constitution, even though it recognized it as theologically acceptable. Instead, the doctrine expressed in that title would be conveyed in equivalent terms by adding a paragraph (now *Lumen Gentium*, no. 53) that acknowledged Mary as the one "whom the Church honors as a most beloved Mother."[47] The official *Relatio* explained that these words were a sufficient expression of Mary's role as mother as well as an adequate compromise in view of the Council's ecumenical concerns.[48]

On 29 October 1964, exactly one year after the initial vote that decided by a slim margin to make the Marian schema an integrated part of the schema on the Church, the final text of the Marian chapter, bearing the title *De beata Maria Virgine Deipara in Mysterio Christi et Ecclesiae*,[49] was voted

---

43. A. Roncalli, 22 April 1954 letter to the Secretariat of the Movement *Pro Regalitate Mariae*, in Angelina and G. Alberigo, *Giovanni XXIII: Profezia nella fedeltà* (Brescia: Queriniana, 1978), 489; as quoted in Mattei, *The Second Vatican Council: An Unwritten Story* (Loreto Publications, 2010), 294.

44. Wiltgen, *The Rhine Flows into the Tiber*, 91–92.

45. *Acta* III/1, 506–8; LG, no. 60: "The Blessed Virgin is invoked by the Church under the titles of Advocate, Auxiliatrix, Adjutrix, and Mediatrix." See also Stacpoole, "Mary's Place in *Lumen Gentium*," 90–92.

46. Wicks, "Recent Scholarship," 549.

47. LG, no. 53; cf. Komonchak, "Toward an Ecclesiology of Communion," 61n206.

48. *Schema Constitutionis De Ecclesia*, 211.

49. *Acta* III/6, 10–23; see also Hontiveros, "The Blessed Virgin Mary," 105.

upon. It received 1,559 votes of *placet*, 521 votes of *placet iuxta modum*, and 10 of *non placet*.[50] The final vote on the Marian chapter took place on 17 November 1964, and the results were near unanimous: 2,096 votes of *placet*, 23 *non placet*, and one abstention.[51] *Lumen Gentium* as a whole was also overwhelmingly approved two days later.

That might have been the grand conclusion to the debates on Mary, but another storm had begun to stir which inevitably involved the Blessed Mother. At the closing of the third session of the Council on 21 November 1964, Pope Paul VI officially proclaimed Mary the Most Holy Mother of the Church. This pronouncement caused much dismay among the Council fathers and was considered the culmination of what was called "the black week."[52] The days preceding the pronouncement had seen multiple instances of papal intervention in the conciliar proceedings. First, the famous *Nota explicativa praevia* appended to *De Ecclesia* seemed to want to reverse the fathers' deliberations on collegiality (it was known that Pope Paul VI had previously commissioned a study of collegiality under Cardinal Ottaviani). Then, the eagerly anticipated vote on *De Libertate Religiosa* was postponed until the last session. The suspicion that this erupted was further heightened by the papal intervention for nineteen amendments to *De Oecumenismo*. Finally, the Holy Father's declaration naming the Blessed Virgin "*Mater Ecclesiae*" capped off what appeared to many to be an ominous imposition of papal authority, since the explicit will of the Council had been to refrain from proclaiming new Marian titles.[53]

A fury of emotions exploded in the aula. Xavier Rynne describes the fathers' reaction to the postponement of the vote on religious liberty as "a wave of grumbling, protests and commotion which spread throughout the hall … [creating] a scene of consternation, outrage, and disarray … [as] the bishops felt cheated, betrayed, insulted, and humiliated."[54] Moreover, the Pope's subsequent proclamation of Mary as Mother of the Church unwittingly associated the Blessed Mother with the consternation resulting from the Pope's recent interventions. The Christotypical emphasis of Mary's preeminent titles and privileges which the majority of the Council fathers had not advocated

50. *Acta* III/6, 49; see also Jelly, "Theological Context and Introduction," 68.

51. *Acta* III/8, 375.

52. For a historical analysis of the Pope's proclamation and the consternation it caused, see Luis Cardinal Tagle's "'The Black Week' of Vatican II," in Alberigo and Komonchak, *History of Vatican II*, 4:444–48.

53. Cf. Riches, "Henri de Lubac and the Second Vatican Council," 136–37.

54. Xavier Rynne, *The Third Session* (New York: Farrar, Straus, and Giroux, 1965), 258.

unfortunately became an expression of the assertion of papal authority over and against collegiality.

De Lubac's own reaction to the Black Week, however, provides a nuanced and valuable perspective. In a letter to Father Bernard de Guibert on 23 November, de Lubac acknowledges the dismay triggered by the events of that week: "November 19, 20, and 21 will remain for a long time, I fear, days of mourning for the Church. It no longer does any good to get indignant over what must well be called a 'robbery.' ... One could see in Saint Peter's a cardinal, one of the most solid members of the council, shedding tears."[55] However, on the specific topic of the Marian title, de Lubac simply comes to the defense of Pope Paul VI. In *Paradoxe et Mystère de l'Église* (1967), he explains that the expression 'Mother of the Church' is founded in tradition and that "each time the Pope saw fit to honour our Lady with the title 'Mother of the Church' ... he hedged it about with a series of qualifying clauses and cautions that tally exactly with the intricate nuances of the conciliar teaching."[56] In de Lubac's view, the Holy Father's speech at the closing of the third session of the Council "shows again and again his intention of stating only that which harmonizes with the text of the Constitution."[57] It would not be far-fetched to suggest, as Chantraine does, that Paul VI actually had de Lubac's writing in mind when he declared Mary "Mother of the Church."[58] And while de Lubac never claimed any such influence, the Marian title represents the best of his own theological instincts on the continuity and significance of Marian *ressourcement*.[59] Moreover, Mary's intimate connection to the Church as *Mater Ecclesiae* will have an important application to our discussion of the relationship of the universal and local Churches, forthcoming in chapter 7.

A Patristic Reintegration

Having surveyed the Council's debate over Mary, a debate that began with an evenly matched opposition between "separated" and "integrated" Mariologies and ended in a balanced synthesis—though not without controversy, we are now poised to consider the essential shift in the Council's theological

55. Letter to Rev. Guibert, as quoted in Figouruex, introduction to *Notebooks*, 26.

56. CPM, 60, with reference to Pope Paul VI, Audience of 18 November 1964.

57. CPM, 60, with reference to Laurentin, *La Vierge au concile*, 40.

58. George Chantraine, "Note Historique," in *Oeuvres complètes* (Paris: Cerf, 1999), 8: xxxi.

59. Riches, "Henri de Lubac and the Second Vatican Council," 139: "De Lubac would have never attributed such influence to himself, but he too must have recognized in the elevation of Mary 'Mater Ecclesiae' a vindication of his own Marian impulse."

outlook. This shift is observed in the evolution of the schemas, with the Council's increased integration of patristic sources. In this light, we next survey the sources deployed in chapter 8 of *Lumen Gentium* in comparison to the sources of the original schema, so as to see in greater relief the patristic *ressourcement* which the Council achieved in its chapter on Mary.

The Initial Schema (1962)[60]

The first schema, spanning only six pages, comprised six sections: (1) on the intimate connection between Christ and Mary according to the will of God; (2) on the role of the blessed Virgin Mary in the economy of our salvation; (3) on the titles by which the association of the blessed Virgin Mary with Christ in the economy of our salvation is accustomed to be expressed; (4) on the singular privileges of the Mother of God and of men; (5) on the cult rendered to the Most Blessed Virgin Mary; and (6) Most Holy Mary, Promoter of Christian Unity. As these subtitles convey, the schema represents a Christotypical perspective: Our Lady is presented principally in relationship to Christ; she is "above the Church" in a certain sense, and her divine prerogative as the Mother of God makes her unlike any other member of the Church. The schema's Marian exuberance—with its emphasis on Mary's titles and privileges—resisted being fitted into a discussion of the Church. On the other hand, the schema's intentional omission of titles such as "Co-Redemptrix" and "Reparatrix"—titles that posed no small challenge to the separated brethren—manifests the Council's ecumenical sensitivity from the very beginning.

The short text of the schema is followed by two pages of prefatory notes and twenty-one pages of endnotes. The *praenotanda* identifies "some erroneous opinions," including both "maximalist" and "minimalist" tendencies in Mariology. The "maximalist tendency" is described as being held by those who err in speaking as if the blessed Virgin is a redeemer paralleled to Christ, or in saying that she did not die or was not herself redeemed. In contrast, the "minimalists" are described as those who err in thinking of Mary as merely a member of the Church in the same way that other descendants of Adam belong to the Church.[61]

A survey of the endnotes—forty-six in total—show twenty-two references to the Fathers of the Church, of both the East and the West. The

---

60. The main text of the schema is provided in English translation in the appendix.
61. See *Praenotanda* IV.2 in *Acta* I/4, 99

most salient feature of the schema's endnotes, however, are the voluminous references to papal documents—a hundred altogether. Leo XIII alone is referenced twenty-nine times, with multiple references to *Iuncunde semper* (1894), *Fidentem piumque* (1896), and *Parta humano generi* (1901). Among other popular sources are eight references to Pius IX's *Ineffabilis Deus* (1854), six to Pius X's *Ad diem illum* (1904), and five to Pius XII's *Fulgens corona* (1953). Most germane to our present discussion are the twenty-two references to the writings of the Church Fathers, catalogued according to authorship as seen in Table 5-1.

Although much fewer in number than papal references, these patristic sources witness to the seeds of Marian *ressourcement* already in place at the start of the Council. Patristic theology offered three major affirmations concerning Mary and the Church, which are each alluded to in the 1962 schema: the idea of Mary as the "type" of the Church (cf. Ambrose); Mary as the New Eve (cf. Irenaeus and Justin); and continuity between Mary and the Church as parallel to the continuity of Christ and His body (cf. Augustine). The most concentrated account of the Church Fathers in the entire schema is found in the third section, "On the titles used to express Mary's association with Christ in the economy of salvation." Footnote sixteen gives a lengthy exposition of both papal and patristic sources for the title of Mary as Mediatrix and Co-Redemptrix. It draws on the parallel between Mary and Eve, as found in the writings of Justin and Irenaeus; then, it attributes to the Council of Ephesus the first formal application of the title "Mediatrix" to Mary and finds further support in the writings of Eastern Fathers such as St. Andrew of Crete (d. c. 740), St. Germanus of Constantinople (d. c. 733), St. John Damascene (d. 749), and St. Epiphanius (d. 403).

Though lesser known in the West, Andrew of Crete and Germanus of Constantinople, alongside John Damascene, are revered in the East as the three great Byzantine Fathers who led the flowering of Mariology in the eighth century after the Iconoclastic controversy. Their ardent defense of Mary's divine motherhood, her corporeal reality, and her role as *Mesites* or *Mesetria*—Greek for "Mediatrix"—are introduced and expounded in the schema's footnote. Moreover, the witness of these Byzantine voices to a fervent devotion to Mary's universal mediation is significant because it locates the debate on Mary as Mediatrix further back in Christian history than the Middle Ages whence the title took root and flourished in the West. The Commission's deployment of these Eastern sources testifies to an awareness of the importance of the Byzantine tradition and its continuity with

TABLE 5-1 Patristic Sources in the Original Marian Schema (1962)

Footnote #	Church Father	Writing	Reference
4	**Ambrose**	*In Lucam II, 7*	PL 15, 1555
31	Ambrose	*De institutione Virginis et S. Mariae virginitate perpetua, c. 8*	PL 16, 334
38	Ambrose	*De virginibus, lib. II, c. 2, n. 15*	PL 16, 210 B
16	**Andrew of Crete**		PG 97, 866
2	**Augustinus**	*De sancta virginitate, VI, 6*	PL 40, 399
3 & 4	Augustinus	*Sermo 25, De verbis Evangelii Matthaei XII 41–50, 7*	PL 46, 938
4	Augustinus	*Sermo 213, 7*	PL 38, 1064
6	Augustinus	*Quaestiones Octoginta tres, q. 11*	PL 40, 14
6	Augustinus	*De Trinitate I, 13, c. 18*	PL 42, 1032
9	Augustinus	*Sermo 215, 4*	PL 38, 1074
24	Augustinus	*De natura et gratia, c. 36, n. 42*	PL 44, 267
31	Augustinus	*Epist. 137 ad Volusianum, c. 2, n. 8*	PL 33, 519
39	Augustinus	*De sancta virginitate, c. 3*	PL 40, 398
16	**Epiphanius**	*Adversus haereses, 78*	PG 42, 727
16	**Germanus** of Constantinople	*In Dormitione Deiparae*	PG 98, 362, 369
33	Germanus of Constantinople	*In Sanctae Dei Genitricis dormitionem, Sermo 1*	PG 98, 346–47
8	**Innocent III**	*Sermo 12: In Purificatione BVM*	PL 217, 506
6	**Irenaeus**	*Adversus haeribus V, 19*	PG 7, 1175 B
16	Irenaeus	*Adversus haereses III, c. 24, 4*	PG 7, 959
31	**Jerome**	*Epist. 48, 21*	PL 22, 510
9	**John Damascene**	*Homilia 1 in Nativ. BVM*	PG 96, 671
16	John Damascene	*In Annuntiatione BVM*	PG 96, 659
33	John Damascene	*Homilia 2 in dormitione BVM, n. 14*	PG 96, 741
16	**Justinum**	*Dialogus cum Triphone, 100*	PG 6, 710
8	**Leo the Great**	*Sermo 21, c. 1*	PL 54, 191
9	Leo the Great	*Sermo 6 in Nativitate Domini*	PL 54, 213
16	**Unnamed author** 5–7th century	*Homilia V de laudibus S. Mariae Deiparae* *Post Concilium Ephesinum*	PG 43, 491
16	Unnamed	*Encomium in Dormitione S. Dominae Nostrae*	PG 86, 3294

the medieval tradition of the West. This witness will continue into the final drafts of the schema.

Lumen Gentium, Chapter 8 (1964)

As we have previously seen, between 1962 and 1964, the draft of *De Beata* underwent significant reconfiguration and refinement in the hands Gérard Philips, its principal architect. The redaction process required considerable work incorporating and responding to hundreds of observations and oral interventions that the Commission received from the Council, and Philips, an adept scholar of conciliatory temperament, was well-suited for the task.[62] Congar describes him as a man of "great intellectual sturdiness ... peaceable [and] pleasant."[63]

The final draft that became the eighth chapter of *Lumen Gentium* is almost twice as long as the text of the original schema, and the two texts differ significantly in their tone and tenor. According to Frederick Jelly, "The initial conciliar *schema* on Our Lady was over 1700 words, roughly half the length of the text that would be approved as chapter 8 of *Lumen Gentium*. It turns out that 300 of these words passed over directly into the final document, and more than 70 words indirectly."[64] The original schema had little to say on the ecclesial dimension of the mystery of Mary except for a few underlying assertions of Mary's unparalleled status over and above all members of the Church. Consequently, the Council's reorientation to a more ecclesiotypical approach demanded an overhaul of significant portions of the text.

The final draft, "The Blessed Virgin Mary, Mother of God, in the Mystery of Christ and the Church," comprises five sections: (1) Introduction, nos. 52–54; (2) The Function of the Blessed Virgin in the Plan of Salvation, nos. 55–59; (3) The Blessed Virgin and the Church, nos. 60–65; (4) The Cult of the Blessed Virgin in the Church, nos. 66–67; and (5) Mary, Sign of the True Hope and Comfort for the Pilgrim People of God, nos. 68–69. In contrast to the content of the original schema, the final version draws directly and liberally from biblical and patristic sources, with scant references to papal documents. For example, the assertion of Mary as "a most beloved

---

62. According to Antonelli, *Il dibattito*, 327–30, Philip methodically had all of the fathers' interventions typed onto index cards with each card corresponding to a numbered paragraph of the schema. This aided both the redaction of the text and Philips's own presentation to the Commission of the changes made.

63. Yves Congar, *My Journal of the Council*, 509.

64. Jelly, "Theological Context and Introduction," 50.

mother" (no. 53) is not made on the authority of papal teaching but on that of Augustine, who states that Mary "is clearly the mother of the members of Christ" and that she partakes in "bringing about the birth of believers in the Church" (no. 53, footnote 3). Similarly, the second section places Mary within the economy of salvation by surveying "the sacred writings of the Old and New Testaments, as well as venerable tradition" (no. 55). These paragraphs of chapter 8 are rich in Scriptural references, tracing Mary's role in salvation history. They also invoke "the Fathers" who "see Mary not merely as passively engaged by God, but as freely cooperating in the work of man's salvation through faith and obedience" (no. 56).

The Council's reorientation to a stronger ecclesiotypical approach is evidenced in the text of the third section, newly introduced to discuss the ecclesial context of the Marian mystery and bearing all the traces of the conciliar debates. Paragraphs 60 and 62 evince a clear focus on the question of mediation. The Council is emphatic that "Mary's function as mother of men in no way obscures or diminishes the unique mediation of Christ.... [Rather,] it flows forth from the superabundance of the merits of Christ, rests on his mediation, depends entirely on it and draws all its power from it" (no. 60). De Lubac is adamant that this perspective is wholly patristic, stating that both the Pope and the Council fathers took pains "to remain in the direct line of patristic tradition (and Scripture too, of course) on the questions of the unique mediation of Christ."[65]

Only after establishing the unicity of Christ's mediation does the text, three paragraphs later, assert that within the mystery of the Church "the Blessed Virgin stands out in eminent and singular fashion as exemplar both of virgin and mother" (no. 63). Here, the draft avails itself of medieval authors to support this close alignment of Mary and the Church, citing in footnote 19 Pseudo-Peter Damien, Godfrey of St. Victor (d. 1195), and Gerhoh of Reichersberg (d. 1169). A fourth medieval figure, Isaac of Stella (d. 1169), whom de Lubac made much use of in his own treatment on the Church and Our Lady in *Méditation sur l'Église*, is referenced in footnote 20 of paragraph 64, alongside Ambrose and Augustine.

Additionally, the preposition "in" in the title of the final schema (*De beata Maria Virgine Deipara in Mysterio Christi et Ecclesiae*) portrays the inspiration the Council wished to convey, namely that Our Lady should always be contemplated in close relationship to both her Son and to the Church. In essence, the treatise sought to revive the patristic perspective that never

___

65. CPM, 61.

spoke of Mary apart from Christ or the Church. This was a fruit of the Council's *ressourcement,* wholly evidenced by the fact that the final text retains only a very small fraction of the references to the papal documents employed in the initial schema, and in contrast, expounds patristic and medieval sources at length. Table 5–2 catalogues these sources.

Of the twenty-four footnotes of the final draft, fourteen make reference to one or more Church Fathers, and the previously one hundred–plus references to various popes are reduced to nine. Many of the patristic sources referenced in the first schema reappear in the final draft, and three references reappear verbatim: Augustine's *de Sancta Virginitate* (PL 40, 399); Ambrose's *In Lucam* II, 7 (PL 15, 1555); and Epiphanius's *Adversus haereses*, 78 (PG 42, 727). These represent both the Christotypical and ecclesiotypical perspectives. Augustine's treatise on virginity—quoted above—employs a Christotypical outlook: Mary "is clearly the mother of the members of Christ ... since she has by her charity joined in bringing about the birth of believers in the Church, who are members of its head."[66] Ambrose's commentary on Luke 2:7 takes a center place in the final presentation and is ecclesiotypically oriented: "As Ambrose taught, the Mother of God is a *type* of the Church in the order of faith, charity and perfect union with Christ."[67] Epiphanius's treatise, which refers to Mary as "Mother of the living," is employed by both the original schema and the final text to link Mary to the figure of Eve.[68]

The continuity between the original schema and the final draft, which is established by these references to Augustine, Ambrose, and Epiphanius, manifests a trajectory of development which adheres to the core of patristic thought concerning Mary and the Church. Irenaeus's famous passage from *Adversus haeresus* referring to Mary as a figure of the New Eve (which was quoted in the original schema) is not quoted in the final draft, but his theology is represented by Epiphanius, who develops the Eve-Mary parallel further, juxtaposing it with the parallel of Eve and the Church.[69] It was, furthermore, through Augustine that the Mary-Church parallel passed on to the theology of the Middle Ages. The deployment of his works in both drafts of the schema *de Beata* highlights the continuity that roots medieval Mariology in Augustine's theology.

66. LG, no. 53n3; 1962 Schema, ch. 1n2.

67. LG, no. 63n18; 1962 Schema, ch. 1n4; emphasis added.

68. LG, no. 56n8; 1962 Schema, ch. 3n16.

69. Cf. Clement Dillenschneider, "Mary, Prototype of Personification of the Church" (1961), *Marian Reprints,* paper 95; accessed online at http://ecommons.udayton.edu/marian_reprints/95, 1–9; here at 3.

TABLE 5-2 Patristic and Medieval Sources of *Lumen Gentium*, Chapter Eight (1964)

Footnote #	Church Father and Writing	Reference
3	Augustine, *De S. Virginitate, 6*	PL 40, 399
5	Cf. Germanus of Constantinople, *Hom. in Annunt. Deiparae*	PG 98, 328 A
5	Germanus of Constantinople, *In Dorm. 2*	Col. 357
5	*Anastasius Antioch, *Serm. 2 de Annunt. 2*	PG 89, 1377 AB
	*Anastasius Antioch, *Serm. 3. 2*	Col. 1388 C
5	Andrew of Crete, *Can. in B. V. Nat. 4*	PG 97, 1321 B
5	Andrew of Crete, *In B. V. Nat. 1*	Col. 812 A
5	Andrew of Crete, *Hom. in Dorm. 1*	Col. 1068 C
5	*Sophronius, *Or. 2 in Annunt 18*	PG 87 (3), 3237 BD
6	Irenaeus, *Adv. Haer. III, 22, 4,* Harvey, 2, 123	PG 7, 959 A
7	Irenaeus, *Adv. Haer. III,* Harvey, 2, 124	PG 7, 959 A
8	Epiphanius, *Haer. 78, 18*	PG 42, 728 CD; 729 AB
9	Jerome, *Epist. 22, 21*	PL 22, 408
9	Cf. Augustine, *Serm. 51, 2, 3*	PL 38, 335
9	Cf. Augustine, *Serm. 232, 2.*	col. 1108
9	*Cyril of Jerusalem, *Catech. 12, 15*	PG 33, 741 AB
9	John Chrysostom, *In Ps. 44, 7*	PG 55, 193
9	John Damascene, *Hom. 2 in dorm. B.M.V., 3*	PG 96, 728
10	Leo the Great, *Epist. ad Flav.*	PL 54, 759
10	Ambrose, *De instit. virg.*	PL 16, 320
13	Cf. John Damascene, *Enc. in dorm. Dei Genitricis, Hom. 2 et 3*	PG 96, 722–762, col. 728 B
13	Germanus of Constantinople, *In S. Dei gen. dorm. Serm. 1*	PG 78 (6), 340–348
13	Germanus of Constantinople, *Serm. 3*	Col. 362
13	*Modestus of Jerusalem, *In dorm. SS. Deiparae*	PG 86 (2), 3277–3312
14	Cf. Andrew of Crete, *Hom. 3 in dorm. SS. Deiparae*	PG 97, 1090–1109
14	John Damascene, *De fide orth., IV, 14*	PG 94, 1153–1168
15	Cf. Andrew of Crete, *In nat. Mariae, Serm. 4*	PG 97, 865 A
15	Germanus of Constantinople, *In annunt. Deiparae*	PG 93, 322 BC
15	Germanus of Constantinople, *In dorm. Deiparae,* III	Col. 362 D
15	John Damascene, *In dorm. B. V. Mariae, Hom. 1, 8*	PG 96, 712 BC–713 A

TABLE 5-2 (*continued*)

Footnote #	Church Father and Writing	Reference
17	Ambrose, *Epist. 63*	PL 16, 1218
18	Ambrose, *Expos. Lc. II, 7*	PL 15, 1555
19	*Cf. Pseudo-Petrus Damien, *Serm. 63*	PL 144, 861
19	*Godefridus a S. Victore. *In nat. B. M.*	Ms. Paris, Mazarine, 1002, fol. 109
19	*Gerhoh Reich., *De gloria et honore Filii hominis, 10*	PL 194, 1105 AB
20	Ambrose, *i.c. et Expos. Lc. X, 24–25*	PL 15, 1810
20	Augustine, *In Io. Tr. 13. 12*	PL 35, 1499
20	Cf. Augustine, *Serm. 191, 2, 3*	PL 38, 1010
20	*Cf. etiam Ven. Bede, *In Lc. Expo. I, cap. 2*	PL 92, 330
20	*Isaac de Stella, *Serm. 31*	PL 194, 1863

*author newly introduced into the schema

In addition to the Church Fathers included in the first schema, the final draft also introduces new patristic texts from Cyril of Jerusalem (d. 386), John Chrysostom (d. 407), and Venerable Bede (d. 735), and it references some lesser-known Eastern Fathers as dominant sources in three particular sections. Germanus of Constantinople, Anastasius of Antioch (d. 599), Andrew of Crete, and Sophronius (d. 638) are invoked in footnote 5 of paragraph 56 as Fathers who "refer to the Mother of God as all holy and free from every stain of sin, as though fashioned by the Holy Spirit and formed as a new creature." Paragraph 59, which speaks of Mary's Assumption into heavenly glory, references John Damascene, Germanus of Constantinople, and Modestus of Jerusalem (d. 634), following after a reference to Pius XII's Apostolic Constitution promulgating the dogma of the Assumption. With the witness of authorities from both the East and West, the Council weds the Christotypical and ecclesiotypical perspectives: Mary's participation in Christ's bodily resurrection anticipates the resurrection of all Christians. Additionally, Andrew of Crete, Germanus of Constantinople, and John Damascene reappear in footnote 15 of paragraph 62 as the main authorities on Mary's Assumption in relation to her intercession from heaven. In continuity with the original schema, the final draft esteems the Eastern witness to Mary's universal mediation from heaven.

The references to Anastasius of Antioch and Modestus of Jerusalem in particular are peculiar because they are relatively obscure figures who are not cited in any other document of the Council. Their introduction into the schema on Mary contributes an important Eastern perspective that links not only the Incarnation but also Mary's bodily Assumption with the restoration of creation, as witnessed, for example, in Modestus's homily: "O most Blessed Dormition of the most glorious Mother of God, through whom the human race has been glorified and called blessed in Christ God ... O most Blessed Dormition of the most glorious Mother of God, through whom all things have been renewed, the things of earth have been united to those of heaven."[70] The Council's use of Modestus thus benefits from his integral perspective: Mary's bodily assumption (a vertical dynamic) has direct implications for the renewal of creation (a horizontal dynamic). Likewise, the Christotypical and the ecclesiotypical approaches are complementary.

This section's itinerary has led us through an overview of the rich patristic and medieval sources for the original schema and the final text of *Lumen Gentium,* chapter 8. We have seen how the currents of renewal at the time of the Council compelled a new grounding for the Council's portrait of Mary in biblical testimony and the patristic tradition so as to reemphasize a central truth: "Mary's place is at the point of departure and the very center of the mystery of salvation."[71]

Three Key Achievements

Lumen Gentium's Marian chapter thus represents a significant theological synthesis rooted in patristic and medieval patrimony. In *Paradoxe et Mystère de l'Église,* de Lubac's commentary on *Lumen Gentium,* he describes the reintegration of patristic sources into the conciliar chapter to be one of the "happy outcomes" of the Council's debates. According to de Lubac, not only did the Council follow "the original intention" of the preparatory doctrinal commission for an integrated presentation, but the final chapter on the Blessed Virgin also "provided a splendid rounding-off for the Constitution," which ensured "continuity with patristic thought."[72] To conclude this study of *Lumen Gentium*'s last chapter, *De beata Maria Virgine Deipara in Mysterio Christi et Ecclesiae,* we assess the achievement of the Council's Mariology, which can be distilled to three key achievements.

---

70. Modestus of Jerusalem, *Homily on the Dormition of the Mother of God* (PG 86), as referenced in footnote 13 of LG, no. 59.

71. Laurentin, *A Short Treatise on the Virgin Mary,* 151.

72. CPM, 55; with reference to U. Betti, OFM, in *L'Église de Vatican II,* ed. Guilherme Baraúna and Yves Congar (Paris: Éditions du Cerf, 1966–67), 2:59, and Laurentin, *La Vierge au concile,* ch. 1.

First, it may be said that the inclusion of the Council's treatment of Mariology within *Lumen Gentium* precluded the development of Mariology as an isolated body of doctrine, thus pivoting away from ahistorical and deductive styles of Mariology that focused solely on Marian privileges and titles, and assuaging the driving ecumenism concerns. The Council's presentation concentrated on Mary's role within the broader context of salvation history rather than on her divine privileges as destined by God's eternal decree. This approach brought into sharp focus Mary's mission within the divine plan of salvation and curbed the excesses of Marian maximalism. It reestablished, for example, that the title *Theotókos* is always to be interpreted in terms of Christ's salvific mission and that the dignity associated with the title is derived precisely from the function for which it was given.[73] In this perspective, the approach seeking primarily to catalog the divine privileges of Mary rightly yielded to a proper integration of the Christotypical and ecclesiotypical views. This integration prevents Mary's union with Christ from being isolated from the Church, and instead links it intrinsically to the Church's own mission and well-being. The ecumenical implications of the vote to integrate *De Beata Mariae Virginae* and *De Ecclesia* is evinced in one Protestant observer's comment: "Close as the vote was and difficult to interpret as it is, the Council fathers have nevertheless taken a step which has the possibility of being ecumenically creative rather than ecumenically divisive."[74]

Moreover, the Council's Marian debates showed that the ecclesiotypical and Christotypical perspectives, although distinct, are not mutually exclusive. Their respective truths are complementary: "Without ever losing sight of the 'Christotypical viewpoint of Mariology,' … the movement to return to the sources entered, with sobriety and equilibrium, upon an 'ecclesiotypical' line."[75] From the Christotypical perspective, Mary rightly stands in a unique relationship to Christ, her son. From the ecclesiotypical perspective, she stands within the Church, not above it. The final text thus speaks of Mary as one who "occupies a place in the Church which is the highest after Christ and also closest to us" (*Lumen Gentium,* no. 54).

Furthermore, the Council's inclusion of Mariology within its ecclesiology establishes a paradigm of integration. Mary and the Church are "mutually

73. Cf. Stefano De Fiores, "Mary in Postconciliar Theology," in Latourelle, *Vatican II: Assessment and Perspectives,* 1:471.

74. Robert McAfee Brown, *Observer in Rome: A Protestant Report on the Vatican Council* (New York: Doubleday, 1964), 125.

75. Charles Moeller, "History of *Lumen Gentium*'s Structure and Ideas," in Miller, *Vatican II: An Interfaith Appraisal,* 143.

inclusive," and this inclusivity coincides with another ecclesiological configuration set forth by the Council, namely the relationship of papal primacy
and episcopal collegiality. The Pope and the College of Bishops are mutually
inclusive because the pope belongs *within* the College of Bishops, albeit as its
head, just as Mary is simultaneously a member and mother of the Church.
The Council's careful and even excessive caution in its articulation—maintaining papal primacy while simultaneously affirming episcopal collegiality—
is evident throughout the third chapter of *Lumen Gentium* on the hierarchical
structure of the Church and is especially conspicuous in the *nota praevia*.[76]
Had the Council fathers chosen to present its Mariology in a separate treatise,
they would have unwittingly reinforced the idea that Mary stands above and
apart from the Church, and by analogous extension, emphasized the Pope's
authority as reigning autonomously and independently of the College of
Bishops as well. On the contrary, the integration of the Marian treatise *within*
the Council's treatment of the Church places her squarely within the Church
as its member while still acknowledging her distinct, divine privileges as its
mother. This specific configuration will come to bear on our analysis of the
relationship between the universal and particular churches in a later chapter.

Second, the placement of the Marian chapter at the end of *Lumen Gentium*, following after the chapter on the eschatological nature of the Church,
reasserts that the Church is not defined by her visible, temporal dimensions
alone but by the *total mystery* of her being, fully realized in her consummate
end. This is a structural achievement, and Ratzinger asserts its significance:
"From the inner logic of their vote [to incorporate *De Beata Virgine* into *De
Ecclesia*], the decision corresponds perfectly to the movement of the whole
constitution; only if this correlation is grasped can one correctly grasp the
image of the church that the Council wished to portray."[77]

The Council's integrated Mariology, presented from the perspective
of the whole economy of salvation, enables the eschatological dimension
of ecclesial existence to emerge with clarity. The seamless insertion of the

---

76. See Heinrich Denzinger and Peter Hünermann, *Enchiridion Symbolorum* (DH), 4356–57.
In paragraphs three and four of the *Nota explicative praevia*, the Council locates the authority of
the Pope *within* the College of Bishops *as its head*. This presupposes an enduring communion—
both explicitly or implicitly—between the Roman Pontiff and the college. Similarly, the College
of Bishops has no authority of its own apart from communion with its head. For a survey of the
main issues of the relationship of papal primacy and episcopal collegiality, see Richard Gaillardetz
and Catherine Clifford, *Keys to the Council: Unlocking the Teaching of Vatican II* (Collegeville, MN:
Liturgical Press, 2012), 124–26.

77. Joseph Ratzinger, *The Essential Pope Benedict XVI: His Central Writings and Speeches*, ed.
John Thornton and Susan Varenne (New York: Harper Collins, 2008), 101.

unanticipated chapter on eschatology and the placement of *De Beata* after it helped to "overcome once and for all the doubts of those who saw the placement of the text on the Virgin 'after those on the laity and religious' as a 'way of banishing and destroying her.'"[78] The historically rooted perspective alternatively "provided a solid biblico-traditional and dogmatic basis for Mary's place and role in the mystery of salvation."[79]

For de Lubac, paragraphs 63–65 of *Lumen Gentium* is of paramount importance. They describe the typological relationship wherein Mary is the "prototype of all perfection" and "the *eschatological figure* of the Church, that is, of the *entire people of God*."[80] In de Lubac's reading, every time the Council "privileged the theme of the people of God, [it] made the biblical image of the daughter of Sion more striking in its double application to Mary and the Church."[81] For the Evangelists, the idea in the Old Testament referring to the remnant of Israel gathered at Jerusalem after the exile, now also refers to Mary as the one who has become "the realization and personal expression of the Church that gives birth to the messianic people."[82] Mary realizes in her own being the full, consummate reality of the Church as bride and mother.[83] She appears as a glorious type of what the Church is in the process of becoming, and she manifests to the Church its own eschatological destiny. Thus insofar as chapter 8 of *Lumen Gentium* presents a particular instance of what chapter 7 describes, the pilgrim Church on earth can look forward in hope to an eschatological fulfillment in Christ as prefigured and realized in Mary.

Third, the Council's integrated treatment underscores the personal and feminine dimension of the Church. As a type and realization of the Church in person, Our Lady is the epitome of ecclesial existence, and she preserves the essential personalism of the Church. When deprived of the personal dimension that Mary brings to the discussion of ecclesiology, what remains is a conception of the Church as an impersonal institution. We will explore the significance of the Church's personal subjectivity in Mary in the last chapter. Here, we note that this personal dimension further reveals the Church to be truly feminine; she is virgin and mother.

The Council's inclusion of the Marian chapter in its schema on the Church revives these two essentially *feminine* dimensions of ecclesial existence. The

---

78. Evangelista Vilanova, "The Intersession, 1963–1964," in Alberigo and Komonchak, *History of Vatican II*, 3:367.

79. Moeller, "History," 141.

80. LG, no. 53; emphases added.

81. CPM, 66.

82. CPM, 66.

83. Moeller, "History," 141.

Church as *spouse* and *virginal mother* constitute patristic themes *par excellence,* and they stand at the fore of de Lubac's understanding of Mary and the Church. This is manifested in the final chapter of *Méditation sur l'Église* and in *Paradoxe et Mystère de l'Église.* In the latter, de Lubac explains that the Constitution on the Church contains four references to the spousal dimension of the Church: *Lumen Gentium,* nos. 6, 7, 9, and 39, and he firmly grounds his interpretation of these passages in early Church Fathers such as Clement the Roman, Origen, Hippolytus, Ambrose, and Augustine.[84] The constant theme of the concrete, mystical union of Mary and the Church accentuates the feminine and personal nature of the Church, a mystery wherein Mary offers to the Church a model of bridal and maternal love. Just as Mary's divine motherhood is the fruit of her own spiritual receptivity, so too, that receptivity becomes "the prototype of the Church's virgin-motherhood with regard to Christians."[85]

These key gains (the integration of the Council's Mariology into its ecclesiology, the comprehensive presentation of Mariology as encompassing the eschatological dimension of salvation history, and the realism of Mary's personal and feminine embodiment of the Church) were achieved in and through the Council's strenuous effort to present a balanced Mariology that acknowledged and addressed the concerns of both the Christotypical and ecclesiotypical approaches. These achievements resonate with de Lubac's long desire to underscore the role of the Blessed Virgin at the heart of the mystery of the Church, as expounded in *Méditation sur l'Église* and reiterated in *Paradoxe et Mystère.* As the virgin bride and mother, Mary's loving union with Christ becomes a model for the Church's own nuptial mysticism and spiritual fecundity. Mary provided the Council with a crowning expression of the Church's nature, and she is justly called Mother of the Church because her spiritual maternity reveals itself to be closely related to the Church's own *sacramental* participation in the work of Redemption. There is a fundamental affinity between Christ's coming to the faithful through the Church's sacraments and his coming into the world through a human mother: Mary's spiritual and virginal motherhood illumines the notion of the Church as a sacrament of salvation. We consider this crucial connection between the Council's Mariology and its *sacramental* ecclesiology in the following chapter which explores postconciliar developments.

84. See CPM, 55.
85. CPM, 57.

CHAPTER 6

Postconciliar Perspectives

While the outcome of the Council's debate and its final Marian synthesis should not be underestimated, neither should it be overestimated. In this chapter, we explore three postconciliar perspectives. First is a historical survey and assessment of the radical decline in Marian scholarship in the decade after the Council. This is followed by a theological analysis that applies the Council's Mariology as an interpretive key to *Lumen Gentium*'s sacramental ecclesiology. Last is a sociological perspective that considers how the Marian question was, at least in part, a real stimulus for the Council's teaching on episcopal collegiality.

Converging Movements and a
Decade without Mary

According to Joseph Ratzinger, "the immediate outcome of the victory of ecclesiocentric Mariology actually was the collapse of Mariology altogether."[1] Writing in 1978, another theologian commented: "Mariology and Marian

---

1. Joseph Ratzinger, "Thoughts on the Place of Marian Doctrine and Piety in Faith and Theology as a Whole," in Hans Urs von Balthasar and Joseph Ratzinger, *Mary: The Church at the Source* (San Francisco: Ignatius Press, 2005), 24; hereafter cited "Marian Doctrine."

devotion are disturbingly close to nil. The choral praise of the Mother of God in the days of Pius XII has been succeeded by a deep silence."[2] In the years following the Council, the theological pendulum had swung to a new extreme. The anemic state of postconciliar Mariology starkly contrasted with the fervor of the Marian spirit of the preconciliar era, of which Yves Congar, an ardent advocate of the ecumenism, had once described as "a situation of over-bidding ... [of] 'raising' it [the bid] still higher and in such a way that tomorrow's bid will only be a step toward higher bids the day after tomorrow."[3] Congar was against the idea of a separate Marian treatise because he predicted that "a conciliar text, with its high authority, even if it is not '*de fide*,' [would] serve as a trampoline for the acrobats of an exaggerating and maximalizing Mariology, even if the text itself is not maximizing ... and that these acrobats will use various expressions in the text to exaggerate it and push it further."[4] However, after the Council had removed the "trampoline" altogether and replaced it with the solid grounds of a balanced synthesis, all "bidding" for Mary seemed to have disappeared as well.

What happened? The Council's Marian-ecclesiological synthesis had sought a balance between the Christotypical and ecclesiotypical approaches, a balance purged of the excesses of Marian maximalism. Along with these excesses, the scaffolding that maximalism had provided for Marian piety and theology had been stripped away too. The exuberance of the Mary-centered devotional life of the Catholic faithful was forced to find a new configuration within a sober ecclesiological approach, and it struggled to do so, yielding a nadir in Mariology in the decade after the Council.

Laurentin offers a nuanced interpretation of the dire postconciliar situation for Mariology and popular devotion. He claims that "the actual crisis is not the result of decadence, but of a reconversion. It is not the result of carelessness, but of adaptation.... Here, as in other places, Vatican II did not create the difficulties but recognized them with the loyalty that the Holy Spirit inspires in the assembled Church."[5] By pointing out the need for "reconversion," Laurentin shifts the blame for the situation away from the conciliar synthesis and to the deficient aspects of preconciliar Mariology. The apparent crisis was a crucial period of rebuilding Marian devotion on more solid

----

2. Wilhelm Beinert, as quoted in De Fiores, "Mary in Postconciliar Theology," 474.

3. Yves Congar, "*Remarques sur le Schéma 'De B. Maria Virgine,'*" as quoted in Komonchak, "The Struggle for the Council," 260.

4. Congar, quoted in Komonchak, 260.

5. René Laurentin, "Mary in the New Age," *The Marian Era* 8 (1967): 29.

foundations: the return-to-the-sources *aggiornamento* recommended by the Council upon the sensitive ecclesiological Mariology of *Lumen Gentium*.

In the years after the Council, the reception of the Council's teaching also manifested a certain misinterpretation of the concept of Tradition and a mistaken idea of the "sufficiency" of Scripture that led to a "biblicist positivism." The plenary sense of Scripture, which drew on both the spiritual and literal senses, soon lost its credibility, and with it, patristic exegesis was cast as more devotional than academic, and thus insufficiently "scientific" (as it did not meet the modern standards of historical and critical exegesis). Biblical positivism not only succeeded in discrediting the symbolic and allegorical dimensions of Mariology, but also undermined the Council's work of *ressourcement* and "condemned the whole patristic heritage to irrelevance."[6]

In retrospect, scholars recognize that the various waves of renewal fomenting within the Church in the decades preceding the Council had clashed with the preconciliar Marian movement. In the time between the First World War and the Council, the ecumenical and Scriptural movements joined the already strong movements in patristics and liturgy.[7] Laurentin describes the impulse of renewal which these movements brought to the workings of the Council: "These movements all proceeded from an irresistible yearning for experiences that the Church had not had in depth for some centuries now. They sprang from the need to make what had become stiff supple again, to lay aside certain artificial elements, to complete what was partial, to enlarge what had become too narrow and tight."[8] However, these new currents, which Ratzinger has described as the "domestic signs of the times for the Church,"[9] appeared to be at odds with the Marian movement. It seemed that the impulse to renewal and a return to the sources demanded a revision of the Marian movement, purging it of the artifice and excesses it had acquired in the previous century. Moreover, the specific relationship of the Marian movement to the other movements of renewal had not yet been clarified when the Second Vatican Council convened, and it appeared as though they represented divergent theological orientations. For example, the liturgical movement described its own piety as objective and sacramental, contrasting itself to the typical characterization of the Marian movement

6. Ratzinger, "Marian Doctrine," 23.

7. For a penetrating analysis on which this account relies in part, see Ratzinger, "Marian Doctrine."

8. Laurentin, *A Short Treatise on the Virgin Mary*, 145.

9. Ratzinger, "Marian Doctrine," 22.

as subjective and personal. The liturgical movement also advocated a piety rooted in Scripture with a theocentric orientation, viewing Christian prayer as adoration addressed to the Father through Jesus Christ. Marian piety, in contrast, was characterized as private, pious devotion *per Mariam ad Jesum.* Whereas the Marian movement had introduced new feasts, vigils, and octaves into the liturgy, the liturgical movement stressed the regular liturgical cycle over the sanctoral cycle that included Marian feasts.[10]

Ratzinger argues that all the debates of Vatican II regarding Mary hinged upon the task of bringing the divergent movements into a fruitful unity, and that "even when there was no explicit awareness of this fact, ... [there was a] struggle to hammer out the right relationship between the ... charismatic currents."[11] The Council, in seeking to return to the sources for a dynamic move forward, sought continuity with the tradition without any superfluity. Its principal discernment with regard to Mariology, therefore, was to distinguish between what was fundamental to Mariology and what was but an expression of the Marian piety of a certain era. This discernment necessitated the renewal of Mariology that brought both Marian theology and devotion in line with the ecclesial movements of the twentieth century. Laurentin gives a positive assessment of the tension: "The new movements flowed from the very life of the church and were geared to a renewed appreciation of aspects of tradition that had remained underdeveloped. Seen from within, these movements were not at all directed against Our Lady. On the contrary, the remarkable fact is that *each* of them in different degrees implied a positive rediscovery of the Virgin Mary in a new light."[12] There are many instances of this "rediscovery." For example, the liturgical movement that arose from the Benedictine reform at Solesmes and the Eucharistic renewal initiated by Pope Pius X both reasserted the soundness of popular devotions and expounded "the ancient traditional root and center of true Marian devotion ... in the mystery of salvation itself."[13] The biblical movement highlighted the biblical foundations of devotion to Mary as the "Daughter of Zion" and the eschatological "Ark of the Covenant," prominent themes from the Hebrew Scriptures. The patristic movement prompted renewed attention to the meaning of the Annunciation and of Mary as the New Eve

---

10. Cf. Ratzinger, "Marian Doctrine," 19–20, and Laurentin, *A Short Treatise on the Virgin Mary,* 147.

11. Ratzinger, "Marian Doctrine," 22.

12. Laurentin, *A Short Treatise on the Virgin Mary,* 148.

13. Laurentin, *A Short Treatise on the Virgin Mary,* 149.

and as a "type" of the Church, thus underscoring the patristic themes of the Church's maternal and spousal nature.

This rediscovery of Mary's proper place in the concrete life of the Church was guided by Pope Paul VI's apostolic exhortation, *Marialis Cultus* (1974), which expounded the compatibility of Marian devotion with the key orientations of Vatican II. Setting forth the Trinitarian, Christological, and ecclesial aspects of devotion to Mary, the document also delineates the biblical, liturgical, ecumenical, and anthropological elements to be taken into consideration in understanding Marian doctrines.

Earnest reception of the Council's Marian ecclesiology has continued through all of the postconciliar pontificates, especially that of Pope Saint John Paul II. In 1987, he proclaimed a Marian year and issued a major Marian encyclical, *Redemptoris Mater*. Subsequent popes have continued to advance the legacy of Vatican II, fostering a rich Marian spirituality focused on Christ and contextualized in the life of the Church. Filial homage to Mary constitutes a vital part of the fabric of Catholic faith and thought today.

In the realm of theology, however, the work of rediscovering the nexus of Mary and the Church *within ecclesiology,* specifically as a theological discipline, has lagged behind other developments. Some attention and fresh scholarship devoted to the ecclesiological dimensions of the Council's *Marian* ecclesiology is emerging today. Brian Graebe, for example, examines the Second Vatican Council's affirmation of the doctrine of Mary's *virginitas in partu* in *Lumen Gentium,* no. 57, and argues for its ecclesiological import. According to Graebe, Mary's perpetual and physical virginity sheds light on *Lumen Gentium's* development of episcopal sacramentality, collegiality, and the apostolic *munus docendi*: as the vessel of the revealed Word, Mary represents the Church's virginal fidelity to divine revelation and to its charge to preserve intact the deposit of faith.[14] Graebe makes an important contribution, not only in reviving discussion on a delicate and oft-misinterpreted topic (one which peaked in the Mitterer/Rahner controversy immediately preceding Vatican II) but also in expounding the theological density of Marian principles applied to ecclesiological doctrine. Graebe's work is a rare gem in the current theological milieu.

Many have the false impression that the Constitution's chapter on the Blessed Virgin Mary is a mere addendum, included to appease the maximalist

---

14. Brian Graebe, *Vessel of Honor: The Virgin Birth and the Ecclesiology of Vatican II* (Steubenville, OH: Emmaus Press), 2021.

tendencies of a minority at the Council. However, the Acts of the Council and our discussion above show that the Council's chapter on Mary is not merely a pious ending to the more important matters of the Council's ecclesiology. Rather, the discussion on the Virgin Mary struck at the heart of the assembly. The Marian question was one that mattered to the Council fathers, and it mattered in the documents they produced as well. The final chapter of *Lumen Gentium* is not a mere appendix but indeed the culmination of the whole Constitution, "bringing its doctrine of the Church to a point in Mariology."[15]

In what follows, we explore the correspondence between key points of *Lumen Gentium,* chapter 8 with the ecclesiology presented in its preceding chapters. Herein we discover the coalescence of the *sacramental* mediation of the Church and the *maternal* mediation of the Blessed Virgin Mary at the crux of their interrelatedness. This discussion, speculative in nature, draws together different strands of de Lubac's thought on the nature of the Church as mystery and sacrament, and as virgin mother and bride, to come to an understanding of the Church's sacramental mediation as analogous to Mary's spiritual maternity. In turn, this correlation will illumine the cogency and coherence of *Lumen Gentium* and the theological weight of its teaching on the Virgin Mary. As Ratzinger has boldly stated, the failure to grasp the connection between Mary and the Church means a failure to grasp correctly the picture of the Church that the Council wanted to portray.[16] De Lubac offers insight into the essential connection between Mary and the Church, and his sacramental theology is an important interpretative key for *Lumen Gentium*'s Marian ecclesiology.

The Inner Logic of *Lumen Gentium*

The Council's Sacramental Ecclesiology

The Council's Mariology represents the climactic point of its ecclesiology. To illumine this point, we begin by examining the basic building blocks of Vatican II's sacramental ecclesiology to grasp how the notions of "mystery,"

15. Hans Urs von Balthasar, "Marian Principle," in *Elucidations* (San Francisco: Ignatius Press, 1998), 101.

16. Joseph Ratzinger, *Pilgrim Fellowship of Faith: The Church as Communion,* trans. Henry Taylor (San Francisco: Ignatius Press, 2005), 150: "Yet from within, this decision [to treat Mariology under the heading of ecclesiology] entirely corresponds to the style of the Constitution as a whole: only when you have grasped this connection will you have correctly understood the picture of the Church that the Council was trying to portray."

"sacrament," and "communion ecclesiology" represent key points of contact with de Lubac's own thinking. These points, in turn, converge with the sacramental/mediatory role of Mary informing the Church's own sacramental/mediatory nature and mission.

The Church as Mystery. By the time the final version of *De Ecclesia* was approved by the Council fathers on 21 November 1964, the initial schema that appeared at the first session had undergone significant revision. Initially, the schema had devoted its first chapter to "*De natura Ecclesiae militantis.*" In contrast, the final version of what would become *Lumen Gentium* begins with a chapter on "*De Ecclesiae Mysterio.*" The change (of title and content) indicates that a fundamental shift in ecclesiological paradigms had taken place in the intervening years. From a political model of the militant Church as a *societas perfecta,* the Council turned its focus to the Church as a mystery of Christ. It is no mere coincidence that this change, as evidenced in the Constitution's first chapter, echoes the title of de Lubac's first chapter in *Méditation sur l'Église* on "L'Église est un mystère" and establishes the context for understanding both Mary and the Church.

The Church as Sacrament. Moreover, *Lumen Gentium*'s teaching on ecclesial *mysterium* is focused on the mystery of Christ and constitutes a sacramental ecclesiology, as expressed in the opening lines of the Constitution: "Christ is the light of the nations ... [and] the Church is in Christ *like a sacrament* or as a sign and instrument both of a very closely knit union with God and of the unity of the whole human race" (LG 1, emphasis added; see also nos. 9 and 48). De Lubac himself considered the idea of the Church's sacramentality in *Catholicisme* (1938): "If Christ is the sacrament of God, the Church is for us the sacrament of Christ; she represents him, in the full and ancient meaning of the term, she really makes him present."[17] Twenty-four years later, when the Second Vatican Council took up the task of examining the Church's profound nature, her essential structure, and her mission in the world, it revived *this* sacramental understanding of the Church and employed it as the Council's principal ecclesiology.

As the sacrament of Christ, the Church is a reality both visible and invisible, divine and human, historical and eschatological. In this sacramental structure, all of the visible elements of the Church are ordered to the invisible reality of Trinitarian communion, as expressed in the biblical notion of *koinonia* (cf. 1 Jn 1:3). In Christ, the Church participates in the communion of God and thus becomes a sacrament of the eternal unity of the Trinity: it

---

17. *Catholicism,* 76.

is "a people made one with the unity of the Father, the Son and the Holy Spirit."[18] Whereas Tridentine ecclesiology focused on the hierarchical reality of the Church and the efficacy of the sacraments, Vatican II's ecclesiology in *Lumen Gentium* goes further in framing these realities within a broader Trinitarian approach.

Communion Ecclesiology. The Church's participation in Trinitarian communion also has horizontal dimensions in which she is not only a sacrament of that "very close knit union with God," but also of "the unity of the whole human race" (LG, no. 1). In 1985, an Extraordinary Assembly of the Synod of Bishops was held in commemoration of the twentieth anniversary of the close of Vatican II. The Synod's final report identified "the ecclesiology of communion … [as] the central and fundamental idea of the Council's documents."[19] While there exists a variety of versions and interpretations of the "ecclesiology of communion"[20] there is also a general consensus that Catholic ecclesiology finds concrete expression in the Eucharist.[21] The centrality of the Eucharist for the life of the Church in the teachings of Vatican II is summed up in *Lumen Gentium,* no. 11: "The Eucharist is the source and summit of the Christian life." This, too, represents a point of contact between the Council's ecclesiology and de Lubac's own work. In his book, *Corpus Mysticum,* on the history of the semantic shift that marked the evolution of Eucharistic theology and its relation to the Church, he coined the saying, "The Eucharist makes the Church."[22] Ratzinger's assessment of de Lubac's influence on the Council's sacramental ecclesiology rings true: "Vatican Council II, in all its comments about the Church, *was moving precisely in the direction of de Lubac's thought.* The Council was not primarily concerned with how the Church envisaged herself, with the view from within, but with the discovery of the Church as sacrament, as the sign and instrument of unity."[23]

This nexus of sacramental mystery and Eucharistic communion is where chapter 8 of *Lumen Gentium* on the Blessed Virgin Mary coalesces with its

18. Cyprian, *De Orat. Dom.* 23 (PL 4, 553); see also LG, no. 4.

19. 1985 Extraordinary Synod, *The Church, in the Word of God, Celebrates the Mysteries of Christ for the Salvation of the World* (1985), II, C, 1.

20. "Communion ecclesiology" has been used to refer to a wide range of theological emphases; Dennis Doyle provides an introductory survey of these meanings in *Communion Ecclesiology: Visions and Versions* (Maryknoll, NY: Orbis Books, 2000).

21. Cf. Congregation for the Doctrine of the Faith, *Letter to the Bishops of the Catholic Church on Some Aspects of the Church Understood as Communion* ('Communionis notio'), 28 May 1992, nos. 5 and 11.

22. *Corpus Mysticum,* 88; cf. also Paul McPartlan, *The Eucharist Makes the Church: Henri de Lubac and John Zizioulas in Dialogue* (Edinburgh: T&T Clark, 1993).

23. Ratzinger, *Principles of Catholic Theology,* 50; emphasis added.

earlier chapters, bringing the Council's ecclesiology to a point in the figure of Mary. The Council's sacramental ecclesiology of communion, which becomes concrete in the Eucharist, further becomes concretely *personal* in the Blessed Virgin Mary, the mother of communion who unites her children.

Like the Church, Mary can be seen as a "Sacrament of Jesus Christ."[24] She is an "efficacious sign" of communion with God and with all Christians. In her unique role as mother of the Redeemer, Mary's spiritual maternity extends to all, and the Council's integration of the Marian chapter within the Constitution on the Church underscores how the Council's sacramental ecclesiology might be illumined by Mary's spiritual maternity: the Church's mediation of grace through the sacraments is analogous to Mary's own maternal mediation. Her motherhood, which is not only bodily but also spiritual, extends to all the faithful and becomes the pattern for the Church's exercise of her own maternal (sacramental) nature.

Mediation and the Council's Mariology

We can begin to draw together the loose strands of our study. The previous survey of the Council's work has already shown how the conciliar text on "The Blessed Virgin Mary, Mother of God, in the Mystery of Christ and the Church" situates the mystery of Mary in her relationship to Christ and the Church. The central concept at work is Mary's maternal mediation: first, of human nature to the Word Incarnate, and second, of grace to the faithful, wherefore, according to *Lumen Gentium*, no. 61, "She is our mother in the order of grace." This is the context in which the Council states that Mary "is invoked by the Church under the titles of Advocate, Auxiliatrix, Adjutrix, and Mediatrix."[25] These titles all refer to her subordinate mediation of grace in and through Christ, her son.

It has already been noted that the topic of Mary's mediation as Mediatrix and *Mater Ecclesiae* had been contentious topics for the Council. The fathers were wary that the title "Mediatrix" would potentially diminish or detract from the truth of Christ's unique mediation, and that "*Mater Ecclesiae*" might be seen as promoting a triumphalistic Mariology and further impeding Christian unification. To preclude such misinterpretations, the Council fathers expanded that part of the *textus emendatus* that eventually became paragraph no. 62 of *Lumen Gentium*. The expanded text explains the

24. *Splendor,* 379.
25. LG, no. 60.

participatory nature of Mary's cooperation in God's plan of salvation, partaking in the unique mediation of Christ:

> For no creature could ever be counted as equal with the Incarnate Word and Redeemer. Just as the priesthood of Christ is shared in various ways both by the ministers and by the faithful, and as the one goodness of God is really communicated in different ways to His creatures, so also the unique mediation of the Redeemer does not exclude but rather gives rise to a manifold cooperation which is but a sharing in this one source.[26]

These lines, the lengthiest of all the emendations, elaborate the statement made regarding Mary's mediation as that which "flows forth from the superabundance of the merits of Christ, rests on His mediation, depends entirely on it and draws all its power from it. In no way does it impede, but rather does it foster the immediate union of the faithful with Christ" (LG, no. 60). The Council wishes to convey concisely the unique and singular mediation of Christ in which Mary and the Church both participate.[27] It is, moreover, on this topic of maternal mediation that de Lubac's earlier writings on Mary, specifically the final chapter of *Méditation sur l'Église,* help shed further light.

We recall that in the preamble to his exposition in "L'Église et la Vierge Marie," de Lubac engaged Karl Barth on the Protestant objections to the Roman Catholic cult of Mary.[28] He acknowledged Barth's fundamental criticism that Catholic Marian cult was the quintessential "heresy of the Roman Catholic Church" consisting in "the doctrine of human cooperation in Redemption"—a "heresy" that is summed up in the person of Mary as "the principle, prototype, and summing up of the dogma of the Church."[29] Barth criticized Catholic Marian doctrine because it, in Catholic terms, was the culminating embodiment of sacramentality and the mediation of grace through a human vessel. At the heart of the dispute in the Protestant Reformation

---

26. Original Latin text: "*Nulla enim creatura cum Verbo incarnato ac Redemptore connumerari unquam potest; sed sicut sacerdotium Christi variis modis tum a ministris tum a fideli populo participatur, et sicut una bonitas Dei in creaturis modis diversis realiter diffunditur, ita etiam unica medatio Redemptoris non excludit sed suscitat variam apud creaturas participatem ex unico fonte cooperationem.*"

27. Cf. Thomas Gaurino, *The Disputed Teachings of Vatican II: Continuity and Reversal in Catholic Doctrine* (Grand Rapids, MI: Eerdmans, 2018), 82–91, for an analysis of the Council's discussion on "mediation" and its understanding of Mary's mediation as a *participation* in the singular mediation of Christ.

28. See *Splendor,* 314–16.

29. Karl Barth, *Die kirchliche Dogmatik* (1938), vol. I.2, 157, 160, as quoted in *Splendor,* 316.

was this issue of the relationship of human nature's free cooperation with grace, and Barth realized that Catholic theology upheld Mary at the center as "the crucial dogma of Catholicism," summing up in her life a particular dual configuration of grace perfecting nature and grace being mediated by nature. Mary meritoriously cooperated with God's grace, and her cooperation continues in time as she still intercedes for the disciples of her Son.

The Council fathers were not ignorant of Protestant concerns. Aware of these real difficulties shared by many other Christian groups, the fathers intentionally articulated a subordination of Mary's mediation to the unique and supreme mediation of Christ (LG, nos. 60–62) and only employed the title of Mediatrix in conjunction with the titles "Advocate, Auxiliatrix, and Adjutrix" in order to temper any ill-perceived prominence regarding her mediatory influence.

Furthermore, our study of the sources deployed at Vatican II noted how the idea of Mary's mediation of grace was expounded by the great Byzantine Fathers of the eighth century. But de Lubac reminds us that the idea of interpreting specifically Mary's motherhood as a form of mediation can be traced back even further. Consider how this is implicit in the title of *Theotókos* as it was proclaimed at the Council of Ephesus in 431 AD. That Council exalted Mary's role as Mother of God, expounding the universal dimension of her maternity with regard to all humankind. A homily given at the conclusion of the Council of Ephesus invokes Mary as not only a particular saint but as the universal saint whose role sums up those of the entire Church:

> We greet you, Mary, Mother of God, venerable treasure of the whole world,
> Light that has never gone out, … never destroyed temple containing the one who cannot be contained, Mother and Virgin …
> By you the Trinity is blessed,
> By you the Cross is venerated throughout the whole world,
> By you heaven is thrown into joy,
> By you the angels and archangels are delighted,
> By you the demons are put to flight,
> By you the devil tempter is thrown from heaven,
> By you the fallen creature is raised to heaven,
> By you the whole world in the grip of idolatry has reached knowledge of truth,
> By you holy Baptism comes to those who believe, …

> By you churches are founded throughout the world,
> By you peoples are led to conversion.[30]

According to Laurentin, the repetition of "by you" provides a "framework of mediation"; it is in and through Mary as *Theotókos* that Redemption comes to humankind.

This ancient witness of Mary's motherhood adds credibility to the debates on Mary as Mediatrix. Her spiritual and universalized motherhood is the unhindered medium for God's bestowal of grace. It is also the nexus of her relationship to the Church, informing the Church's own maternal nature and sacramental mission. Our Lady and the Church each partake in the sole mediation of Redemption by Christ—Mary, by way of her spiritual maternity, and the Church, by way of the sacraments. Mary's divine maternity and the Church's sacramentality are thus analogous modes by which Christ is mediated to the world.

It is not surprising that the ecumenically-minded Council fathers had so strongly objected to the promotion of new Marian doctrines and the inflation of Marian devotions. Ironically, though, the resolution to their concern was neither to be found in a dialectical opposition between Mariology and ecclesiology, nor in a disregard of Mariology altogether, but in a balanced integration. The Council's decision to incorporate the chapter on Mary into its Constitution on the Church fostered this balanced synthesis and, given the parallels of sacramental and maternal mediation in the Church and Mary, respectively, the Council's ecclesiology is indeed brought to a climax in that final chapter of *Lumen Gentium*. The Church's mission as the universal sacrament of salvation is to bring forth the life of Christ in all humankind. It is a mission exemplified in Mary's maternal mediation of Christ. The Blessed Virgin epitomizes the perfection of nature elevated by grace and of human cooperation in the divine work of Redemption. As such, Mary prefigures the nature, mission, and destiny of the Church, and the Council's treatment of her is fittingly integrated into its Constitution on the Church.

In his discussion of the Marian mystery of the Church in the *Dogmatic Theology* textbook series he coauthored with Joseph Ratzinger, Johann Auer

---

30. *Hom. 4 Ephesi in Nestorium habita quando septem ad sanctam Mariam descenderunt* 4 (PG 77:992bc), in E. Schwartz, *Acta Conciliorum oecumenicorum* I, vol. 1, fasc. 8, p. 104; as quoted in Laurentin, *A Short Treatise on the Virgin Mary*, 88–89. See also *Splendor*, 341n141. Laurentin notes that the homily, which is commonly attributed to Cyril of Alexandria, was actually pronounced by an unknown author, and that attempts to confirm its authorship as Cyril's have been met with reserve in academic circles. It nonetheless appears in the Office of Readings for the August 5th feast of the Dedication of the Basilica of St. Mary Major, attributed to Cyril.

proposes a similar thesis on the relatedness of Mary and the Church when he states: "The chapter on Mary in *Lumen Gentium* proceeds from an understanding of the Church as the sacrament of salvation."[31] Auer's statement proffers an essential perspective highlighting the organic unity of *Lumen Gentium*. The link between chapter 8 of *Lumen Gentium* on Mary and its earlier chapters is forged in the sacramental nature of both Mary and the Church: Mary is like a sacrament of the Church, and the Church is the sacrament of salvation. Although de Lubac never makes any explicit statement comparable to Auer's, his ideas can be employed to confirm the link between the Council's sacramental ecclesiology and its Mariology, to which Auer alludes.[32]

The Council's chapter on Mary is not an appendage to its discussion on the Church. On the contrary, chapter 8 of *Lumen Gentium* brings into concrete focus the sacramental nature of the Church as coming to a culmination in Our Lady and opening up to Christ. She personally embodies the reality of communion with God and humankind in her very being as mother of Jesus Christ. When the Church exercises her sacramental function, acting as a mother giving birth to Christians from the womb of the baptismal font and nurturing them with the food of the Eucharist, she fulfills her mission as the sacrament of salvation, participating in the maternity of Mary who first gave birth to Christ. While de Lubac does not spell out these specific connections, his theological and methodological principles move in this direction and are consonant with Tradition. His accounts of the Council's sacramental ecclesiology and of the Church's motherhood elucidate the Council's ecclesiology and explain how the final chapter of *Lumen Gentium* is the climax of the Constitution. In carrying out the mission of sanctifying its members through the sacraments, the Church participates in the spiritual maternity of Mary.

Collegiality and the Marian Question

In review, the previous chapter traced the evolution of the Council's Mariology, a development rife with tension. The current chapter has proffered an analysis of the final synthesis, the fruit born of the Council's struggles. It has postulated that the Council's Mariology is the culminating point, an

---

31. Auer, *The Church: Universal Sacrament of Salvation*, 480.

32. A final discussion on the notion of sacramentality and its significance for the Council's Marian-ecclesiological synthesis will be taken up in the concluding chapter of this book.

interpretive key, of the Council's sacramental/communion ecclesiology, as put forward in *Lumen Gentium*. One further sociological analysis will round out our study of postconciliar perspectives on the Council's Mariology. It will show how the Marian vote in 1963 occasioned the Council's teaching on episcopal collegiality.

We recall that the topic of Mary made three substantial appearances in the first three periods of Vatican II. In the first session, the fathers' refusal to hastily approve the Marian schema marked the beginning of a change of guard, from the Curia's control over the commissions to a greater voice accorded to the universal episcopate. Then, core deliberations on the Marian schema took place during the second session, following an indicative vote which revealed the divergent Christotypical and ecclesiotypical tendencies of the Council fathers. The tension between the constituents of these two parties resurfaced in the third session with Pope Paul VI's unexpected proclamation of the Marian title, *Mater Ecclesiae*. This act appeared as an endorsement of the Christotypical Mariology that a majority of the Council fathers had labored intensely to moderate and as a rejection of the ecclesiotypical integration of Mary that the fathers did embrace. Charles Moeller describes the event in this way.

> Two positions confronted each other. Both curiously intervened in the same way regarding the pope and the Blessed Virgin. One group considered the pope as superior to and a part of the Episcopal college, like the head of a body. The other considered him as superior to but apart from the college, and felt that papal primacy was diminished, run down, compromised in the other position.... The same thing happened when the question of the Virgin Mary came up: some saw in her an eminent and singular member of the Church, the summit of its communion with Christ; the others tended to place her in opposition to the rest of the Church, sometimes even going to the point of considering her as predestined with Christ independently of the Church and prior to it, endowed with a grace specifically different from the others.[33]

The bone of contention was the revival of episcopal collegiality and the extent of the College's authority. Both topics were perceived by some to be in contest with the authority of the Supreme Pontiff. The Council's retrieval of the ancient configuration of synods and episcopal collegiality

---

33. Moeller, "History," 141.

was, perhaps unwittingly, associated with the Marian debates in two ways. First, the Marian vote of the second session took place just one day before the indicative vote regarding the episcopacy. Second, the slim victory was achieved through the real collaboration of the bishops, what one might call episcopal collegiality in action. We conclude this chapter exploring how the Council's decisive vote on the Marian question was the result of a lived experience of collegiality.

On one level, the close Marian vote of 29 October 1963 is indicative of the Council's initial deep divide and lack of consensus on the topic of Mary. On another level, however, the vote reveals another dynamic at work. Hilari Raguer's study of the "Initial Profile of the Assembly" surveys the composition of the assembly and probes the question of how, over the course of the Council, a "reversal of positions and forces" came about—namely, how the authority concentrated in the Roman Congregations shifted toward the universal episcopate.[34] He argues that the Council provided a real opportunity—even a necessity—for the unified action, not only of individual bishops with one another but also of the entire episcopate through the effective collaboration between episcopal conferences. This collaboration, moreover, was fostered by numerous informal but organized collegial exchanges that took place outside of the aula of St. Peter's Basilica. Interestingly enough, the Marian vote represents a direct outcome of this organic development.

Early on, the Council fathers realized the need for a broader interaction and exchange of ideas outside of the official conciliar gathering. Of the various informal groups that emerged, the Conference of Delegates that met at the *Domus Mariae* on Via Aurelia made a lasting impact as an engine of change. This group—also referred to simply as the *Domus Mariae*—was initiated by Cardinal Roger Etchegaray who served as its secretary throughout the time of the Council.[35] The *Domus Mariae* has been described as "a gathering of Council fathers from various episcopates, who come together

34. Hilari Raguer, "An Initial Profile of the Assembly," in Alberigo and Komonchak, *History of Vatican II,* 2:168.

35. At the beginning of Vatican II, Cardinal Liénart asked Etchegaray to make contacts with other conferences. The latter thus made connections with Dom Hélder Câmara and Manuel Larraín of CELAM, and this later expanded to the heads of the Federation of African Episcopal Conferences (FACE) and developed into the group of twenty-two bishops from their respective conferences. See also Jan Grootaers, "Une forme de concertation épiscopale au Concile Vatican II: La 'Conférence des Vingt-deux' (1962–1965)," *Revue d'Histoire Ecclesiastique* 91 (1996): 66–112; Pierre C. Noël, "Gli incontri delle conferenze episcopali durante il concilio: Il 'gruppodella Domus Mariae,'" in Maria Teresa Fattori and Alberto Melloni, *Evento e decisioni: studi sulle dinamiche del concilio Vaticano II* (Bologne: Il Mulino, 1997), 95–133.

periodically, in a spirit of friendship and brotherhood, to exchange impressions on the general progress of the Council."[36] Every Friday afternoon during the months the Council was in session, twenty-two delegates from various episcopal conferences gathered for collegiality and theological conferences on conciliar topics. The lectures were given in French and English, and the slate of speakers was coordinated by Antonio Guglielmi, a Brazilian *peritus* residing at the *Domus*. The lecturers included leading figures such as Cardinals Bea, Lercaro, Ruffini, and Suenens, along with *periti* such as Küng, Vogt, Häring, Rahner, Ratzinger, Schillebeeckx, Congar, and de Lubac.[37] Throughout the Council's working sessions, a total of ninety-one such conferences were held.[38]

Melissa Wilde's sociological study attributes the close vote on 29 October 1963 to the collaborative work of the bishops at the *Domus Mariae*. Wilde has documented the connections between the delegates to the *Domus Mariae* meetings and the episcopal conferences to which they reported, and she posits that over time, these meetings reached a broad audience of approximately 1,900 Council members—approximately 75 percent of the Council.[39] Moreover, the meetings were more than just information sessions; they were ripe opportunities for building consensus and promoting collegiality, both in theory and in practice. The concrete organizational strategy of the *Domus Mariae* brought together episcopal delegates from the diverse national and transnational conferences (such as CELAM or the Pan-African FACE) who otherwise might not have had substantial contact with each other. Moreover, by providing invaluable theological perspectives from the greatest experts of the day, the *Domus Mariae* exercised a powerful influence, informing and guiding the votes of a large number of bishops. Jared Wicks confirms: "What

36. Msgr. Cantero Cuadrado to Gómez de Arteche, as quoted in Raguer, "Initial Profile," 208. For a list of the twenty-two participants, see Table B.3 in Melissa Wilde, *Vatican II: A Sociological Analysis of Religious Change* (Princeton, NJ: Princeton University Press, 2007), 136. See also Jan Brouwers, "Derniers préparatifs et première session," in *Vatican II commence: Approches francophones* (Leuven: Bibliotheeck van de Faculteit der Godgeleerdheid, 1993), 367–68.

37. According to Jared Wicks, "Further Light on Vatican II Council," *Catholic Historical Review* 95, no. 3 (2009): 554, de Lubac gave at least fifteen different conferences, especially during the first and last periods of the Council, "to bishops of France, Madagascar, and francophone Africa, and Argentina, and to Brazilians and others at the *Domus Mariae*."

38. José Oscar Beozzo, "Le Concile Vatican II (1962–1965). La Participation de la Conférence Épiscopale du Brésil–CNBB," *Cristianesimo nella storia* 23 (2002): 121–96; see also Wicks, "More Light on Vatican Council II," *Catholic Historical Review* 94, no. 1 (2008): 81–82.

39. Cf. Wilde, *Vatican II: A Sociological Analysis*, 61–68. See page 65 for an illuminating map of the *Domus Mariae*'s organizational structure and the extent of its influence. See also Rock Caporale, *Vatican II: Last of the Councils* (Baltimore: Helicon, 1964); and Wicks, "Further Light," 562.

the delegates heard from the episcopal conferences of the northern pluralist lands at the *Domus Mariae* meetings in 1962 and 1963 were largely the views first expressed by *periti* in afternoon episcopal conference study sessions and then appropriated by a conference majority or even unanimously."[40] In this way, many "reformist positions" (on topics such as the Marian schema, ecumenism, collegiality, and religious liberty) solidified, as the Council's votes evince.

The *Domus Mariae's* sophisticated network of communication enabled a lived experience of episcopal collaboration that, in turn, translated into a lived experience of episcopal collegiality, with the organizational structure of the *Domus* mirroring the network of local, particular churches in communion with one another. Bishop Ernest Primeau, the American delegate to the *Domus Maria,* states, "Contact with the bishops of the world has widened my horizons, made me more appreciative of the ideas and problems of others, more sensitive to their needs, spiritual and material.... *Before collegiality [was formally approved by the Council] ... I had already profoundly experienced [it].*"[41] Moreover, as the bishops encountered one another, they experienced a renewed awareness of the catholicity of the Church and the diversity of the challenges it faces in a pluralistic and modern world. As a result, the votes at the Council were swayed in the direction of greater ecumenical awareness, and this further served to alter the vote on Mary.[42]

Wilde's complex analysis traces the voting patterns of the bishops and distinguishes between the conservatives (mostly bishops from Italy, Portugal, Spain, and Ireland) and the Northern European and North American constituency that tended to be more progressive. She shows how the reform agenda of the latter increasingly gained ground amongst the fathers over the minority group, particularly on issues related to the liturgical, biblical, and ecumenical movements, winning adherence from among the Latin American, African, and Asian episcopate. Wilde attributes the success of this group in shifting the vote of the Council, at least in part, to the organizational effectiveness and the culture of collegiality that the *Domus Mariae* practiced and sought to formalize.

---

40. Wicks, "Further Light," 565. Also worth noting is the fact that once the decisions moved from the aula to the drafting phase by the respective Commissions, the same *periti* who aided the bishops in formulating their positions would very often also provide essential aid in the revision of the schemata.

41. Ernest Primeau to Tirot, 4 February 1966, PC 21 (7), as quoted in Wilde, *Vatican II: A Sociological Analysis,* 68; emphasis added.

42. Wilde, *Vatican II: A Sociological Analysis,* 107.

To illumine by way of contrast, the *Coetus Internationalis Patrum* (CIP) that promoted a conservative agenda was especially circumspect about the workings of episcopal conferences and openly opposed the doctrine of episcopal collegiality. Associated with the Curia, it was organized by Geraldo de Proenca Siguad, Archbishop of Diamantina; Marcel Lefebvre, Titular Bishop of Sinnada, Phrygia; and Luigi Carli, Bishop of Segni, Italy. The CIP has been described as representing "the conservative line in all its purity, both in its fundamental attitudes (zeal for the precise formulation of truth; a suprahistorical or triumphalistic outlook, and therefore a mentality of caution in the face of change; scant interest in and even apprehension about ecumenism) and in its more important concrete choices."[43] At the beginning of the second session, Siguad, the founder of CIP gave a forceful speech against collegiality, expounding how it poses a veritable threat to papal primacy. This is in stark contrast to how the episcopal delegates to the *Domus Mariae* prioritized collegiality and practiced it in the course of the Council.[44]

The tension on the topic of papal authority and episcopal collegiality peaked on the occasion of Pope Paul VI's promulgation of the Marian title, *Mater Ecclesiae*, manifesting the intense consternation around the Marian question. Most significant for our study is the evidence that the *Domus Mariae* had a direct impact on the Marian vote. Bishop Manuel Larraín, one of the first collaborators of Cardinal Etchegaray, says of the Council's Marian debate: "We have rethought our theology ... in the vision of Mary's function." Bishop Câmara corroborates Larraín's assertion: "We have developed our ecumenical sense of respect for all.... It is a question of avoiding ... scandalizing our faithful, while giving Mary the right place."[45] For Wilde and Wicks, the vote of 29 October 1963 is indicative of the influence of the *Domus Mariae* and the wide acceptance of its reform proposal.

T. William Coyle, an American Redemptorist who accompanied Bishop Thomas Murphy, CSsR, to the Council, offers another corroborating perspective in his account of the "American Influence on the Conciliar Decision Regarding BVM Schema."[46] According to Coyle, on 28 October 1963,

43. Salvador Gómez de Arteche y Catalina, *Grupos "extra aulam" en el II Concilio Vaticano y su influencia III*, Appendix II, 241, as quoted in Raguer, "Initial Profile," 195. Gómez de Arteche's lengthy 2,585-page-long work is an unpublished doctoral dissertation, Biblioteca de la Facultad de Derecho de la Universidad de Valladolid.

44. For more on the struggle to revive the concept of episcopal collegiality, see Gilles Routhier, "Vatican II: The First Stage of an Unfinished Process of Reversing the Centralized Government of the Catholic Church," *The Jurist* 64 (2004): 247–83.

45. Wilde, *Vatican II: A Sociological Analysis*, 68.

46. Coyle, "American Influence," 266–69.

one day before the close vote on the Marian schema, four American experts, Frs. Barnabas Ahern, Eugene Maley, Godfrey Diekmann, and William Coyle himself, addressed the American bishops at their weekly meeting at the North American College. The invitation to address the bishops came from Cardinal Meyer of Chicago who, only a few days earlier, asked Father Ahern to put together a panel of theologians to provide input on the schema *De Beate Maria Virgine.*[47] Coyle states that after studying the schema, he and the other panelists "agreed that we would urge the rejection of the current [separated, Marian] schema and favor its incorporation into the document on the Church."[48] Cardinal Lawrence Shehan of Baltimore attests to the fact that the American bishops followed through with the panel's recommendation the next morning: "As a result of their talks and the discussion that followed, most of us were convinced that it [the doctrine on Mary] should be included in the Constitution on the Church."[49]

Monsignor Vincent Yzermans states, "[The presentation of the experts] succeeded in convincing a good part of the American hierarchy to vote in favor of incorporating the Marian schema into the schema on the Church." He even suggests that the close result of the indicative vote on Mary is to be attributed to the American bishops and their 28 October meeting: "If they [the scholars] had not had the opportunity of making this presentation, perhaps the forty-vote difference in the voting would have resulted in favor of a special Marian decree."[50] Another American prelate states emphatically, "I am convinced that a number of the United States bishops would have voted with the conservatives if they had not had the benefit of the presentation made by this panel on the subject of Mariology.... I feel quite sure that at least twenty votes of the United States bishops were switched as a result of that meeting."[51]

While no single variable can completely explain the dynamics and outcome of the vote on 29 October 1963, and the twenty deciding votes were

47. The invitation was extended "about October 22" (more likely the next day, 10/23), and this corroborates the timeline of the Council's debate concerning the Marian schema. Meyer's plan for the presentation and discussion was a timely follow-up to Cardinal Döpner's announcement on 23 October of the Council's presentations by Cardinals König and Santos the following day.

48. Coyle, "American Influence," 267.

49. Lawrence Shehan, *A Blessing of Years* (Notre Dame, IN: University of Notre Dame Press, 1984), 155.

50. Vincent Yzermans, *American Participation in the Second Vatican Council* (New York: Sheed and Ward, 1967), 25. See also Michael Novak, *The Open Church* (New York: Macmillan, 1964), 200.

51. Testimony of an unnamed American prelate, as quoted in Yzermans, *American Participation*, 25–26.

not limited to the votes of the American bishops alone (for they could have come from any constituency), at least one point is clear: The Marian question touches upon crucial aspects of the Church. As Hermann Pottmeyer has argued, the practice and experience of communion and collegiality at the Council were necessary for a corresponding ecclesiology to develop and to be accepted.[52] The Marian question was interwoven with the bishops' experience of collegiality, and the struggle for it gives us a glimpse, at least in part, of the inner workings of the Council and what the results of the vote in 1963 really represent. What appeared as a divided council was actually a council moving toward greater collegiality.

The day after the Council voted on the Marian question, another indicative vote was made on five propositions, three directly on the question of collegiality. The results were overwhelmingly in favor of recognizing the College of Bishops: 2,049 placet votes (95 percent) in favor of recognizing the sacramental nature of episcopal consecration; 1,808 placet votes (84 percent) in favor of recognizing the succession of the College of Bishops from the Apostolic College; and 1,717 placet votes (80 percent) in favor of recognizing the College's full and supreme authority (in union with the Pope as its head).[53]

While the debates on collegiality would become the most protracted of all the debates of the Council, this initial straw vote on 30 October 1963 was a crucial turning point. And as if the Council was riding the momentum that began the previous day with the close Marian vote, episcopal collegiality won the day.

52. Cf. Hermann Pottmeyer, "Continuité et innovation dans l'eccléssiologie de Vatican II" in G. Alberigo, *Les Églises après Vatican II* (Paris: Beauchesne, 1981), 93, as quoted in Routhier, "The First Stage," 248.

53. Alberto Melloni, "The Beginning," 105–8.

CHAPTER 7

The Marian Dimension of the Universal and Particular Churches

The foregoing chapters have considered the rich aspects of de Lubac's writings on the topic of Mary and the Church in connection with conciliar and postconciliar developments. Emphasis has been laid on de Lubac's retrieval of the maternal and virginal aspects of the mystery of the Church, which informed the Council's debates on Mary's ecclesial motherhood and mediation of grace. De Lubac's Marian thought extends to every aspect of his work: from the nuptial dimension of Christian mysticism embodied by a Marian exegesis of the Song of Songs to the success of episcopal collegiality at the Council; from the cosmic finality of Teilhard and Monchanin's evolutionary outlook to the concrete sacramental nature of the Church. The present chapter addresses the question of the relevance and practical application of de Lubac's multifaceted Marian thinking: What might de Lubac's ideas on the Marian mystery of the Church contribute to contemporary ecclesiology? Focusing on the particular issue of the relationship of the universal Church to particular churches—an issue directly related to papal primacy and episcopal collegiality, a central plank of the Council's institutional re-forms[1]—we will examine how de Lubac's Marian thought positively informs the contemporary problematic. To this end, this chapter will proceed in five sections. Section 1 provides a historical overview of the development of the theologies of the local church and of the universal Church. Section 2 exam-ines the postconciliar development of an ecclesiology of communion and the recent debate between Cardinal Walter Kasper and then-Cardinal Jo-seph Ratzinger on the topic of the relationship of the particular churches to the universal Church. Section 3 then considers de Lubac's own writing on the topic of *Les églises particulières dans l'Église universelle* (1971). Section 4 analyzes the ways Kasper and Ratzinger each employ de Lubac's thought, and section 5 employs de Lubac's insights so as to consider a possible Marian dimension of the relationship of particular churches to the universal Church and, hence, offer some light on the issues of controversy between Kasper and Ratzinger. Here we discover how distinctive features of de Lubac's Ma-riology, namely the notions of "mutual interiority," the "concrete universal," and bridal mysticism, all come together to enable a nuanced reconfiguration of the local-universal church problematic.

An Overview of the Theology of the Church as Local and Universal

In the post-apostolic era, the Church existed as a network of local churches under the direction of their bishops.[2] Amongst this body of Churches, the Church of Rome held prominence in political standing and historical im-portance as the place of the martyrdom of Peter and Paul, and deference was given to Rome as the Church that "presided in charity" among the church-es.[3] A theology of the universal Church emerged in the late Middle Ages when a *universalist* ecclesiology that stressed the central authority of the pope was developed; the departmental form of the Roman curia came into

1. For an illuminating assessment of the Church's reception of the Council's reform agenda, see Hervé Legrand, "Forty Years Later: What Has Become of the Ecclesiological Reforms Envis-aged by Vatican II?" *Concilium* 4 (2005): 57–72.

2. See Avery Dulles, "The Church as Communion," in *New Perspectives in Historical Theology: Essays in Memory of John Meyendorff*, ed. Bradley Nassif (Grand Rapids, MI: Eerdmans, 1996), 129.

3. Cf. Ignatius of Antioch, Salutation to the *Letter to the Romans*, in which Ignatius greets the Church of Rome as "*prokathēmenē tēs agapēs*," or "preeminent in charity'; see Michael Holmes, *The Apostolic Fathers: Greek Texts and English Translations*, third edition (Grand Rapids, MI: Baker Academic, 2007).

being under Pope Sixtus V in 1588.[4] Yves Congar describes this development that began at the turn of the first millennium as a transition from an "ecclesiology of communion" to an "ecclesiology of powers,"[5] and he comments that under Pope Leo IX and Pope Gregory VII, the Church had become "a single society subjected to the authority of the pope," understood as "the universal bishop."[6]

This universalist ecclesiology reached its peak in the nineteenth and early twentieth centuries with the teaching of the First Vatican Council on Petrine primacy and papal infallibility, a teaching that was further reinforced by the Code of Canon Law of 1917.[7] While this centralization of authority strengthened the Church's identity and mission in the world, it also lent itself to a universalist perspective with a tendency toward triumphalism on the one hand and neglect of the relative autonomy and creative initiative of local churches on the other.

The Second Vatican Council reexamined the Church's self-understanding from a *ressourcement* perspective. While reiterating the teaching of Vatican I, it also sought to give a fuller account of the local church, drawing on patterns from the early Church. Called by some a "Copernican revolution,"[8] the revival of episcopal collegiality and the sacramental nature of episcopal ordination are fruits of this initiative, undergirded by a theology of the local church.[9]

Paragraphs 23 and 26 of *Lumen Gentium* and paragraph 11 of *Christus Dominus* are the key conciliar texts providing a fundamental theology of the local church. They assert that a local/particular church gathered in the name of Christ manifests the full reality of being the Church, particularly when its

---

4. See John W. O'Malley, *Vatican I: The Council and the Making of the Ultramontane Church* (Cambridge, MA: Harvard University Press, 2018).

5. Yves Congar, "L' 'Ecclesia' ou communauté chrétienne, sujet integral de l'action liturgique," in *La Liturgie après Vatican II*, ed. J.-P. Jossua and Y. Congar (Paris: Cerf, 1967), 261, as quoted in Paul McPartlan, *A Service of Love: Papal Primacy, the Eucharist, and Church Unity* (Washington, DC: The Catholic University of America Press, 2016), 30.

6. Yves Congar, "De la communion des églises à une ecclésiologie de l'Église universelle," in *L'Épiscopat et l'Église universelle* (Paris: Cerf, 1964), 238, as quoted in McPartlan, *A Service of Love*, 31.

7. Cf. Vatican I's *Pastor Aeternus* (1870); see also Patrick Granfield, "The Church Local and Universal: Realization of Communion," *The Jurist* 49 (1989): 450.

8. Emmanuel Lanne, "L'Église locale et l'Église universelle: Actualité et portée du theme," *Irénikon* 43 (1970): 490.

9. Cf. McPartlan, *A Service of Love*, 34–36, wherein the author provides an account of Vatican II's understanding of the sacramental basis of episcopal collegiality following its eclipse beginning in the twelfth century, in which the episcopacy lost its part in the sacrament of holy orders and collegiality was subordinated to papal authority with the Pope as the "universal ordinary."

members are assembled with their bishop around the altar in the celebration of the Eucharist. In other words, the local churches are communities formed by the Gospel and the Eucharist under the presidency of the bishops. In these particular churches, the "one, holy, catholic, and apostolic Church of Christ is truly present and active" (*Christus Dominus*, no. 11).

These conciliar statements, underscoring a theology of the local church, are among the Council's most significant teachings. The formula in paragraph 23 of *Lumen Gentium* has been called "the most important ecclesiological formula of the Council."[10] It states: "Particular churches … are constituted after the model of the universal Church; it is in these [particular churches] and formed out of them that the one and unique Catholic Church exists" (LG, no. 23). The universal Church and the local churches are related as two aspects of one reality of the Church of Christ: the particular churches are "constituted after the model of the universal Church," but at the same time, the one and only Catholic Church comes into being "in and from" these particular churches. The local church and the universal Church exist in and from each other.

However, it has also been noted that the "council's theology of the local church is a small, mostly implicit chapter of its ecclesiology of communion and catholicity."[11] In Louis Bouyer's estimation, Vatican II provides a "rather poorly developed doctrine of the local church."[12] The teaching of *Lumen Gentium*, no. 26, for example, was a late interpolation in the development of the conciliar text, and as such it "exercised little explicit structural or thematic influence upon the council's ecclesiology," which remained "predominantly universalistic and pontifical."[13] Moreover, the Council did not provide any theological explanation for its affirmation of what has subsequently been considered the mutual inclusion and interiority of local churches and the universal Church.[14] Scholars have noted that "the two statements [of *Lumen Gentium*, no. 23] are simply juxtaposed, without any attempt to clarify their

10. Eugenio Corecco, "Aspects of the Reception of Vatican II in the Code of Canon Law," in *The Reception of Vatican II*, ed. G. Alberigo, J.-P. Jossua, and J. A. Komonchak (Washington, DC: The Catholic University of America Press, 1987), 274.

11. Christopher Ruddy, *The Local Church: Tillard and the Future of Catholic Ecclesiology* (New York: Crossroad, 2006), 49.

12. Louis Bouyer, *The Church of God* (Chicago: Franciscan Herald Press, 1982), 177.

13. Ruddy, *Local Church*, 49.

14. A theological explanation would potentially involve the integration of ecclesiology and Trinitarian theology in which the communion of the Triune God, three-in-one, exhibits no ontological priority between oneness and threeness because all three Persons of the Trinity are co-eternal and equally divine.

logical and temporal relationships. One is left wondering *how* such inclusion occurs."[15] Without further theological explanation of the mutual inclusion of the local and universal Church, the question of ecclesial priority was neither asked nor addressed at the Council, thus leaving room for the debates that would arise decades later.

Post-Vatican II Communion Ecclesiology

In the years following the Council, reception of the Council's ecclesiology led to the distilling of its principal ideas and to the growing prominence of "communion ecclesiology." The Scriptural term *koinonia* became a valuable concept for understanding the simultaneous multiplicity of churches within the unity of the one Church of Christ.[16] Communion ecclesiology brings together the essential qualities of the Church as at once universal and particular, affirming the legitimacy of both. However, efforts to retrieve this *communio* model of the early Church have not been without their challenges.[17]

In 1992, the Congregation for the Doctrine of the Faith, whose Prefect at that time was Cardinal Joseph Ratzinger, issued a *Letter to the Bishops of the Catholic Church on Some Aspects of the Church Understood as Communion* (*'Communionis notio'*).[18] It sought to address "some approaches to ecclesiology [that] suffer from a clearly inadequate awareness of the Church as a mystery of communion" (no. 1). With regard to the relationship of the universal Church to particular churches, it rejected the view "that every particular Church is a subject complete in itself, and that the universal Church is the result of a reciprocal recognition on the part of the particular Churches" (no. 8). According to *Communionis notio,* such an "ecclesiological unilateralism, which impoverishes not only the concept of the universal Church but also that of

---

15. Ruddy, *Local Church,* 51.

16. Cf. Dulles, "The Church as Communion," 125–39. For a succinct summary of the various uses of "communion" in the documents of Vatican II, see also Ruddy, *The Local Church,* 47, which lists some of the dimensions of ecclesial communion as vertical or Trinitarian, horizontal or human, Eucharistic, local, universal, ecumenical, incarnational, eschatological, visible, and invisible.

17. For discussions on the relationship of the local and universal churches in contemporary ecclesiology, prior to the Ratzinger-Kasper debate, see William Henn, "Historical-Theological Synthesis of the Relation between Primacy and Episcopacy during the Second Millennium," *Il Primato del successore di Pietro Atti del simposio teologico* (Roma, 1996; Vatican City: Editrice Vaticana, 1998), and Joseph Komonchak, "The Local Church and the Church Catholic: The Contemporary Theological Problematic," *Jurist* 52 (1992): 416–47.

18. Congregation for the Doctrine of the Faith (CDF), *Letter to the Bishops of the Catholic Church on Some Aspects of the Church Understood as Communion* (*'Communionis notio'*), 28 May 1992, *Origins* 22 (June 25, 1992): 108–12, also available at http://www.vatican.va/roman_curia/congregations/cfaith/doc_doc_index.htm.

the particular Church, betrays an insufficient understanding of the concept of communion" (no. 8).[19]

In contrast to this unilateral view (that gave precedence to the local church over the universal Church), paragraph nine of *Communionis notio* states:

> In order to grasp the true meaning of the analogical application of the term *communion* to the particular Churches taken as a whole, one must bear in mind above all that the particular Churches, insofar as they are "part of the one Church of Christ," have a special relationship of "mutual interiority" with the whole, that is, with the universal Church, because in every particular Church "the one, holy, catholic and apostolic Church of Christ is truly present and active." For this reason, "the universal Church cannot be conceived as the sum of the particular Churches, or as a federation of particular Churches." It is not the result of the communion of the Churches, but, in its essential mystery, it is a reality *ontologically and temporally* prior to every *individual* particular Church.[20]

The first sentence of this oft-quoted passage reiterates the interpenetrating realities of the particular churches and the universal Church and defines their relationship as one of "mutual interiority." The second sentence further clarifies that the universal Church thus cannot be viewed as a sum or federation of particular churches. The third sentence, however, makes a relatively new and unexamined claim that the universal Church, in its essential mystery, is "*ontologically and temporally* prior to every *individual* particular Church."

The Ratzinger-Kasper Debate (1999–2001)

The last statement caused consternation and triggered an ongoing debate between two leading Church prelates, Cardinal Walter Kasper and Cardinal Joseph Ratzinger.[21] The controversy—stemming from the statement of

---

19. This critique of ecclesial unilateralism (i.e., a bias to the local church, based on the self-sufficiency of the local church) might be read as a critique of the ecclesiologies which were emerging at that time, namely, liberation theologies of Latin America as well as the Eucharistic ecclesiology developed by Nikolai Afanasiev in Eastern Orthodoxy, both of which, in their own distinctive ways, emphasized the local church over the universal Church.

20. *Communionis notio*, no. 9.

21. The main texts of the debate, as enumerated and examined in Paul McPartlan, "The Local Church and the Universal Church: Zizioulas and the Ratzinger-Kasper Debate," *International Journal for the Study of the Christian Church* 4, no. 1 (2004): 21–33, are fivefold: (a) In 1999, Walter

Communionis notio, no. 9, that the universal Church "is a reality *ontologically and temporally* prior to every *individual* Church"—attests to the perennial tension between the universal church and the particular churches, between central authority and local autonomy. These tensions have far-reaching consequences in the pastoral and ecumenical realms.[22] As we will see in the final analysis, Mary suffuses these ecclesial realities and can prove to be helpful in illuming the problematic.

In the course of the debate, Ratzinger and Kasper both clarified and refined their arguments. Some of the relevant points are as follows. Kasper's initial critique of the *Letter*, argued from a pastoral perspective, was that the CDF's emphasis on the priority of the universal Church belies a tendency to restore Roman centralism. Moreover, because the phrase "temporal and ontological priority" had already been used by Ratzinger in earlier works, its appearance in the CDF's *Letter* bore the obvious hallmark of the Congregation's prefect himself.[23] Kasper also took issue with how the *Letter* in-

---

Kasper, then-Bishop of Rottenburg-Stuttgart, gave a critique of the CDF's letter, *Communionis notio*, in an article, "Zur Theologie und Praxis des bischöflichen Amtes," in *Auf neue Art Kirche Sein Wirklichkeiten—Herausfoderungen—Wandlungen* (Munich: Bernward bei Don Bosco, 1999); (b) Ratzinger, in turn, replied to Kasper's critique in an address at the Vatican in February of 2000; an English translation is found in "The Ecclesiology of the Constitution *Lumen Gentium*," in *Pilgrim Fellowship of Faith*, 123–52. A subsequent debate ensued, consisting of two replies from Kasper and a counterreply from Ratzinger, all of which were published in the Jesuit journal *America*, consisting in: (c) Walter Kasper, "Das Verhältnis von Universalkirche und Ortskirche," *Stimmen der Zeit* 125, no. 12 (December 2000); English translation by Ladislas Orsy, SJ, "A Friendly Reply to Cardinal Ratzinger on the Church," *America*, 23 April 2001; (d) Joseph Ratzinger, "A Response to Walter Kasper: The Local Church and the Universal Church," *America*, 19 November 2001; and (e) Kasper, "Letter of Reply," in *America*, 26 November 2001. My account relies on McPartlan's chronological and thorough examination of the key texts. See also Kilian McDonnell, "The Ratzinger/Kasper Debate: The Universal Church and Local Churches," *Theological Studies* 63 (2002): 227–50.

22. One might note, for example, that the recent discussion on the possibility of offering communion to divorced Catholics stems, in part, from this tension between a universal norm and the pastoral concerns of a particular church in a particular sociohistorical setting. Kasper's comments in his reply to Ratzinger are made in this context; already in the year 2000, he spoke of "how a gap was emerging and steadily increasing between norms promulgated in Rome for the universal church and the needs and practices of our local church.... The adamant refusal of Communion to all divorced and remarried persons and the highly restrictive rules for Eucharistic hospitality are good examples" (Kasper, "Reply to Ratzinger," 8). For a discussion which draws out the implications of the local-universal Church theology for ecumenical dialogue, in addition to McPartlan's essay, see Richard DeClue, "Eucharistic Ecclesiologies of Locality and Universality in John Zizioulas and Joseph Ratzinger, *Nova et Vetera* 12, no. 1 (2014): 77–103.

23. Cf. Joseph Ratzinger, *Church, Ecumenism and Politics* (New York: Crossroad, 1989), 75: "The priority of the universal church always preceded that of particular churches"; the German edition dates from 1987. See also *Called to Communion* (San Francisco: Ignatius Press, 1996), 44: "The temporal and ontological priority lies with the universal Church"; the German edition dates to 1991. Both references predate the CDF's Letter, *Communionis notio* (1992).

terpreted the Pentecostal event as a manifestation primarily of the universal Church, an event that would only later lead to the founding of the local churches. For Kasper, "The correct history of the beginnings of the church is found comprehensively in the narrations of its initial expansion and not in Luke's isolated passage about Pentecost."[24] Both the content and structure of the Acts of the Apostles attest to the growth of the Church, called to be the new Israel, a worldwide community joined by the Spirit, through the witness of the Apostles "in Jerusalem and in all Judea and Samaria and to the ends of the earth" (Acts 1:8).

Kasper also pointed out that the CDF "went beyond the limits of the council's doctrine, which is that the universal church exists 'in and from' the local churches. The congregation stated that the local churches exist 'in and from' the universal church."[25] Paragraph no. 9 of *Communionis notio* quotes both formulas: the first, taken from *Lumen Gentium*, no. 23, states that the one Catholic Church exists in and from the local churches; the second, taken from an address of Pope John Paul II to the Roman Curia in 1990, additionally asserts the inverse reality, namely that the particular churches exist "out of and in the universal Church" (*ex et in Ecclesia universali*).[26] The logic of the *Letter* develops from the latter statement, assigning ontological priority to the universal Church. While Kasper did not reject either statement, he contended that the conclusion the *Letter* made did not strictly follow. He, instead, asserted a relation of mutuality and simultaneity in which the universal Church and the particular churches perichoretically interpenetrate one another.[27]

In his written response in 2001, Ratzinger denied any political agenda, arguing that "the inner precedence of God's idea of the one church, the one bride, over all its empirical realizations in particular churches has nothing whatsoever to do with the problem of centralism."[28] "The fears voiced by Kasper are groundless,"[29] he said, and the Church of Rome "is a local church and not the universal Church—a local church with a peculiar, universal responsibility, but still a local church."[30] Ratzinger conceded to Kasper's

24. Kasper, "Reply to Ratzinger," 13.

25. Kasper, 11.

26. See Pope John Paul II, "Address to the Roman Curia," 20 December 1990, no. 9, in *Acta apostolicae sedis* 83 (1991): 746.

27. Kasper, "Reply to Ratzinger," 13.

28. Ratzinger, "Response to Kasper," 8, 10.

29. Ratzinger, 8.

30. Ratzinger, 8, 10.

"thesis of simultaneity" but asserted that "it misses the actual point at issue as seen in the reference to the 'pre-existence' of the church."[31] He explained that according to the Fathers' theology of creation, "the basic idea of sacred history is that of gathering together, ... uniting human beings in the one body of Christ.... There is only one bride."[32] Ratzinger explains that this patristic development is "a continuation of rabbinic theology" in which the Torah and Israel were conceived as preexistent and in which the Church, standing in continuity with Israel, could veritably be said to preexist in God's will, which is to gather all creation in Himself through the Church.[33] Hence, for Ratzinger, the "superordinate principle is ultimately unity," and there must exist an "inner priority of unity, of the one bride to her essential variety."[34]

Among other points, Ratzinger defended his position on the ontological priority of the universal Church as scripturally warranted, relying on the Lucan account of Pentecost and on Galatians 4:26: "The Jerusalem above ... is our mother."[35] Through the sacramental reality of baptism, one is not simply born into a particular local church, but directly born into the universal Church from this heavenly mother who necessarily comes before her children. Ratzinger writes: "In baptism the door to the one church is opened to us; it is the presence of the one church and it can come only from her—from the Jerusalem that is above, our new mother. In baptism the universal church continually precedes and creates the local church."[36] Moreover, "what comes first in Saint Luke's account is not any original community at Jerusalem; what comes first is that, in the Twelve, the old Israel, which is one, becomes the new and that through the wonderful gift of tongues, this new Israel of God is then shown ... to be a unity encompassing every time and place."[37] Ratzinger later clarified his initial stance on the "ontological and temporal priority"[38] of the universal Church as referring to a "priority of

31. Ratzinger, 10.
32. Ratzinger, 10.
33. Ratzinger, "Ecclesiology of the Constitution *Lumen Gentium*," 134.
34. Ratzinger, "Response to Kasper," 10.
35. Ratzinger, "Ecclesiology of the Constitution *Lumen Gentium*," 135–37.
36. "Response to Kasper," 11; see also Ratzinger, "Ecclesiology of the Constitution *Lumen Gentium*," 142. The reference to the universal Church as that which "continually precedes and creates the local church" is an odd claim, and a similar statement can be found in paragraph no. 9 of *Communionis notio*: "According to the Fathers, ontologically, the Church-mystery, the Church that is one and unique, precedes creation, and *gives birth to the particular Churches as her daughters.*"
37. Ratzinger, "Ecclesiology of the Constitution *Lumen Gentium*," 137–38.
38. Ratzinger, "Response to Kasper," 8.

inner unity," by which he meant "the inner precedence of God's idea of the one church, the one bride, over all its empirical realizations in particular churches."[39]

On the other hand, as seen above, Kasper maintained the principles of simultaneity and perichoresis over ontological priority. For Kasper, if there is a preexistent Church, it must involve both the universal Church and the particular churches; otherwise, as he said, with reference to de Lubac, an ecclesiology of preexistence that did not involve the Church as it exists throughout history would be merely an ecclesiological abstraction.[40]

Both Kasper and Ratzinger, at different points in the debate and in different ways, refer to de Lubac to support their respective positions.[41] It seems appropriate, therefore, to probe more deeply de Lubac's writing on the topic, *Les églises particulières dans l'Église universelle*.

De Lubac's *Les églises particulières dans l'Église universelle*

The Centrality of the Eucharist and the Episcopacy

Written decades prior to the debate between Ratzinger and Kasper and free of those polemics, *Les églises particulières dans l'Église universelle* anticipates many of their respective concerns. The book was de Lubac's first work directly on what he called "the subject of institutions," and in it, de Lubac examines the topics of catholicity, unity, episcopal collegiality, and the relationship of the universal and particular churches. On the last topic, de Lubac focuses on the centrality of the Eucharist and the episcopate in the constitution of the particular churches. The bishop, gathered with his priests and faithful at the altar in celebration of the holy Eucharist, becomes "a living cell 'in which the whole vital mystery of the one Body of the Church is present, each one ... open on all sides through the bonds of communion and preserves her existence as Church only through this openness.'"[42] In his characteristic way, de Lubac marshals evidence from a wide array of sources. He references the New Testament studies of Heinrich Schlier to underscore the centrality of the Eucharist in the early Church: "According to the

---

39. Ratzinger, 10.

40. Kasper, "Reply to Ratzinger," 13, with reference to de Lubac, MC, 208.

41. See McPartlan, "The Local Church and the Universal Church," 24.

42. MC, 202, quoting Joseph Ratzinger, "The Pastoral Implications of Episcopal Collegiality," *Concilium* 1 (1965): 44–45.

writings of the New Testament, it is certain that the community is built up principally in worship, ... the active center of the divine service."[43] De Lubac is clear that each local eucharistic community is "the real actualization of the entire universal Church."[44] Even more emphatically, he states: "No more than the local Church is a mere department of the universal Church, is the latter simply a federation composed of the local churches. For there is but one Eucharist, as there is but one baptism and one episcopate."[45] De Lubac's statements provide an important focus and will have significant implications for implementing the institutional reforms initiated by Vatican II.

The Mutual Interiority of the Particular Churches to the Universal Church

Based on the Eucharistic-episcopal constitution of each particular Church, de Lubac posits that the universal and particular churches are "mutually interior" to each other. In *Paradoxe et Mystère de l'Église,* de Lubac comments on *Lumen Gentium,* no. 23, saying: "If, in chapter 3, no. 23, the local church is called '*portio Ecclesiae universalis*,' such an expression ... does not pretend to be a full definition; nor is it said that the sacramental communities are *only* parts of the Church."[46] In *Les églises particulières dans l'Église universelle,* he develops this idea further, positing a "radical correlation" between the universal and particular churches such that the Church is one, mystical body:

> Since there is a mutual interiority or inclusion, there is a radical correlation, so that it is not enough to say that the particular churches have to be inserted into the universal Church: they are so by their very existence. The universal Church is therefore not one of a "federative" unity—as if particular churches were at first able to establish themselves, each one separately, and then were free to join together; she is the Spouse of Christ. Her unity is "organic and mystical."[47]

With regard to this dense passage, it is worth noting that the "radical correlation" or mutual inclusion of the particular and universal churches involves more than a simple insertion of the former into the latter. On the contrary, "by their very existence" the particular churches are interior and

43. MC, 349.
44. CPM, 36.
45. CPM, 36–37.
46. CPM, 37.
47. MC, 203; de Lubac is quoting from Charles Journet, *Primauté de Pierre dans la perspective protestante et dans la perspective catholique* (Paris: Alsatia, 1953), 76.

inclusive to the universal Church.[48] Conversely, the unity that constitutes the universal Church is not a "federative unity" of separate entities that enter into a federation. Rather, says de Lubac as he switches gears to the mystery of the Church as a whole, the Church is "the Spouse of Christ" and "her unity is organic and whole." This is not to say that the particular churches are espoused to the universal Church, but rather, that their mutual interiority, "organic and mystical," constitutes one mystery of the Church as the one Spouse of Christ. De Lubac makes an emphatic statement on this radical correlation of the particular churches and the universal Church: "Just as the universal Church does not result, in a second 'moment,' from an addition of particular churches or from their federation, neither could these churches be considered the result of the division of a universal Church alleged to be anterior to them."[49] He also speaks unambiguously of the Church of Jerusalem as primarily a "particular concrete church" and again rejects the idea of any universal Church "anterior" to it: "They [particular churches] all proceed from a prior, *particular, concrete church*, that of Jerusalem; they came from her, 'as it were, by cutting and planting.' An anterior universal Church, or one alleged to exist on her own, apart from all others, is only a creation of the mind."[50] De Lubac's point is that every church proceeds from the concrete, particular gathering of the disciples in Jerusalem at Pentecost (Acts 2:1–13). This event in the Upper Room—the Holy Spirit's descent manifested in tongues of fire and a strong driving wind, accompanied by the gift of tongues—traditionally marks the birth of the Church. It is not without significance that Luke reports Mary's presence in the first community in Jerusalem (Acts 1:14).

De Lubac's point that all particular churches proceed from the Church of Jerusalem as a concrete and particular church, carries great significance for the debate that ensued between Cardinals Kasper and Ratzinger decades after *Les églises particulières dans l'Église universelle* was written. We are now poised to examine that debate anew and to consider how de Lubac's writings help to illumine the key issues of the debate and to arrive at a true rapprochment.

48. MC, 203.
49. MC, 207.
50. MC, 207–8.

Kasper's Resonance and Dissonance
with de Lubac

In the course of that spirited exchange between Kasper and Ratzinger, the former makes three direct references to de Lubac. The first is found in his affirmation of three "Common Foundations in Ecclesiology" on which he believes Ratzinger and all Catholic theologians must concur.[51] Kasper enumerates these points as follows: (a) Christ willed but one Church, a church that "subsists" in the Roman Catholic Church; (b) this one Church of Christ exists "in and from" the local churches that are interior to the universal Church; and (c) the mystery of this inclusivity constitutes the unity of the Church, a unity that includes diversity. After a brief explanation of each point, he says: "In affirming these three points, I think I am in substantial agreement with Henri de Lubac, who expressed such essentials in a concise formula: 'Whenever there is mutual presence and inclusion, there is a perfect relationship.'"[52]

Two further references to de Lubac are made. The first is found in the subsequent section on "Controversy: Points of Disagreement," in which Kasper reasserts his position that "the pre-existence of the church must be understood as the concrete church that exists 'in and from' particular churches" and says, as noted above, that: "No less a scholar than Henri de Lubac stated, 'A universal church which would have a separate existence, or which someone imagined as existing outside the particular churches, is a mere abstraction.'"[53] Another reference to de Lubac is made in Kasper's final reply to Ratzinger at the conclusion of the debate, when he says: "In any case I can invoke for my position a witness as prominent as Henri de Lubac, whom both Cardinal Ratzinger and I highly respect as one of the 'Church Fathers' of present-day theology."[54]

In consideration of where there is substantial agreement between de Lubac's views and those of Kasper, it might be said that Kasper's fundamental aim to bolster the standing of the local church finds a consonant aim in de Lubac's own concern to expound the proper nature and importance of the particular church with its bishop as pastor. Three further points of affinity

---

51. See Kasper, "Reply to Ratzinger," 12.

52. Kasper, 12; the source of the internal quotation is not specified, but it appears to be alluding to MC, 203.

53. Kasper, 13; again, the internal quotation is not specified, but appears to be alluding to MC, 207–8.

54. Kasper, "Letter of Reply," 28.

can be delineated. The first point of note is de Lubac's statement, given in his commentary on *Lumen Gentium* in *Paradoxe et Mystère de l'Église*: "To oppose … 'the local church, foundation of primitive ecclesiology' to 'Roman universalism' would be to adopt a one-sidedness equally out of harmony with the Fathers as with *Lumen Gentium*."[55] Kasper actually accused Ratzinger of doing this (i.e., that he promoted the priority of the universal Church over the local church in order to advance Roman universalism), an accusation that Ratzinger claimed was unfounded. Second, de Lubac's statement, "Between the particular church and the universality of the church 'there is, as it were, a mutual interiority,'"[56] resonates fully with Kasper's own position (as well as the CDF's). In the same vein as de Lubac, Kasper wrote: "There can be no local church in isolation, for its own sake, but only in communion with all other churches.… The local churches and the universal church *mutually include* each other."[57] Third, de Lubac's emphatic statement that the particular churches cannot be "considered the result of the division of a universal Church alleged to be anterior to them"[58] makes clear his view that the Church of Jerusalem is primarily a "particular concrete church" and that there is no such thing as some "anterior universal Church." For de Lubac, "An anterior universal Church, or one alleged to exist on her own, apart from all others, is only a creation of the mind."[59] These three points: the objection to positioning local churches against Roman universalism; the mutual interiority of the particular and universal churches; and the concrete particularity of the Church of Jerusalem at Pentecost, bespeak the significant continuity between de Lubac's and Kasper's views.

Additionally, Kasper develops an idea of his own when he posits the simultaneous pre-existence of the local/particular churches with the universal Church: "The Pauline texts about the pre-existence of the church do not at all support the thesis about the pre-existence of the universal church. They do support, however the doctrine defended by me and many others of the *simultaneous pre-existence* of the universal church and the particular church-es."[60] Kasper's argument can be considered a development that is not found explicitly in de Lubac's writings. When de Lubac explores the Pauline texts,

---

55. CPM, 37, with reference to Meyendorff, *Orthodoxie et catholicité* (1965), 97–98, 146, and Dom Burkhard Neunheuser on "*Église universelle et Église locale*," in *L'Église de Vatican II*, 607–38.

56. MC, 201, with quotation from Yves Congar, *La collégialité de l'épiscopat*.

57. Kasper, "Reply to Ratzinger," 12; emphasis added.

58. MC, 207.

59. MC, 207–8; this point was expounded by Kasper in "Reply to Ratzinger," 13.

60. Kasper, "Reply to Ratzinger," 13; emphasis added.

he says: "According to Paul, the Church, which is the Spouse of Christ, both virgin and fruitful at the same time, is the mother of all those who are born (reborn) in the Spirit and for whom she proclaims and maintains the pure authentic doctrine of Christ" (cf. Eph 5; Gal 4; 2 Cor 11:2–4).[61] De Lubac's statement is made with reference to the Church without distinguishing the particular churches from the universal Church. Furthermore, de Lubac's statements, previously quoted, that the particular churches "all proceed from a prior, particular, concrete church, that of Jerusalem" and that "an anterior universal Church, or one alleged to exist on her own, apart from all others, is only a creation of the mind,"[62] show unambiguously that de Lubac considered the Church of Jerusalem to be, not simultaneously particular and universal, but a particular, concrete church. The mariological underpinnings of de Lubac's stance will be explored in a later section.

Ratzinger's Resonance and Dissonance with de Lubac

Ratzinger's writings on the relationship of the universal and particular churches express an affinity to de Lubac's thought, although he rarely quotes de Lubac directly in support of his own views.[63] Three points in particular appear to bear traces of de Lubac's influence. The first is the importance of Eucharistic ecclesiology for both de Lubac and Ratzinger. De Lubac posited in *Paradoxe et Mystère de l'Église* that the Constitution, *Lumen Gentium*, "owes its strength to a central doctrine of our faith…. Thomas Aquinas summed it up when he said that the mystical body which is the Church is the *res* of the sacrament of the Eucharist."[64] Ratzinger also expounds Eucharistic ecclesiology, inherited from the Council and the works of Orthodox theologians in the twentieth century, as a key aspect of communion ecclesiology.[65] Moreover, de Lubac's warning against a narrow Eucharistic ecclesiology neglecting the correlation of the particular churches and the universal Church, also finds an echo in *Communionis notio*, no. 11: "The rediscovery of

61. MC, 41.

62. MC, 207–8.

63. See Ratzinger, "Response to Kasper," 10. Of the few explicit references to de Lubac in the course of his debate with Kasper is Ratzinger's reference to Kasper's use of de Lubac's thought: "The term 'universal church' is understood to refer only to the pope and the Curia. It seems, as Kasper says in his response, echoing Henri de Lubac, to be a pure abstraction." A second reference is examined in following.

64. CPM, 36.

65. See Ratzinger, "Ecclesiology of the Constitution *Lumen Gentium*," 131.

a eucharistic ecclesiology, though being of undoubted value, has however sometimes placed unilateral emphasis on the principle of the local Church."

Second, it is also worth noting that de Lubac's explanation of the mutual interiority of the particular and universal churches anticipates the statement of *Communionis notio,* no. 9, that "the universal Church cannot be conceived as the sum of the particular churches, or as a federation of particular churches." Although the *Letter* itself attributed the statement to Pope John Paul II,[66] the idea had already been asserted by de Lubac when he wrote, as previously quoted: "Since there is a mutual interiority or inclusion, there is a radical correlation.... The universal Church is therefore not one of a 'federative' unity—as if particular churches were at first able to establish themselves, each one separately, and then were free to join together."[67]

Third and most significantly, de Lubac's statement that the universal Church is "the Spouse of Christ" whose unity is "organic and mystical"[68] resonates deeply with Ratzinger's own argument, which centers on the unity of the bride of Christ when he later writes:

> The basic idea of sacred history is that of gathering together, ... the union of human beings and through human beings of all creation with God. There is only one bride, ... [who is], as the fathers of the church said, drawing on Psalm 44, dressed in many-colored robes; the body has many organs. But the superordinate principle is ultimately unity. That is the point here. Variety becomes richness only through the process of unification. [69]

Throughout the debate, Ratzinger adamantly maintains this argument for an "inner priority of unity, of the one bride to her essential variety."[70]

It was earlier shown in an exposition of *Les églises particulières dans l'Église universelle* that de Lubac draws on the works of Heinrich Schlier to posit the unity of the Church in the New Testament as a unity founded in the Eucharist presided over by the bishop. Ratzinger employs the same author in expressing his views of the Church's primordial unity as a unity embodied in the reality of the one bride of Christ. The joint use of Schlier's writings by

---

66. Pope John Paul II, Address to the Bishops of the United States of America, 16 September 1987, no. 3; accessible at http://w2.vatican.va/content/john-paul-ii/en/speeches/1987/september/documents/hf_jp-ii_spe_19870916_vescovi-stati-uniti.html.

67. MC, 203, with quotation from Journet, *Primauté de Pierre,* 76.

68. MC, 203.

69. Ratzinger, "Response to Kasper," 10.

70. Ratzinger, 10.

both de Lubac and Ratzinger underscores the continuity of their views on the witness of the New Testament to the unity of the Church. Moreover, in his essay, "The Ecclesiology of the Constitution *Lumen Gentium*," Ratzinger also quotes Schlier for his interpretation of Galatians 4:26:

> In the heart of the great Pauline letters, in the Letter to the Galatians, the Apostle talks to us about the heavenly Jerusalem, and indeed not as an eschatological entity, but as one that comes before us: "The Jerusalem above ... is our mother" (Gal 4:26). H. Schlier observes in this connection that, for Paul as for the related Jewish tradition, the Jerusalem above is the new age. But for the Apostle the new age is already present "in the Christian Church. This is for him the heavenly Jerusalem in its children."[71]

Ratzinger's main concern is principally with "the inner beginning of the Church in temporal existence,"[72] which, in his reading of Luke, belongs to the power of the Holy Spirit. Specifically citing Kasper's characterization of the CDF's position, he says:

> It is not being fair to Luke's account if we say that the "original community at Jerusalem" was at one and the same time the universal Church and local Church. What comes first in Saint Luke's account is not any original community at Jerusalem; what comes first is that, in the Twelve, the old Israel, which is one, becomes the new and that through the wonderful gift of tongues this new Israel of God is then shown, before there is any question of constituting a local community in Jerusalem, to be a unity encompassing every time and place.[73]

Ratzinger seems to be introducing a new configuration when he draws an explicit distinction between the community of believers gathered at Jerusalem on Pentecost day and the local community of Jerusalem of which James, the Elder, assumed leadership, positing that the former was principally a manifestation of the New Israel, the Jerusalem coming from above and the first earthly manifestation of the universal Church. From this line of reasoning, which posits the Church of Jerusalem at Pentecost to be the primordial experience of the universal Church, Ratzinger further asserts the ontological and temporal priority of that universal Church.

71. Ratzinger, "Ecclesiology of the Constitution *Lumen Gentium*," 135–36, with reference to H. Schlier, *Der Brief an die Galater,* 12th ed. (Göttingen, 1962), 223.

72. Ratzinger, "Ecclesiology of the Constitution *Lumen Gentium*," 137.

73. Ratzinger, 137–38, as previously quoted.

Moreover, Ratzinger explicitly refers to de Lubac in defense of his views of the "inner priority of unity, of the one bride to her essential variety,"[74] a view he adamantly holds:

> The priority of the one Church, of the one Bride of Christ, in which the heritage of the people of Israel, of the "daughter" and "bride" of Zion, is carried forward, as against the empirical realization of the people of God in practice, is in fact so obvious, in Scripture just as in the writings of the Church Fathers, that I find it difficult to understand the oft-repeated views disputing this. One need only read again de Lubac's *Catholicisme* (1938) or his *Méditation sur l'Église*.[75]

In *Catholicisme*, when de Lubac examined the interpretation of Scripture and considered the unity of the soul and the Church according to Scriptural exegesis, he cited St. Gregory the Great whose homilies show that "the Bride is revealed in the fullness of her mystery—'the only one, the dove, the perfect, the chosen one,' appears as the very unity of all Christ's members, the *Corpus Christi* spoken of by St. Paul."[76] Herein, the coalescence of de Lubac and Ratzinger's thought is evident: the unity of the Church as Christ's members is revealed in the mystery of the Bride.

While it may be inferred that de Lubac would fundamentally concur with Ratzinger's position on the preexistent inner unity of the Church as the bride of Christ, there remains a significant point of difference in the details of their articulation of that mystery of the Church as bride and as mother. It has already been noted that while de Lubac identifies the Church of Jerusalem at Pentecost as a concrete, particular Church, Ratzinger adamantly asserts the contrary, saying that the Church of Jerusalem at Pentecost is universal. In view of what both theologians hold pertaining the mystery of the Church as the bride of Christ, however, it seems that whether one chooses to call that gathering in Jerusalem upon which the Spirit descended a particular church or the universal Church, their views essentially convey the same mystery and acknowledge the primordial unity of that mysterious Bride.

A point of difference, however, is found in Ratzinger's assertion that in

---

74. Ratzinger, "Response to Kasper," 10.

75. Ratzinger, "Church Movements and Their Place in Theology," in *Pilgrim Fellowship of Faith*, 188n5. This article, originally published in 1998 as "Movimenti ecclesiali e loro collocazione teologica," in *Il Regno* 43 (1998): 399–407; in *Orientamenti pastorali* 6/98, 8–30; and in *Communio* 27 (1998): 65–83, lays bare Ratzinger's position on the priority of the Church as the one bride of Christ.

76. *Catholicism*, 214–15, quoting Gregory the Great, *In Cant.*, hom. 15 (PG 44, 1116–20).

"baptism the universal Church always takes priority over the local Church and is creating her."[77] *Communionis notio*, no. 9, makes a similar statement, asserting: "Indeed, according to the Fathers, ontologically, the Church-mystery, the Church that is one and unique, precedes creation, and gives birth to the particular Churches as her daughters." For the CDF, all particular churches are born from the Church-mystery as their mother, and although it claims that this point is made "according to the Fathers," the *Letter* does not provide any reference to the Fathers. The concept of the particular churches as "daughters" born from the Church-mystery is actually a novelty.[78]

The subtle but significant difference of speaking of the Church as mother to its Christian members and as mother to particular churches, per se, emerges with greater clarity when contrasted with de Lubac's patristic perspective on the maternity of the Church. In his *La maternité de l'église*, he considers the notion of ecclesial maternity as a notion that has always been understood in the context of the universal Church and posited with regard to *Christian persons*, and never to particular churches per se. De Lubac draws readily from the testimony of Tradition. Tertullian, for example, comforts the imprisoned confessors of the faith, saying that Mother Church will provide for their spiritual needs from her maternal breasts.[79] St. Cyprian writes: "There is only one single Church, [and] we are born from her womb, nourished by her milk, animated by her spirit."[80] St. Augustine beckons the Donatists to "come back to the Mother Church, to the Catholic mother."[81]

In each of these examples, reference to "Mother Church" is reference to the "Church-mystery" and to the reality of the new *Christians* as her offspring. There is no reference to *particular churches* as the "daughters" of a Mother Church (or Church-mystery). While this may seem to be a subtle and pedantic distinction, it is essential to the discussion of the relationship of the particular churches to the universal Church. Are the particular churches properly the offspring, "born" of the Church-mystery, as the CDF's *Letter* states?[82] Is it, strictly speaking, the universal Church that "creates the

---

77. Ratzinger, "Ecclesiology of the Constitution *Lumen Gentium*," 142; see also "Response to Kasper," 11, in which he argues, "In baptism the universal church continually precedes and creates the local church."

78. This subtle point was brought to my attention in conversation with Paul McPartlan.

79. MC, 48, with reference to Tertullian, *De monogamia*, c. 7, n. 9 (CSEL, 4:58).

80. Cyprian, *De Ecclesiae catholicae unitate*, c. 5, *Epist.* 46, c. 1 (2:604); as quoted in MC, 48.

81. Augustine, *Contra Cresconiun* (PL, 43, 550–55; 581); as quoted in MC, 51.

82. *Communionis notio*, no. 9: "Ontologically, the Church-mystery, the Church that is one and unique, precedes creation, and gives birth to the particular Churches as her daughters."

local church" in baptism, as Ratzinger states?[83] It seems more in keeping with patristic theology to say, as de Lubac says, that "the Church, which is the Spouse of Christ, both virgin and fruitful at the same time, is the mother of all those who are born (reborn) in the Spirit."[84]

It is certainly more common to speak of the Church as mother of *new Christians* than of *particular churches* in themselves,[85] and Ratzinger employs this sense as well when he says, for example: "Baptism springs from this [universal] Church and by it, *people* are born into her."[86] In baptism, it is the faithful who are born, not particular churches per se. It seems that Ratzinger inadvertently equates the birth of new Christians with the creation of the local church. Such a move might be considered a logical semantic development on the premise that in birthing, like begets like, and so, it follows logically that one can speak of the Church as a mother begetting daughter (or local, particular) churches. If this be the case, then, Ratzinger has conceptually conflated the two realities of the birthing of new Christians and that of the constitution or building up of the particular churches (in these new Christians).

Problems arise when this conflation, made on the basis of the evident priority of Mother Church to her Christian children, leads to the further assertion of an ontological and temporal priority of the universal Church over particular churches. While it is true that the Church-mystery, as mother, precedes her children, it does not necessarily follow that she is to be identified exclusively with an earthly, universal Church (i.e., the Church of Jerusalem at Pentecost). Nor does it follow that her direct progeny are, strictly speaking, the particular churches. Spiritual maternity is an undifferentiated quality of *both* the universal and particular churches: The Church-mystery is a mother who gives birth to Christians in baptism.[87]

When de Lubac considers the motherhood of the Church, it is always of the *entire* Church; he neither distinguishes between the particular and universal churches in this regard nor does he say that the former are born from the latter. Contrarily, he underscores how it is the *entire* Church, not just the hierarchy, that exercises spiritual maternity: "The whole Church, the entire

83. Ratzinger, "Response to Kasper," 11; see also Ratzinger, "Ecclesiology of the Constitution *Lumen Gentium*," 142.

84. MC, 41.

85. See de Lubac's account of the Scriptural and patristic witness to the idea of the motherhood of the Church in the first two chapters of MC, 39–58, in which reference to the Church as the mother of Christians is made as a matter of fact.

86. Ratzinger, "Ecclesiology of the Constitution *Lumen Gentium*," 142.

87. Cf. MC, 55–58.

Christian community is mother. 'In carnal marriage, … the mother and child are distinct; in the Church, on the contrary, mother and child are one.'"[88] Hence, for de Lubac, it is "immediately consistent with patristic thought to consider this maternity as that of the entire Church, which all the faithful living the life of Christ participate in spreading."[89] Ecclesial maternity belongs to neither the universal Church nor the particular churches principally, but to that communion of *Christian persons* who constitute the mystery of the one body of Christ. This communion comprises both the universal and particular churches.

As the title of these two subsections indicate, there is both resonance and dissonance in Kasper's and Ratzinger's use of de Lubac's thought. He was an important source for both, and this exposition has shown that while de Lubac agrees on some points with Kasper and other points with Ratzinger, both Kasper and Ratzinger polarized de Lubac's ideas and created an opposition where there was none for de Lubac. It has been the goal of this chapter to return to the writings of de Lubac and seek in him a higher perspective free of the polemics of the controversial debate. To this end, the following section aims to show that it is, in fact, de Lubac's Marian ecclesiology that endows him with a unique perspective that ratifies aspects of Kasper's and Ratzinger's views and brings the various notes of resonance and dissonance of their debate into harmony.

Marian Dimensions

We now take up the charge of employing the Marian principles, which de Lubac's writings provide, to consider how Mariology might illumine and advance the discussion of the relationship of the particular and universal churches. Proceeding in three sections, the first considers how the Council's Marian teaching manifests a parallel, conceptual structure of mutual interiority between Mary and the Church and how this parallel might illumine the relationship of the local and universal churches. The second examines de Lubac's own considerations of the Virgin Mary as a concrete universal and explores how this conception allows de Lubac to take a perspective on the local-universal church relationship that precludes the controversial points of the Kasper-Ratzinger debate and helps to resolve their conflict. The third section considers that the idea of the Church as *sponsa Christi* is best

---

88. MC, 77, with quotation from Augustine, *Psalm* 127, 12 (PL 37, 1684).
89. MC, 83.

understood in light of Mary whose Assumption into heaven is an icon of the Church's own consummate union with Christ at the eschaton.

Mutual Interiority and the Council's Mariology

De Lubac, Kasper, and Ratzinger all agreed that the relationship of the local church and the universal Church is one of mutual inclusion or interiority. This idea of "mutual interiority" presents a fundamental point of contact between the Council's Mariology and its teaching on the communion of the local and universal churches, as presented in *Lumen Gentium,* no. 23: the particular churches are "formed in the image" of the universal Church, which in turn is realized "in and from" the particular, local churches.

As noted above, the Council posited this relationship of mutual interiority without providing any in-depth theological explanation of *how* this mutual inclusion takes place. Nevertheless, an illuminating structural similarity can be found in the Council's Marian teaching in which the relationship between Mary and the Church might also be described as a relationship of "mutual interiority." The Council's decision to treat Mariology within its Constitution on the Church was a decisive one with profound theological implications. Overall, by its integrated treatment, the Council taught that Mary is to be considered "interior" to the Church. Based on this structural inclusivity, it might thus be said that Our Lady exists "in and from" the Church and that the Church is "formed in the image" of Mary.

Pope Paul VI's proclamation of the Marian title, *Mater Ecclesiae,* on 21 November 1964, underscored the dynamic of the Church as born from Mary: the Church comes into existence "in and from" Our Lady. In other words, the ecclesio-Marian synthesis of *Lumen Gentium* itself embodies a relationship of mutual interiority, and the formula of *Lumen Gentium,* no. 23 regarding the relationship of the local and universal churches might also be applied to the relationship of Mary and the Church in which each interpenetrates the other, existing in and from each other. Mary, who is the Church's "mother in the order of grace" (LG, no. 61), also "occupies a place *in* the Church that is the highest after Christ and yet very close to us" (LG, no. 54; emphasis added).

When one considers this mutual interiority of Mary and the Church, the heart of the relationship is illumined: *faith* is the key to their mutual interiority. It is Mary's faith that identifies her with the People of God (and hence makes her a *member* of the Church), and it is by her faith, virginal and fruitful, that she is a *mother* to Christ and to the Church. Similarly, a fundamental unity of faith is what unites all Christians in one body of Christ.

Furthermore, given the structural parallel between the Council's teaching on the relationship of Mary and the Church and on that of the local and universal churches, it can be said that one finds a real exemplification of this church-constituting faith, not simply in either the local or the universal church per se, but, primordially and concretely in Mary. Her faith is no mere abstract principle but one that is concrete and personal; it is fully realized in Our Lady's own *fiat* and lifelong discipleship. She is the epitome of Christian faith and she thus exemplifies the nexus of the mutual interiority of the local and the universal churches, a relationship constituted *in faith*. Because she who is the concrete realization of faith is also the concrete realization of what it means to be *church*, it might even be said that the faith that constitutes the church as a communion of believers and as disciples of Christ is precisely a *Marian* faith.

In summary, the twofold dynamic of the Council's determination of a Marian-ecclesiological synthesis and Pope Paul VI's subsequent proclamation of Mary as *Mater Ecclesiae* indicates a mutual interiority that illumines the element of faith at the core of the relationship of the local and universal churches, a faith that is made concrete in Mary. However, this analogy of the mutual interiority of Mary and the Church and of the local and universal churches is primarily a *structural* analogy, and it has a limited application as such. In other words, it only illumines a structural similarity and does not say much about the content of the analogy beyond its constitution in faith. De Lubac's Marian thought offers yet another paradigm for considering the substance of *how* this interpenetration of the local churches and the universal Church might be conceived. The next section thus returns to the conception of Our Lady as a concrete universal and explores how it might clarify the inner dynamics of the mutual interiority of the local and universal churches.

Mary as a Concrete Universal

De Lubac's commentary on Teilhard's poem *"L'Éternel féminin"* expounded the notion of the concrete universal as an expression employed by Teilhard and Blondel.[90] As previously noted, the idea of the concrete universal relies on the idea that a given concrete being is so personal that it has universal

90. See EF, 120.

effect. In his commentary on Teilhard's works, de Lubac explained that the most concentrated personality contains a simultaneous universal dimension because "universality is the prerogative of the strongest personality."[91] In Paul McPartlan's words: "What is most unique and specific has, by that very fact, the greatest effect on others, colouring and sustaining them."[92]

De Lubac's conception of the concrete universal provides a unique perspective and framework in which to consider the relationship of the local and universal churches. The identification of the universal and the particular aligns rather remarkably with Kasper's idea that the Church is simultaneously "universal and local in its single reality."[93] However, de Lubac's conception of the concrete universal explains more than just the coincidence of local and universal realities; it adds two substantial points that help explain, at least in part, the relationship posited. First, in de Lubac's conception of the concrete universal, the universal is always defined as supremely personal (or particular). In this light, the Church of Jerusalem at Pentecost may be thought of as universal precisely *because* it is supremely local and concrete. Second, de Lubac is emphatic that the concrete universal is not the personification of a principle; rather, the personal must always come first, and only thereafter does it assume the dimension of a universal.[94] In this sense, it might be said that the notion of a concrete universal brings together the best aspects of Kasper's and Ratzinger's respective positions: the Church gathered at Jerusalem on Pentecost day is indeed a local gathering, and in the utter uniqueness of its composition and spiritual significance, it is a manifestation of the universal Church.

Furthermore, considered in light of the mutual interiority of Mary and the Church (which, as previously discussed, is analogous to the mutual interiority of the local and universal churches), the notion of Mary as a concrete universal shows her to be *ontologically* related to the Church as "the essence of the Church, the quintessential 'us-ness' of the bond between Christ and the Church."[95] In other words, the analogous predication of Mary and the Church, and of the local and universal churches, as mutually interior or

---

91. EF, 118, with reference to Teilhard's "Sketch of a Personalistic Universe," 65.

92. McPartlan, "Mary for Teilhard and de Lubac," 4.

93. Kasper, "Zur Theologie und Praxis des bischoflichen Amtes," 44.

94. Cf. EF, 118: "It is not the universal which takes on for us the appearance of the personal in order that it may make itself apprehensible by giving itself mythical expression; the universal does not become more or less personal and so acquire an added attribute. It is the personal which becomes universal, to the degree in which (subject to certain conditions) it realizes more profoundly its own specific character."

95. McPartlan, "Mary for Teilhard and de Lubac," 5.

inclusive to one another, contains the dynamic of a particular entity becoming universalized—the same dynamic alluded to in *Lumen Gentium,* no. 23, which describes the universal Church as "formed in and out of" the particular churches. It may thus be said that Mary exemplifies the structure of the communion of local and universal churches as a concrete universal. Just as her (concrete) historical existence is essential to her (universal) role in the work of Redemption, the particular dimension of the local churches is an essential part in the Church's being. Moreover, the intriguing convergence of universality and locality in Mary is manifest in the countless titles which associate her to the nations of the world and even depict her as a native of those respective cultures. These depictions express the universal dimension of Mary's being in which the local dimension endures.

Furthermore, Mary's maternal relationship to Christ and her particular role in the economy of salvation are unique and exceptional. In light of the Christian tradition that has employed the term *specialiter* to denote that coalescence of Mary's concreteness and her universality as the unique and exemplary form for the Church and for all Christians, the Church of Jerusalem at Pentecost—that gathering of disciples with Mary present—might also be considered the Church-mystery *specialiter.* It is, as de Lubac argues, a concrete, *particular* Church, but not just any particular Church. On the contrary, it is *the* concrete particular Church from which all other Churches are founded, and as such, it is both universal and unique in that it reveals the form of the Church as animated by the Spirit. "*Specialiter*" allows one to conceive a balanced relationship of both particularity and universality.[96] Mary is a concrete universal in whom the universal essence of the Church and its inner unity as the one bride of Christ is concretely realized. One final question flowing directly from this reality remains: might an ontologically and temporally prior, universal Church be found in the Blessed Mother?

Mary as *Sponsa Christi*

The CDF's letter, *Communionis notio,* concludes on a Marian note positing the intimate connection between Our Lady and the Church in an ecclesiology of communion. It states that the Blessed Virgin Mary is essential for understanding the Church because she "is the model of ecclesial communion in faith, in charity and in union with Christ." Moreover, it refers to "the

---

96. Cf. de Lubac's discussion of Isaac of Stella's trio of terms with *specialiter* applied to Mary in *Méditation sur l'Église.*

Church … congregated in the upper part (of the Cenacle) with Mary who was the Mother of Jesus, and with his brethren" (*Communionis notio*, no. 19). Returning, then, to that event of Pentecost, an event that posed the crucial question of whether the Church of Jerusalem at Pentecost was the universal Church or a particular one, one encounters Mary's unobtrusive but definitive presence in that initial community of faith (cf. Acts 1:14). It is here, in the Church of Jerusalem at Pentecost, that Mary's significance for the Church can be considered in light of the idea of the Church as the bride of Christ.

A previous chapter has considered how de Lubac's (and Teilhard's) notion of Mary as the concrete universal shows her to be a universalized figure whose personal history has a unique bearing for all of salvation history. As also shown in de Lubac's spiritual exegesis on the Song of Songs, Our Lady is the complete fulfillment of the symbol of the figure of the bride. De Lubac's Mariology not only associates Our Lady with the bride of the Song of Songs but also with the bride of Revelation. Her words, "Come, Lord Jesus!" (Rev 22:17) echo through the ages to the consummation of time, announcing the advent of a new creation.

The meaning of this "wonderful parallelism" between the Song and Revelation,[97] which de Lubac explores, can be expounded further in connection with two other Scriptural references, underscoring how Mary's presence in the Upper Room at Pentecost is not without salvific significance. The first is the brooding of the Spirit of God over the waters of creation in the first chapter of Genesis. The second is Mary's own reception of the Spirit at the Annunciation. In accord with the first allusion to the Spirit (in Genesis), Pentecost may be seen as the beginning of a new creation. As regards the second allusion to the Spirit (at the Annunciation), the Church at Pentecost—as a new creation at the coming of the Spirit—can further be likened to that *overshadowing of the Spirit* (cf. Lk 1:35) upon Mary at the moment of the Incarnation.[98] Taken together, these three allusions to the Spirit (brooding over the waters of creation in Genesis; overshadowing Our Lady at the Annunciation in Luke's Gospel; and coming upon the disciples gathered in Jerusalem in

---

97. *Splendor,* 373.

98. Cf. Sarah Jane Boss, *Mary: The Complete Resource* (London: Continuum, 2007), 2–3, in which Boss considers the connections between creation and the Annunciation, between Mary and the Ark of the Covenant: "When we turn to the presentation of Mary in Luke's Gospel, we find that she too is presented as if she were the Ark, or perhaps Tabernacle, of the Lord's presence, and that she may also be seen as the being out of whom the world is created, and certainly as the one in whom it is re-created." Developing the parallel that Boss draws between the Spirit as it hovered over the formless waters at creation and over Mary at the Annunciation, the further connection of the Spirit as it descended upon the Apostles in the "new creation" of the Church at Pentecost is my own.

chapter 2 of the Acts of the Apostles) confirm that the Church of Jerusalem with Mary at the center is indeed an event of "re-creation;" it is the New Jerusalem with Mary as a figure of the bride of the Lamb (cf. Rev 19:7; 21:2, 9; 2 Cor 11:2).

Ratzinger explained his position on the ontological priority of the Church as one that centers on the inner unity of the mystery of the Church as the New Israel. In the course of the debate with Kasper, he refined his position, arguing for an "inner priority of unity, of the one bride to her essential variety."[99] By this, he was referring to the essential unity of the Church as the one Body or one Bride of Christ, and he explains that the idea is based in patristic theology. The Fathers adopted the bridal imagery and developed it in continuity with a rabbinic theology of creation, a theology that perceived creation to be the sphere for the exercise of God's will, the Torah and Israel to be preexistent, and the Church to be the continuation of Israel, the chosen People of God. Like Israel, called to live according to God's will and to be a light to all the nations, the Church of Christ is the extension of the sphere in which God's will would be achieved. This implies, for Ratzinger, a preexistent unity willed by the Creator. In this sense, the universal Church preexists the local churches.

Furthermore, Catholic theology teaches that Redemption is characterized by unity.[100] Its essence is the healing of the disunity that resulted from sin and the restoration of the order and unity intended by God, a "recapitulation of the whole of humanity under the headship of Christ" (*Lumen Gentium*, no. 13). Ratzinger states: "The basic idea of sacred history is that of gathering together, of uniting—uniting human beings in the one body of Christ, the union of human beings and through human beings of all creation with God."[101] The Church, as a universal sacrament of salvation, herself possesses God's gift of unity, a gift that preexists as willed by God from the foundation of the world. It seems that this idea is what leads Ratzinger to a thesis of the Church's ontological precedence.

---

99. Ratzinger, "Response to Kasper," 10, as previously quoted.

100. Cf. LG, no. 13, which describes the Catholic and unifying character of the Church of Christ: "This characteristic of universality which adorns the people of God is a gift from the Lord Himself. By reason of it, the Catholic Church strives constantly and with due effect to bring all humanity and all its possessions back to its source in Christ, with Him as its head and united in His Spirit. In virtue of this catholicity each individual part contributes through its special gifts to the good of the other parts and of the whole Church. Through the common sharing of gifts and through the common effort to attain fullness in unity, the whole and each of the parts receive increase."

101. Ratzinger, "Response to Kasper," 10.

When de Lubac takes up a discussion of unity and plurality in his chapter on "Pluralism or Harmony?" in *Les églises particulières dans l'Église universelle*, he states, "The concrete and living unity of the Church is not a uniformity. It is … a 'pluriformity' … a harmony."[102] For this harmony to be fully realized, moreover, "all diversity must be taken up into the *essential movement toward unity*."[103] The diffusion of the Spirit at Pentecost inaugurated this "essential movement toward unity" into which all diversity is subsumed and by which harmony is realized. According to de Lubac, the disciples' experience at Pentecost was "not merely a '*yearning* for unity'" but rather, "a *consciousness* of the unity given by God."[104] The unity for which the Church strives is a preexistent unity willed by God from all eternity and gifted to the Church at Pentecost.

This allusion to an "essential movement toward unity" is indicative of precisely that reality of the priority of the "inner unity" of the Church that Ratzinger emphasizes. The "end" of this movement must, at least in principle, preexist the movement itself; otherwise, such movement would be haphazard and aimless. Furthermore, this end is characterized by Ratzinger as an *inner* unity, "the inner precedence of God's idea of the one church, the one bride, over all its empirical realizations in particular churches."[105]

Ratzinger's main point can be verified in light of de Lubac's analysis of the contrasting movements denoted by the terms "universal" and "catholic." By emphasizing the *inner* dimension, Ratzinger underscores the centripetal movement of the latter term, "catholic," which, for de Lubac, denotes "the idea of an organic whole, of a cohesion, of a firm synthesis, of a reality which is not scattered but, on the contrary, turned toward a center which assures its unity."[106] It is the center or inner core that provides the unity for the whole and takes ontological precedence. This inner core can be identified as the New Israel, the one bride of Christ underscored in Ratzinger's reading of the Pentecost event of Acts 2:

> What comes first in Saint Luke's account is not any original community at Jerusalem; what comes first is that, in the Twelve, the old Israel, which is one, becomes the new and that through the wonderful gift of tongues this new Israel of God is then shown, before there is

102. MC, 218, with reference to Neunheuser, "*Église universelle et Église locale*," 637.
103. MC, 219; emphasis added.
104. MC, 219; emphasis added.
105. Ratzinger, "Response to Kasper," 10.
106. MC, 174.

any question of constituting a local community in Jerusalem, to be a unity encompassing every time and place.... [F]rom the very first moment, [it] bears universality within itself.[107]

This New Israel is the one bride of Christ, and Ratzinger reaches this thesis based on a Christological and nuptial reading of the Old Testament. He writes:

> On the basis of Christology the picture can be extended and developed: history is interpreted—again, following the example of the Old Testament—as a love story involving God and man. God finds for himself a bride for his Son, the one bride who is the one Church. On the basis of the saying in Genesis, that man and wife shall "become one flesh" (Gn 2:24), the image of the bride blends in with the idea of the Church as the body of Christ, which is in turn anchored sacramentally in Eucharistic piety.[108]

The idea of the Church as *sponsa Christi* finds support in Pauline texts that speak of the Church as that bride for whom Christ died, sanctifying and cleansing her so that she might be "without spot or wrinkle ... holy and without blemish" (Eph 5:27). Because the Church Fathers developed the idea in continuity with the Rabbinic notion of the Torah and Israel seen as preexistent, Ratzinger considers that the concept of the Church as the New Israel and *sponsa Christi* points to that preexistent reality of the people chosen by God "before the creation of the world, to be holy and without blemish before him" (Eph 1:4). God's plan from all eternity is to bestow the fullness of his grace upon the Church as the bride won by and for his Son.

It may be said that Ephesians and other corresponding texts that refer to Christians as those loved by the Father before the foundation of the world (cf. Jn 17:23–24) and predestined in Christ (cf. Rom 8:29) as the first fruits of salvation (cf. 2 Thes 2:13) can be read in reference to both the Church and Mary. The Blessed Virgin is the preeminent bride, full of grace and chosen by God before the creation of the world. Moreover, as the Immaculate Conception, she constitutes the primordial core of the bridal Church. Preserved from the stain of original sin in order to be *mater Christi* and a figure of the spotless *sponsa Christi*, Mary is the fullness of the Church in person. Mark Miravalle posits, regarding Mary's "preservative redemption"[109] in the

---

107. Ratzinger, "Ecclesiology of the Constitution *Lumen Gentium*," 138, as previously quoted.
108. Ratzinger, 134.
109. "Preservative redemption" was proposed by Bl. John Duns Scotus to explain that "Mary's

Immaculate Conception, that "Mary, rather than being the exception, fulfills in a real sense the original intention of what God wanted for all his human children: to be members of his family from the first moment of their existence."[110] Our Lady is the bride God intends for his Son, a bride who is not closed up on herself, but one who fosters communion in providing the inner unity and centering core of the universal Church and who, as a result, might be considered as ontologically prior. The "end" of that "essential movement toward unity"[111] preexists in Mary.

If, as previously suggested, the constitution of the Church at Pentecost can be likened to that overshadowing of the Spirit upon Mary at the Annunciation (cf. Lk 1:35), then the coming of the Spirit upon those gathered in Jerusalem with Mary at the center is assuredly the creation of a New Israel as the bride of Christ. Mary's decisive presence among the Twelve in the Upper Room confirms her "universalized" role in the constitution of the New Jerusalem. Furthermore, there is a direct connection between Mary's universalized personhood and the notion of her as *sponsa Christi*: Our Lady's motherly, universal influence stems from what might be called her "concentrated personality," a perfect personhood untainted by sin, holy and unblemished in God's sight.[112]

The one bride of Christ who preexists in God's will for all creation thus preexists also in the eschatological reality presently and fully realized in the person of Mary. Ratzinger's idea of the inner unity of the Church can thus be said to come to a point in this human person, resplendent with grace. Mary is the proleptic icon of the eschatological Church in that she is the New Israel, the final reality already here present. The patristic and scriptural testimonies confirm that the mystical bride of Christ is, in a spiritual sense, Mary herself.

In summary, the Pentecost event in Jerusalem might thus be considered

---

preservation from original sin was an application by God of the saving graces merited by Jesus Christ on Calvary" at the first moment of her existence. As immaculately conceived, she is in no less need of redemption than other human beings. She is truly a member of the Church as one who is redeemed through the grace and merits of Christ (Mark Miravalle, *Introduction to Mary: The Heart of Marian Doctrine and Devotion* (Goleta, CA: Queenship Publishing, 2006), 71. See also Pope Pius IX, Apostolic Constitution *Ineffabilis Deus* (8 December 1854); DH 2800–804.

110. Miravalle, *Introduction to Mary*, 70.

111. MC, 219.

112. It might also be said that Mary's own being exemplifies an analogous "priority of inner unity." She is constituted by paradox—being at once mother and virgin—and yet she possesses perfect unity and integrity of being. It is only with a view to the principle of inner unity that one might, in faith, hold together the mystery of grace at work in Our Lady in the paradoxical realities of her perpetual virginity and divine motherhood.

the primordial experience of the Church, and there is an inner unity to this experience when viewed in the light of Our Lady as a concrete universal. The eschatological mystery of the Church is a reality presently embodied in Mary who possesses perfect faith, hope, and love. Consequently, the relationship of the local and universal churches is positively illumined when examined with reference to her. By considering the Marian dimensions of that relationship with reference to the event of Pentecost, moreover, the birth of the Church emerges as a true Marian event, wherein the nuptial dimension of the Church's inner unity is most evident.

A Final Analysis of Kasper, Ratzinger, and de Lubac

Although Ratzinger and Kasper eventually arrived at a rapprochement, both continued to critique the other and to assert the validity of their own positions. For example, while Kasper came to acknowledge the notion of the preexistent mystery of the Church (of which Ratzinger argued in favor), he continued to insist that such preexistence does not justify granting priority to the universal Church alone.[113] He suggested, instead, that the preexistent mystery of the Church must somehow consist of both the universal Church and the local churches in their socio-historical dimensions—a thesis of the simultaneous preexistence of the universal Church and the particular churches. Ratzinger, on the other hand, acknowledged Kasper's thesis of simultaneity, but he adamantly maintained the inner priority of unity in the Church-mystery with reference to the unity of salvation history as preexistent in the figure of the one bride of Christ.

It is perplexing that Kasper and Ratzinger, who each draw on aspects of de Lubac's writings, come to conflicting positions where de Lubac found no opposition. His study of the topic (made antecedently to the debate between Kasper and Ratzinger) maintained a delicate, judicious balance. It has been shown that while certain points from both sides of the debate can be found in de Lubac's writings, the incompatible aspects stem from developments that go beyond what de Lubac himself espoused. Hence, a true rapprochement can be established by considering de Lubac's views once again. In particular, it is perhaps his view of Mary as "*specialis*" and as a concrete universal that allows de Lubac to understand the relationship of the local and universal churches in all its nuanced complexity.

In the final analysis of the debate, one might ask: Why is Kasper so

---

113. See Kasper, "Reply to Ratzinger," 13.

adamant in arguing that the local Church is essential, and Ratzinger, that the universal Church is ontologically prior? How does the idea of Mary as the concrete universal respond to these respective concerns? To the first question, a direct answer is found in Kasper's own articulation of his goal. His critique of Ratzinger and the CDF's statement of the ontological and temporal priority of the universal Church is based on his pastoral experience and observation of "how a gap was emerging and steadily increasing between norms promulgated in Rome for the universal church and the needs and practices of our local church."[114] Kasper wants to emphasize the local church in order to preserve its relative autonomy and to preclude the Church's potential regression to mere abstract constructions and bureaucratic structures. De Lubac shares Kasper's fundamental concern. His *Les églises particulières dans l'Église universelle* is driven by the goal "to restore ... the true idea of episcopal collegiality, traditional and conciliar"[115] and to promote "a decentralization that gave back to the episcopacy, with the full awareness of its responsibilities, the full exercise of its charge."[116] De Lubac's perspective of Mary as the concrete universal promotes this emphasis on the concrete particularity that becomes universal only in as much as it is concretely particular.

Ratzinger, on the other hand, maintains an unyielding position on the ontological and temporal priority of the universal Church, and this is deeply rooted in his theology. As noted above, he had argued for this particular position in his theological writings as early as 1987 and reasserted it in 1991.[117] For Ratzinger, it is essential that the Church is, first and foremost, one universal Church that only subsequently makes itself present in many local churches: "What *first* exists is the one Church, the Church that speaks in all tongues—the *ecclesia universalis;* she then generates Church in the most diverse locales, which nonetheless are all always embodiments of the one and only Church."[118]

The ontological value that Ratzinger assigns to the universal Church, viewing it as a primordial, self-subsisting reality apart from particular churches, is fundamentally consistent with a key principle in his thought, namely the principle of receptivity. For Ratzinger, Christian faith and existence are

---

114. Kasper, 8.

115. ASC, 133.

116. ASC, 136, from the German edition preface.

117. See Ratzinger, *Church, Ecumenism and Politics*, 75 (first German edition, dated 1987), and *Called to Communion*, 44 (first German edition, dated 1991).

118. Ratzinger, *Called to Communion*, 44.

gratuitous gifts from God that can only be *received from without*; they are never made. The priority of "receptivity" is a leitmotif that runs throughout Ratzinger's thought.[119] In his discussion of the Council's ecclesiology, he writes: "The element of *receiving* belongs essentially to the Church.... We call this structure of receiving and encountering 'sacrament.'"[120] Similarly, with regard to the Eucharist, Ratzinger says: "The fact that the sacrament of priestly service is requisite for the Eucharist is found upon the fact that the congregation *cannot give itself* the Eucharist; it has *to receive it* from the Lord by the mediation of the one Church."[121] It is in keeping with this fundamental principle of receptivity that Ratzinger emphasizes that the local Church *must receive* its existence from outside itself, namely from the universal Church. It seems that this logic undergirds his adamant assertion of the ontological and temporal priority of the universal Church over the local churches.

Although Ratzinger does not employ a Marian lens in his discussion of the priority of the inner unity of the one bride over her essential variety in local realizations, the idea of Mary herself as the bride of Christ corresponds to his conviction of the receptive nature of the Church and is not at all foreign to his thought. Ratzinger recognizes Mary's unique relationship to the Church and appreciates that, in her, the Church *receives* its existence. In his comments on the ecclesiology of the Council, Ratzinger states: "Only by being Marian can we become the Church. At its very beginning the Church *was not made, but given birth*. She existed in the soul of Mary from the moment she uttered her *fiat*."[122] The Church preexists in Mary.

De Lubac's conception of Mary is consistent with Ratzinger's own Mariology and the principle of receptivity that underlies much of his theology.[123] Akin to Ratzinger's emphasis on universality, de Lubac sees in Our Lady a

119. See, for example, Ratzinger's critique of *techne* in chapter 1, "Belief in the World Today," in *Introduction to Christianity*, trans. J. R. Foster (San Francisco: Ignatius Press, 2004).

120. Ratzinger, "The Ecclesiology of the Second Vatican Council," trans. Stephen W. Arndt, *Communio* 13 (1986): 244; emphasis added.

121. Ratzinger, "Ecclesiology of the Constitution *Lumen Gentium*," 143; emphasis added.

122. Ratzinger, "The Ecclesiology of Vatican II," *L'Osservatore Romano*, 23 January 2002, weekly English edition, no. 4, 7; emphasis added.

123. For an excellent work examining the question of the relationship of the particular churches to the universal Church in light of an ecclesiology of reception, see Derek Sakowski, *The Ecclesiological Reality of Reception Considered as a Solution to the Debate over the Ontological Priority of the Universal Church* (Rome: Gregorian & Biblical Press, 2014). Although Sakowski does not identify an ecclesiology of reception as specifically Marian, there is deep affinity and harmony between his analysis and the thesis of this present chapter on the Marian dimension of the Church as particular and universal.

cosmic, or universal, figure of the eternal feminine and an epitome of receptivity: she *received* the Word of God so perfectly that the Word becomes flesh within her. There is nothing in Mary that is not received from God, and her virginal receptivity constitutes her as a true figure of that spotless bride of Christ, an idea central to Ratzinger's argument for the preexistent universal Church. In contrast to Ratzinger, however, de Lubac is not compelled to make any explicit assertion of the temporal and ontological priority of the universal Church. Rather, his conception of Mary specifically as a concrete universal seems to provide him with a model for thinking about the Church-mystery in which the particular churches and the universal Church are not ordered in terms of ontological priority, but co-inhering, they mutually constitute one rich mystery.

When applied to the discussion of the local and universal Churches, de Lubac's concept of Mary as a concrete universal illumines the structural and substantive similarities between the relationship of Mary and the Church as well as the simultaneity and inner unity of the universal Church and the particular churches. Insofar as the notion of the concrete universal underscores the character of the local and concrete, ecclesiological abstraction (of which Kasper was so wary) is curtailed without undermining the universal (upon which Ratzinger insisted). The concrete universal brings to a new level of appreciation the significance of the Marian mystery of the Church as expounded by the Council. It preserves the essence of both universality and particularity, uniting them in a person who is simultaneously concrete and universal. It provides a human face, a real personal identity, to the Church-mystery.

William Henn has argued that "the more adequate harmonization of primacy and episcopacy, of the church universal and the local church, is widely considered to be one of the most pressing theological tasks of the Church today."[124] Having laid hold of the Marian dimensions of this ecclesiological problematic, we've discovered how de Lubac's writings give a new impulse to the theological task at hand. His own mariological perspective on the Church had already presented to him the complete ideal of a "more adequate harmonization" by which we might better mediate the divergent theological positions of Kasper and Ratzinger. Moreover, the application of de Lubac's Marian perspective to the particular-universal Church problematic helps us to see and to appreciate the fruitful correlation between the Council's

---

124. William Henn, "Historical-Theological Synthesis," 219–20.

synthesis on Mary and the Church and de Lubac's understanding of their perichoretic relationship: the universal and particular churches are mutually interior just as Mary and the Church enjoy mutual interiority. The Church can thus be said to preexist *in* Mary—she who is simultaneously particular and universal. And although Our Lady might not exhaust the entire mystery of the Church, the quintessence of the consummate ecclesial existence as *sponsa Christi* can indeed already be found in her.

CHAPTER 8

Marian Subjectivity

Karl Adam famously said that the "I" of the Church is Christ.[1] To what degree and in what respect, then, might the Church be considered truly "Marian" in essence? In other words, does the Church simply venerate in Our Lady an outstanding example of holiness—indeed, the most outstanding in the whole communion of saints—or, can one perceive in her personal being, her holiness, something essential to this communion, something *defining* with respect to the entire mystery of the Church? These are the questions before us as we consider what a more complete reception of Vatican II's Marian ecclesiology might entail.

Of the many attributes by which de Lubac refers to Mary, he calls her the "*prototype* of all perfection,"[2] and reiterating *Lumen Gentium,* no. 63, he also says that she "occupies the first place" in the mystery of the Church, "offering, to an eminent and singular degree, the *model* of the virgin and the mother."[3] She is the Church's "*pre-eminent* and altogether *unique* member."[4] "Prototype," "model," "pre-eminent and unique member": each of these

---

1. Karl Adam, *The Spirit of Catholicism,* trans. Dom Justin McCann (London: Sheed & Ward, 1934), 17.

2. CPM, 58; emphasis added.

3. CPM, 57, with reference to LG, nos. 63–65; emphasis added.

4. LG, no. 53, as referenced in CPM, 59; emphasis added.

predications emphasize Mary's exemplary status in relation to the Church. Yet in no way does she ever detract from the Church's Christocentric subjectivity. Rather, Mary always directs our attention to her Son. This Christocentric focus is evidenced in the early controversies in which the Church taught about Mary in light of its teaching on Christ. The dogmatic development in the teaching on Mary as *Theotókos* preserved the Christological truth of Christ's divine personhood precisely by affirming Our Lady's divine motherhood.[5] The Son of God can be seen as truly human, truly belonging to the human race, because he was born of a human mother. Marian doctrine helps maintain the orthodoxy and realism of Christology. With that in mind, the question for our investigation is: In what sense might the *personhood* of the Church be considered "Marian"?

Personhood and Personality

The Marian mystery inserts a personal realism into ecclesiology. As personal and feminine, Mary realizes the bridal consciousness of the Church and preserves the identity of the Church as a true spousal subject focused on Christ, her bridegroom. She sustains this essential focus and reminds the Church that it exists to bring about the life of Christ in all persons. The Church is not an abstract political entity nor an impersonal institution, but a real communion of persons in Christ, partaking in the communion of the Trinity through faith, hope, and charity. Mary preserves the personal identity of the Church in that it is her disposition of faith and receptivity that allows the "I" of Christ to emerge.

Emphasis on the receptivity of Our Lady and of the Church as the body of Christ draws upon the distinction between the bride and bridegroom. Here, we see how the Marian mystery also enriches this distinction. Louis Bouyer has posited that Christian anthropology should be recognized as a specifically *Marian* anthropology because one is "entitled to see in her, and in her alone, all that grace was able to make of a creature, of human nature, while still leaving it in its order as a created being."[6] While Christian anthropology focuses on the person of Christ as the perfect man who "fully reveals man to himself" (*Gaudium et Spes*, no. 22), it is only *in Mary* that one learns

---

5. Cf. "Second Letter of Cyril of Alexandria to Nestorius," Council of Ephesus, Session I (22 June 431); DH 251.

6. Louis Bouyer, *The Seat of Wisdom: An Essay on the Place of the Virgin Mary in Christian Theology* (New York: Pantheon Books, 1962), viii; with reference to Bérulle, *Élévation à la Très sainte Vierge* in *Oeuvres*, ed. Migne (Paris, 1856), 526.

of the redemption of a human person qua *human person*. Christ is indeed fully human and fully divine, possessing two natures in one *divine* Person, but He is not a human person. Thus, although He alone is the complete revelation of the Father and the defining lens of Christian anthropology, it is in Mary that Redemption is first received by a human person in the order of a created being.

The perennial question of the Church's identity has re-emerged in modern ecclesiological circles and elicited diverging views.[7] Yves Congar has noted that "the title of Spouse traditionally given to the Church ... supposes in her a certain quality of personhood [*personnalité*], *altera persona*."[8] Prominent in both Scripture and Tradition, this bridal image evokes the idea of an "other" who enters into union with her bridegroom, becoming one body with him. Contrary to this conception of the Church as an *altera persona,* the prominent Orthodox theologian John Zizioulas argues that the Church *as Church* does not have any "hypostasis of its own" and is indistinguishable from Christ in its corporate personality.[9] On the other hand, theologians such as Alexander Schmemann,[10] Vladimir Lossky,[11] and Sergius Bulgakov[12]—in the East, and Louis Bouyer[13] and Hans Urs von Balthasar—in the West, all recognize this spousal subjectivity of the Church as one which expresses a Marian subjectivity. Balthasar, for example, constructs a robust ecclesiology on this basis. In a programmatic essay, "Who is the Church?," he states that "in so far as she [i.e., the Church] makes to him [i.e., Christ] the response of a woman and a bride, she has her supreme, normative subjectivity in Mary," and "all ... converge in a single consciousness, opening in Mary to Christ."[14]

7. A penetrating analysis which guides much of this section's exposition is offered by Paul McPartlan, "Who Is the Church? Zizioulas and von Balthasar on the Church's Identity," *Ecclesiology* 4 (2008): 271–88. Other helpful works include: Benoît-Dominique de la Soujeole, "The Question about the Personality of the Church," chapter 12 of *Introduction to the Mystery of the Church* (Washington, DC: The Catholic University of America Press, 2014), 504–11; and Charles Journet, "De la personnalité de L'Église," *Revue Thomiste* 69 (1969): 192–200.

8. Yves Congar, "La personne 'Eglise,'" *Revue Thomiste* 71 (1971): 625.

9. John Zizioulas, "The Mystery of the Church in Orthodox Tradition," *One in Christ* 24 (1988): 302.

10. Alexander Schmemann, "On Mariology in Orthodoxy," *Marian Library Studies* 2 (1970): 25–32.

11. Vladimir Lossky, *The Mystical Theology of the Eastern Church* (Cambridge and London: James Clarke, 1957), 192–93.

12. Sergius Bulgakov, *The Bride of the Lamb* (Grand Rapids, MI: William B. Eerdmans; Edinburgh: T&T Clark, 2002), 264–65 and 411.

13. Louis Bouyer, *Woman and Man with God* (London: Darton, Longman & Todd, 1960), viii, 129–30, 196–201, and *The Seat of Wisdom,* as referenced above.

14. Hans Urs von Balthasar, "Who Is the Church?" in *Explorations in Theology II: Spouse of the Word,* trans. Alexander Dru (San Francisco: Ignatius Press, 1991), 179; emphasis added; see

De Lubac's own writings on the relationship of the Church to the individual Christian contain a profound anthropological insight that tends to identify the Church's subjectivity or personhood as specifically Marian. In *Catholicisme*, de Lubac states that "to be a person ... is fundamentally to enter upon a relationship with others so as to converge upon a Whole."[15] Prior to this, he asserted that the Whole "is not the antipodes, but the very pole of Personality,"[16] and that the "most complete expression of Personality appears ... in the Being of whom every being is a reflection."[17] In the latter statement specifically, he is referring to the eternal Being of the three divine Persons of the Trinity, and elsewhere, he draws from Teilhard to say that God is the "Personality personalizing."[18] Walter Kasper similarly asserted in his work on the Trinity that "'person' is the highest category we have at our disposal."[19] De Lubac writes: "It is in his divine vocation that man learns to know himself. God reveals himself to him in a more and more sharply contoured personal form, but also one that is more and more mysterious, whose correlative is the increasing personalization of the one who receives his revelation."[20] In other words, personhood is truly understood only in light of God's manifestation to human beings, revealing his personhood in divine condescension. Moreover, in grappling with the ontological content of this analogous association of the human person to the divine Persons of the Godhead, one discovers that Mary can be seen as the epitome of created personhood, and she thus informs, at least in part, the Church's subjectivity (as a human-divine institution). For these reasons, it is necessary to make a brief foray into de Lubac's thoughts on the Trinity.

De Lubac asserts that there is a "radical divine humility" in God that "is native to his eternal being." This humility consists in the "excentration (ecstasy) of each Person sharing himself completely with the other two."[21] It marks the inner processions of the Trinity and also characterizes the mission of the Son and the Spirit. Hence, it is in the kenosis of the Incarnation that divine personhood is most fully revealed: "God's humility" is manifested in

---

also Stephan Ackermann, "The Church as Person in the Theology of Hans Urs von Balthasar," *Communio* 29 (2002): 238–49.

15. *Catholicism*, 331.

16. *Catholicism*, 330, with reference to Teilhard de Chardin.

17. *Catholicism*, 329.

18. MC, 154; de Lubac does not provide the exact reference for Teilhard's statement.

19. Walter Kasper, *The God of Jesus Christ* (New York: T&T Clark, 2012), 153.

20. MC, 154.

21. *A Brief Catechesis on Nature and Grace*, trans. Richard Arnandez (San Francisco: Ignatius Press, 1984), 61n15; parenthesis is de Lubac's own.

that, "although sovereignly free in his transcendence, [God] makes himself partially immanent in his creatures by that *kenosis*, that 'excentration,' that 'movement of descent' which is the Word's Incarnation."[22] This divine ecstasy that pours itself out for the other is the basis for Christian humility and the mold of true personhood. By analogy with divine Personhood, the anthropological notion of "person" must therefore be fashioned according to the humble condescension of the second Person of the Trinity.

It may be said that Mary's essential role in the mystery of the Incarnation and her presence at the foot of the cross give her a pivotal place in a theological anthropology that is based on Christ's kenotic self-revelation to man. De Lubac's writings on Mary show that she not only stands at the center of the mystery of the Incarnation, but also that she personally embodies the Trinitarian dynamic of excentration. Just as Christ's self-emptying delineated his eternal "yes" to the Father, an oblation completed on the cross, wherein the Church was born (cf. LG 3; Jn 19:34), Mary, in her own creaturely way, exemplifies complete self-effacement in carrying out God's will in the plan of salvation. As handmaid of the Lord, she epitomizes the spirituality of the *ani*[23]—the poor and lowly who remain faithful to God and rely entirely on Him. Having nothing to boast of except what God has done for her, Mary embodies the disposition of perfect humility, a fundamental anthropological stance of man before God and the defining posture of receptivity to grace.[24]

The Virgin Mary thus exemplifies the Christian notion of "person" as referring to a creature made in the image of a self-emptying God, who is a communion of three Persons united in love. The creaturely "personhood" that constitutes the human subjectivity of the Church as a whole in its bridal response to the incarnate and kenotic Word is exemplified in Our Lady. Furthermore, if it can be said that Mary possesses this personhood in perfect form, might it also be said that she defines the essence of the loving communion of self-effacing souls called forth by God?

As we have seen, *L'Éternel féminin*, de Lubac's eponymous study of Teilhard's poem, highlighted Mary's supreme personhood.[25] It applied to her the notion of a concrete universal, basing the attribution on her close

---

22. *A Brief Catechesis*, 61.

23. *Ani* is the singular of *anawim*, the Hebrew word from the Old Testament which refers to the faithful and poor "remnant of Israel"; humble, needy, and oppressed, they depend solely on God.

24. Cf. *A Brief Catechesis*, 55–64, in which de Lubac expounds the virtue of humility as the first consequence of an understanding of grace as a supernatural quality infused into the soul (nature).

25. Cf. EF, 121–22.

association with the personal and universalizing work of her Son.[26] De Lubac also notes: "In seeing all the 'chaste essence of the Feminine' realized in Mary, Teilhard thereby attributes to the Virgin, considered in what is most concrete, individual, and intimately her own in her personality, a sort of universality which is analogous to the universality he recognizes in Christ."[27] Teilhard recognized the epitome of femininity in Mary's perfect and chaste love. Her perpetual virginity, through which her personhood is totally given over to Christ, is so intricately related to Christ's mission that it is also mysteriously *universalized*.

In view of this notion of the universalized personality, Mary's Immaculate Conception might be considered as having ever greater significance. It refers not simply to her preservation from the sin to which all other human beings are subject as a result of the Fall. Contrarily, the fact of Mary's sinless fullness of grace bespeaks her integrity and self-possession, the necessary condition for her complete self-gift to God and to His people in the plan of salvation. Sin can be seen as taking away from authentic personhood insofar as it opposes the dynamic of "excentration" and seeks only its own good in a kind of self-referential egotism. Mary is preserved from such depersonalization in order to be able to give the primordial assent of faith on behalf of the human race and thus, also, to be perfectly conformed to the Personhood of God as "excentric." In giving herself completely and freely to God in his divine plan of salvation, Mary's personhood is perfected in grace.[28]

Interpreting Teilhard, de Lubac emphasizes that "it is the personal which becomes universal, to the degree in which (subject to certain conditions) it realizes more profoundly its own specific character."[29] In other words, universality correlates with what is most particular to personhood, and de Lubac has shown that personhood, in the light of the dynamic of Trinitarian communion, is characterized by excentration, a going out of self to another in a relationship of love. His statement that "universality is the prerogative of the strongest personality,"[30] can be appreciated as most applicable to Mary,

---

26. See EF, 122, in which de Lubac states: "The Virgin (and this is where we meet the boldness of Teilhard's Mariology) is closely associated with the personal and universalizing work of her Son. To understand this association is to 'universalize Our Lady' and at the same time to understand how much she is 'truly unique: *Virgo Singularis*.'"

27. EF, 124.

28. Cf. de Lubac's discussion of human cooperation in the work of redemption in *Splendor*, 315–16.

29. EF, 118.

30. EF, 118.

whose personality is purely concentrated because she is sinless and fully "excentrated." Her openness to the Incarnate Word anchors the openness of the entire human race to Christ.

It might therefore be said that Our Lady stands at the summit of created *personhood*. Her perfected personality does not exist for her own sake but rather for the sake of all persons. Her personhood, which is free of sin and marked by complete excentration, is universalized and benefits all. This is not to say that the Church and its members are necessarily, nor immanently, sinless themselves, but it does reveal that our final union with Christ is a union purged of sin. Mary's Immaculate Conception is therefore the prolepsis of the new heavens and new earth. Her personal integrity represents the personal wholeness God intends to restore to every human person.

There is no conflict between universality and particularity in Mary. Her preeminence in grace exists in the service of all, and her *fiat* is to be replicated in the hearts of all the faithful until the consummate, nuptial banquet of the Lamb is realized. De Lubac states that Teilhard's bold Mariology consisted in the application of this idea of the concrete universal to Mary, grounding it in Ephesians 4:7–10.[31] According to de Lubac, Teilhard likened Mary's Assumption to Christ's Ascension, saying that she, like Christ, also "ascended on high" so as to "fill all things"; Mary fulfills a mysterious function that is complementary to Christ's in enabling the world to be filled with God's glory by way of her own self-effacing abandonment.[32] It may thus be said that she occupies the first place in the mystery of the Church, closest to Christ, and that she offers to the Church not only a *model* of ecclesial existence in her own discipleship as virgin and mother, but that she also *informs* the subjectivity of the Church, the ecclesial consciousness that empties itself to receive all from Christ, its head. She is, in a sense, the person of the Church in its response to Christ who imparts his own personhood to His mystical body.

De Lubac's consideration of Mary as a concrete universal, corresponding as a kind of receptive complement to Christ himself as *the* concrete universal, suggests that she indeed substantially informs the ecclesial existence of each and every member of the Church. Her primordial assent of faith is the universal form of ecclesial existence, par excellence.

31. EF, 122.
32. EF, 125.

Sacramentality

The "perichoresis"[33] by which "Mary is figured in the Church, and the Church is figured in Mary,"[34] is a fundamental mystery that has found expression in the Church's enduring veneration of the Mother of God. However, it eludes precise dogmatic definition. In *Méditation sur l'Église*, de Lubac explored the profusion of patristic and medieval images that associated Mary with the Church, and he advised against positing a mere external and "functional analogy" between the two.[35] With regard to what the Christian tradition says about Mary, we have seen how adamant he is in asserting that "there is in all this something much more than a case of parallelism or the alternating use of ambivalent symbols."[36] He continues: "As far as the Christian mind is concerned, Mary is the 'ideal figure of the Church,' the *'sacrament'* of her, and the mirror in which the whole Church is reflected."[37] Let us consider the extent to which the sacramentality of the Church might be related to the personhood of Mary.

As previously shown, de Lubac sees an intrinsic existential link between a figure and its type, such that "there is between the two an 'inner continuity' and 'ontological bond.'"[38] Similarly, his reference to Mary as a "sacrament" of the Church seems to propose an existential link, an *ontological* bond, between Mary and the Church—she being the ideal figure of the latter. Sacraments are efficacious signs of grace; they point to a reality beyond themselves and confer the grace they signify. Recalling de Lubac's words in *Catholicism* that "[i]f Christ is the sacrament of God, the Church is for us the sacrament of Christ,"[39] one might apply the dynamic of sacramentality further and say that Mary might also be considered, in an analogous way, a sacrament of the Church. She points beyond herself to the consummate reality of the Church's own motherhood and virginal, loving assent.

De Lubac considers the Church's spiritual motherhood by which it

33. De Lubac applies this theological term to the relationship of Mary and the Church in *Splendor,* 328, 336, and in EF, 29, acknowledging Scheeben for the original application.

34. Serlo of Savigny, *In nativitate B.M.* (p. 117 in Tissier's edition), as quoted by de Lubac in *Splendor,* 328.

35. *Splendor,* 316.

36. *Splendor,* 320.

37. *Splendor,* 320, with reference to Clement Dillenschneider's *Le Mystère de la corédemption mariale* (1951); a thirteenth-century hymn, *Mariae praeconio*; and Pierre Ganne's "La Vierge Marie dans la vie de l'Église" (1950); emphasis added.

38. *History and Spirit,* 462.

39. *Catholicism,* 76.

generates sons and daughters to new life in Christ as a participation in Mary's divine motherhood.[40] The idea of Mary as a sacrament of the Church further implies that Mary's own mothering of Christ can be seen as a sign and instrument by which the Church recognizes and exercises its own motherhood with regard to Christian souls. Moreover, in revealing the perfect countenance of the Church's virginal assent to God, Mary embodies that spousal union by which the Church is the bride of Christ. In particular, de Lubac's discussion of the apocalyptic image of the bride of Revelation and the banquet of the Lamb can be seen to allude to this consummate reality, sacramentally signified in Mary. Scripture and Tradition both speak of the Church as Bride, an image that consists of an "other"—a Bride—who, in becoming one with her Bridegroom, is mystically united to him as his body. This mystical union includes a Marian dimension in which the Bridegroom's gift of himself is met with complete receptivity, the kind of receptivity that is consonant with the "excentration" of the Trinitarian Persons and the "kenosis" of the Word.

The link between Mary and the Church evades precise definition and requires a nuanced and careful explanation. Mary's relationship to Christ is irreducibly inscribed in the mystery of the Church as Christ's bride. While it must be maintained that the being of the Church is decisively Christocentric, Mary is mysteriously linked to the Church in such a way that the latter might be said to *participate* in Mary's own *fiat*, in her motherhood and virginal union with Christ.

Furthermore, sacramentality is an important notion in de Lubac's theology, and what he writes of it in *Méditation sur l'Église* also underscores the hidden and quasitransparent nature of Mary's relationship to the Church. In a chapter entitled "The Sacrament of Christ," de Lubac describes sacramentality as follows:

> That which is sacramental—"the sensible bond between two worlds"—has a twofold characteristic. Since, on the one hand, it is the sign of something else, *it must be passed through*, and this not in part but wholly. Signs are not things to be stopped at, for they are, in themselves, valueless; by definition a sign is something *translucent*, which *dissolves* from before the face of what it manifests—like words, which would be nothing if they did not lead straight onto

---

40. See *Splendor*, 333, in which de Lubac quotes Scheeben, who says, "The maternity of the Church acts on the basis and by the virtue of that of Mary, and that of Mary continues to act in and by that of the Church" (Matthias Scheeben, *Dogmatik*, bk. 5, no. 1819).

ideas. Under this aspect it is *not something intermediate but something mediatory*; it does not isolate, one from another, the two terms it is meant to link. It does not put a distance between them; on the contrary, it unites them by making present what it evokes.[41]

De Lubac's description of the sacrament as a means, a medium through which one must pass, closely matches Teilhard's description of the Eternal Feminine as "the air"[42] we breathe, and it reveals the possible ontological link between Mary and the Church, explaining also why that bond is somewhat elusive. This image also coincides with Gerard Manley Hopkins's poem, "The Blessed Virgin compared to the air we breathe," and it conveys the evanescence of Mary's being and personhood: she resists the limelight and exists principally as a diaphanous medium of life, like the air we breathe, impalpable yet vital. Like the sacraments of the Church, Mary's role in the economy of salvation is to be a "translucent" medium for encounter with Christ, a sacramental sign that "dissolves" before the reality it mediates.

Although de Lubac does not develop the idea of Mary considered as a sacrament of the Church beyond the passing reference he makes to it in *Méditation sur l'Église*,[43] the link between what he says there of sacramentality and what he says later of Mary in *L'Éternel féminin* consolidates the idea of Mary as a sacrament, or more precisely, of Mary as a key to a deeper understanding of the Church's own sacramentality. Moreover, he alludes to sacramental realities in other contexts that can also be applied to Our Lady. For example, when de Lubac studies the meaning of *Mater Ecclesia*, he quotes Scheeben's words stating that "the motherhood of the Church is not an empty title; ... [rather,] this motherhood is as real as the presence of Christ is real in the Eucharist, or as real as the supernatural life that exists in the children of God."[44] Underlying Scheeben's assertion is an understanding of the ontological reality of the Real Presence, mediated in the sacrament of the Eucharist.[45] His principal point, though, is to maintain the *ontological* reality of the *motherhood* of the Church when he says that it is as real as the

41. *Splendor*, 202; emphases added.

42. EF in WTW, 201; the Feminine speaks of her elusive nature: "When you think I am no longer with you—when you forget me, the air you breathe, the light with which you see—then I shall still be at hand, lost in the sun I have drawn to myself."

43. Cf. *Splendor*, 379.

44. Scheeben, as quoted in MC, 39, although de Lubac does not provide the exact reference for Scheeben's words.

45. It can also be noted that the sacraments of baptism, confirmation, and holy orders each confer a sacramental character that is *ontological*.

ontological presence of Christ in the Eucharist. Although he does not expound how it (the motherhood of the Church) comes into being, one might connect the dots further in saying that just as the Eucharist sacramentally mediates the real presence of Christ, so too, ecclesial motherhood is mediated by a real mother; she is none other than Mary, and the manner of her mediation can be considered sacramental.

Furthermore, the significance of such sacramental mediation is even more pronounced when one considers that a sacramental sign, in de Lubac's words, "is not something intermediate but something mediatory; it does not isolate, one from another, the two terms it is meant to link."[46] This description might also be applied to Mary, who does not stand as an intermediary between Christ and his Church. Just as the sacraments actualize the unity of Christ, the Head, with his body, the Church, the same can also be said about Mary who unites Christ and his Church in her own (Mary's) divine and spiritual maternity. By virtue of her motherhood and perfect discipleship, Mary makes Christ present in the Church and unites Christ and his disciples by forming in them the proper Marian attitude of radical openness and receptivity to Christ. In other words, she makes present the spiritual maternity and virginal realities that she embodies and sacramentally expresses.

One sees, then, how Mary illumines, and, in a way, encompasses the efficacy of the Church's sacraments. Without Marian receptivity, there is a danger of misunderstanding the sacraments in an abstract or technocratic way as a mechanical production of grace. Such a view even risks isolating the sacraments from the mystery of the Church. Conversely, the notion of Mary as Mother of the Church expresses the Church's intuition that Mary's receptive disposition is reflected in the faithful, and her maternal presence is effective wherever the Church's works of prayer and sacraments are fruitful in begetting union with Christ. In other words, it may be said that Mary's subjectivity (defined by her complete self-gift to God) is an essential requisite in the fruitful mediation of sacramental grace and thus informs ecclesial subjectivity.

In the end, however, as helpful as the concept of sacramentality may be for understanding the elusive and mysterious link between Mary and the Church, it has not found much development in the Christian tradition. Moreover, it would be overly simplistic to suggest that the deep mystery the Council espoused regarding the link between the Church and Mary might be completely defined or contained in this single category. Nonetheless,

---

46. *Splendor,* 202, as previously quoted.

recognition of the convergence of the mystery of Mary and the mystery of the Church in their sacramental dimensions yields helpful insights. One better understands, for example, that enigmatic statement, which Auer made but never explained, that "the chapter on Mary in *Lumen Gentium* proceeds from an understanding of the Church as the sacrament of salvation."[47] In this perspective, the final chapter of the Constitution, devoted to Our Lady, should not be read simply as a compromising resolution to the heated debates of the Council on whether to incorporate Mary into the treatise on the Church. Nor should it be interpreted as a mere addendum appeasing the maximalist tendencies of certain Council fathers. On the contrary, it should be studied with the complete trajectory of the Constitution in mind, as the culmination of the Council's sacramental ecclesiology, illumining the sacramental/maternal nature of the Church as a participation in Mary's divine motherhood in the order of grace.

First in the Communion of Saints

The questions of ontology, of subjectivity and personhood, are fraught with philosophical difficulties. An alternative and decisively theological category for considering the Marian mystery of the Church's personhood as the bride of Christ is the notion of the communion of saints, a tenet of faith professed in the Apostles' Creed; the *sancta ecclesia* is a communion of saints.[48] This communion is real and can be considered "ontological" in a nontechnical sense, in which grace elevates and transforms nature.

The proper category for speaking of the substance of the Church's being is the category of grace.[49] In baptism, there is indeed an *ontological* change wherein a *new being* comes into existence. The new Christian who has renounced his sinful self for new life in Christ is infused with divine life through sanctifying grace and the theological virtues of faith, hope, and love. Moreover, he is incorporated into the Church and shares in the communion of saints through the Spirit who indwells, vivifies, and unites all the members of Christ's body. This communion in one body of Christ is

47. Auer, *The Church: Universal Sacrament of Salvation*, 480; previously examined in chapter 6.

48. Cf. *Splendor*, 338, in which de Lubac states that "our Lady is like the Church ... under her second aspect—that is, as the community of saints, the community of the sanctified.... [She] is the first cell of the organism of that restored paradise."

49. Cf. de la Soujeole, *Introduction to the Mystery of the Church*, 509. In his discussion of the ontological personality of the Church, de la Soujeole delineates a twofold supernatural ontology in which grace constitutes the Church as a mystical body by way of the *created* graces of virtues and gifts and the *uncreated* grace of the Spirit's indwelling.

mediated through Christ's salvific human nature, united to the Godhead in the mystery of the Incarnation.[50] It is a mediated reality, though without an intermediary, and insofar as it is mediated through Christ's humanity, it bears a decisive Marian character.[51]

Mary stands as first within the communion of saints in one mystical body. Therein, the good of each member is communicated to all in the bonds of charity. Communion in the Spirit of love means that each of the members is united to all the others; each participates in the sufferings and rejoices in the merits of all the others (1 Cor 12:26).[52] This is how the "I" and the merits of Christ are communicated to the Church, and it means that the same bonds of charity give one a share also in Mary's personhood, perfectly conformed to Christ. All Christians share in Our Lady's receptivity, of faith, hope, and love, and because Mary's "excentration" is the greatest in the communion of saints, it encompasses all the saints who have appropriated—always, only to some degree—the ideal of her excentration, her holiness. This is why Our Lady is venerated in the Church with a special devotion above all the saints (*hyperdulia*).[53]

De Lubac's writings show that Mary exemplifies the paradoxical notion of being as a kind of negation of being—an excentration or complete self-donation in love. It is this dynamic of kenosis, of losing oneself, that positively defines personhood, and this paradox is in accord with the biblical message that only he who loses his life for the sake of Christ will find it anew (cf. Mt 10:39). It is this same self-emptying dynamic that constitutes the being of the Church:[54] she is the body of Christ only insofar as she is the Bride who empties herself to receive all from her Bridegroom. Though it is constituted of sinners, the Church can act as a virgin bride by participating

50. Cf. Adam, *Spirit of Catholicism*, 138, in which he describes the communion of saints as a "fellowship of love" and says that Christian charity is "the lifeblood of the Body of Christ, which, welling forth out of the heart of the God-man, flows through the whole Body and gives it form and strength and beauty."

51. It may seem contradictory to speak of "mediation with an intermediary." However, in the order of grace, mediation happens by way of *participation* and is thus immediate (i.e., non-intermediary).

52. 1 Cor 12:26: "If one member suffers, all suffer with it; if one member is honored, all share its joy."

53. *Hyperdulia* is the term used to denote the special measure of veneration due to Mary as distinguished from both the veneration of the saints (*dulia*) and the cult of adoration due to God alone (*latria*); cf. B. Neunheuser, "Adoration," in *New Catholic Encyclopedia*, vol. 1 (New York: McGraw Hill, 1967), 141–42. For what the Council says on the pious veneration of Mary, see LG, no. 66.

54. There is a striking affinity between this idea of kenotic "excentration" and what de Lubac says of the ideal *homo ecclesiasticus* as one who is "dispossessed" of himself; see *Splendor*, 258.

in the pure faith, hope, and love of the woman who stands as first in the communion of saints.

In the final analysis, de Lubac's writings on Mary underscores the mystical dimension of the Church as the bride of Christ in a way otherwise inconceivable. The faith of the Church is not something abstract; it is founded on a personal encounter with Jesus Christ. Having offered her own being as the place of that supreme encounter between God and man, Mary's loving consent to God's message is the exemplary bridal consent that informs the nuptial mystery of love between Christ and his Church, between the Holy Spirit and every Christian soul. This exemplarity is ontologically dense because it refers to the perfect concentration of Mary's personhood as "full of grace" (cf. Lk 1:28). Her particular and personal being is, furthermore, universalized in such a way that it might be said that, precisely as exemplar of ecclesial existence, Mary's "fullness of grace" overflows to inform the being of the Church and of all Christians. She veritably constitutes the heart of ecclesial existence as one of mystical love, and all subsequent acts of faith, hope, and love are participations in her proleptic holiness.

In this light, it is evident that the Marian chapter of *Lumen Gentium* contributes something substantial, unique, and indispensable to ecclesiological reflection. The Constitution would fail to provide the best possible description of the Church if it did not consider Our Lady. It would neglect the innermost core of the Church if it omitted consideration of the woman who mysteriously embodies the reality of the Church. Mary exemplifies how the Church is the object of divine love in every human soul; she is the archetype and the quintessence of "excentrated" personhood. In Mary, the Council offers a person, a spouse and mother, as the best explanation of what it means to be the Church.

Avenues Forward

Having come to the conclusion of this study of de Lubac's writings on the relationship of Mary and the Church, one might echo the words of T. S. Eliot, "We shall not cease from exploration, and the end of all our exploring will be to arrive where we started and know the place for the first time."[1] This study has endeavored to show how the writings of Henri de Lubac, a leading proponent of *ressourcement*, help to uncover the riches of the Christian tradition on the Marian mystery in relationship to the Church. We have traced the lines of his patristic *ressourcement*, his attention to nuptial mysticism and spiritual exegesis, and his thought on the mystical identification of Mary and the Church, to come to a more complete appreciation of the Church's defining attributes of virgin bride and mother, attributes shared with Our Lady. In the spirit of *ressourcement*, de Lubac directed our attention to the heart of the Christian Tradition, built on the inexhaustible richness of the mysteries of faith. In the corresponding spirit of *aggiornamento*, he also gave us insight into current discussions on Mary as a concrete universal. With regard to the Marian mystery of the Church, there is no new revelation to be had, but rather, a deepened understanding and renewed appreciation

1. T. S. Eliot, "Little Gidding," from the *Four Quartets*, IV.5 (1943).

of the mystery of the communion that we call the Church. In a real sense, we've "arrived where we started," only to discover the delight of "knowing the place for the first time." We gaze anew upon the beloved countenance of Holy Mother Church.

A singular theme that has consistently emerged from this study is de Lubac's conception of the relationship of Mary and the Church as a *mystical* identification. Mystery is the context for understanding that Mary is the eschatological icon of humankind's collective destiny. De Lubac's writings, in which he favored a sacramental understanding of the Church, help to explain why the final chapter on Mary in *Lumen Gentium* is not a mere addendum but the apex and culmination of the Church's self-understanding. The mystery of the Church finds its climactic expression in the mystery of Mary. She magnifies the Lord and her praise overflows to the Church, animating it with the same Spirit by which the eternal Word of God came to dwell in her and among humankind.

Mary stands at the center of salvation history, within a communion of the saints bridally united to Christ. As the bridal figure of the Song of Songs, of Revelation, and ultimately, of salvation history, she is the most concrete expression of the Church as virgin bride and mother. The Council's decision to integrate its discussion on Mary within its Dogmatic Constitution on the Church highlighted the inextricable role Mary plays in salvation history. Our Lady indeed informs the Church's identity and mission, and de Lubac's writings enable postconciliar theology to take cognizance of this reality.

The contemporary complex of the relationship of the universal Church to local churches served as a test case of how Marian theology might potentially enrich contemporary ecclesiology. De Lubac's own consideration of the Virgin Mary as a concrete universal allowed him to take a perspective on the local-universal church relationship that precluded the controversial points of the Kasper-Ratzinger debate, a debate instigated by Ratzinger's assertion of the "ontological priority" of the universal Church. Alongside the idea of Mary and the Church as *sponsa Christi,* the configuration of their *mutual interiority,* understood by de Lubac as both *concrete universals,* positively elucidated the difficult question of the relationship of the universal and particular churches. This study thus sheds light on the structural and substantive similarities between the relationship of Mary to the Church and that of the universal Church to particular churches, positing that the latter relationship coincides in Mary in such a way that underscores how she enjoys an ecclesial and ontological priority. Without claiming to resolve the problematic, de Lubac's writings helped bring clarity to many facets of the issue and his insight into the Marian mystery of the Church proved illumining.

Vast horizons continue to open before us when we view the Church through the lens of Mariology. Insofar as Our Lady occupies a first place in the mystery of the Church such that all that is said of her can also be said of the Church, Mary must indeed have something important to offer to a systematic reflection on the Church. She is a *"nexus mysteriorum*—the intrinsic interwovenness of the mysteries [of faith] in their irreducible mutual otherness and their unity."[2] By way of a conclusion, I outline three broad categories in which a full cognizance of the Marian mystery of the Church opens up new vistas for further investigation. These include ecclesial reform, ecumenical dialogue, and the role of women in the Church.

First, *ecclesial reform.* In Pope Francis's Christmas address to the Roman Curia in 2019, he spoke of personal conversion as a fundamental requisite for institutional reform.[3] De Lubac similarly spoke of the priority of spiritual renewal at the heart of all structural reform. He asserted in *Les églises particulières dans l'Église universelle* that he had never been very interested in the subject of institutions because *"structural reforms . . . are never the main part of a program that must aim at the only true renewal, spiritual renewal."*[4]

There is not—nor will there ever be—any simple formula for ecclesial renewal, be it reform of the curia or some program to expunge corruption from the Church's structures. Although Mary does not directly inform the hierarchy of the Church, she plays an essential role in its renewal. Mary provides the Church with an unwavering focus on Jesus Christ, the source and impetus of ecclesial vitality and the crucial focus in a healthy configuration of ecclesial authority.

Mary represents the quintessence of the Church's nature and mission, the end that the hierarchical structures must serve. By always pointing to her Son, Our Lady highlights how the hierarchical communion of the Church

2. Ratzinger, "Thoughts on the Place of Marian Doctrine," 29. The phrase *"nexus mysteriorum inter se"* was employed by the First Vatican Council (1869–70) to assert the interrelatedness of the mysteries of faith (DH 3016).

3. *Christmas Greetings to the Roman Curia, Address of His Holiness Pope Francis* (21 December 2019), accessed online at http://www.vatican.va/content/francesco/en/speeches/2019/december/documents/papa-francesco_20191221_curia-romana.html.

4. MC, 33.

can only be understood in Him, in the order of faith and of service in love. Through the lens of faith, the greatest authority in the Church is recognized not as one wielding power for profit, but one whose supreme authority rests in charity. The Church's effectiveness is gauged by the measure of the faith, hope, and love that animate and inspire its members to be true servants of the Gospel (cf. Mk 10:45). Mary exemplifies this dimension of faith-filled service and reminds the Church that hierarchical communion exists for this main purpose.

Pope Francis's apostolic constitution on curial reform, *Predicate Evangelium* (2022), redefines the role of the Curia, locating the Church's mission of preaching the Gospel to be at the core and center of its governing structures. The Constitution's shift of the power of governance away from the power of orders, allowing any member of the faithful (lay or ordained) to preside over a dicastery, highlights how the power of governance is essentially a service of charity. Herein we again discover the implicit but pervasive Marian significance. The mission of the Church flows directly from her nature as the bride of the Lamb (Rev 21:2). In the work of evangelization, the Church's bridal fertility is realized, and she acts as a mother: all ecclesial ministries are expressions of the Church's motherhood and flow from her feminine nature, enlivened and fructified by the Spirit, in the likeness of Mary's divine motherhood.[5] Pope Francis's statement that "the reform of the Roman Curia is to be viewed in the context of the Church's missionary nature" (Predicate Evangelium, no. 3), might thus be read as implying that the institutional structures of the Church must become more Marian!

Second, *ecumenical dialogue*. For Christian Churches to progress toward ecumenical unity, the difficult questions regarding Mary must be seriously reckoned with. The Vatican Council's own contentious debates over Mary show its struggle to moderate the excesses that were introduced into Catholic Marian devotion over time and perdured in certain maximalist tendencies, which were counterproductive to ecumenical aims. Robert Brown, a Protestant observer at the Council, reflected in his journal on the significance of the indicative vote on Mary in 1963, saying: "Close as the vote was and difficult to interpret as it is, the Council fathers have nevertheless taken a step which has the possibility of being ecumenically creative rather than

---

5. Cf. MC, 75–84. St. Paul exemplified this maternal dynamic when he spoke of his mission explicitly in maternal terms: "My children, for whom I am again in labor until Christ be formed in you!" (Gal 4:19).

ecumenically divisive."[6] The Council's final synthesis constituted a positive step forward; it was ecumenically sensitive and theological constructive.

De Lubac's attention to *ressourcement* on Mary proffers a way forward. In returning to biblical revelation as well as the early Church Fathers, Christians meet on common grounds. It is evident, for example, that the idea of Mary as a type of the Church was conceived prior to the breach of ecclesial unity. The patristic formulation signifies that Mary is not a type of any singular Christian denomination but of the Church in unity, both on earth and in eschatological glory. Moreover, the theology of Mary underscores that insofar as she was the chosen locus of the divine-human encounter, Mary can also serve as the personal context and catalyst for the transformation of all human encounters with God and with one another.

Additionally, a Marian perspective could potentially mediate between different denominational theologies. Contemporary theological circles tend to assign a binary association to current Baptismal and Eucharistic ecclesiologies: The Reformed/Protestant traditions emphasize baptismal ecclesiology while the Orthodox and Roman Catholic churches emphasize a Eucharistic theology. A Marian perspective highlights how these distinct ecclesiological approaches are but expressions of *one* ecclesial maternity. *Lumen Gentium* did not hesitate to consider "devotion toward the Virgin Mother of God" a personal "force impelling toward Catholic unity" (LG, no. 15 and 8).[7] Marian theology is potent for rich conversation and new ecumenical initiatives.

Moreover, de Lubac also makes a point of ecumenical value when he asserts in his commentary on *Lumen Gentium* that the bond between Mary and the Church "represents the convergence of a twofold application of the same sapiential texts in the Western liturgical tradition to Mary and in the writings of the Eastern Fathers of the Church."[8] This statement provides an ecumenical nod to the rich Sophiology of Orthodox theologians such as Sergei Bulgakov, Vladimir Soloviev, and Pavel Florenski, drawing out their connection to Western thinkers such as Teilhard de Chardin and Monchanin who also expound the symbol of Lady Wisdom. The topic is potent for rapprochement between Eastern and Western thought.

Third, *the role of women in the Church*. As shown in the discussion of the Church's Marian subjectivity in the previous chapter, there are far-reaching

6. Brown, *Observer in Rome*, 125.

7. Although *Lumen Gentium* refers specifically to the elements of sanctification and truth as forces impelling toward catholic unity, those elements are found in an exemplary degree in Mary and, therefore, the same can be predicated to her.

8. CPM, 66.

implications for a Christian anthropology built on Marian principles. Mary represents a theology in which woman—in all her femininity—encompasses all creation while remaining open upwards to God, first in a creature-Creator relationship, and then in the nuptial relationship of bride and bridegroom.[9] This perspective finds its warrant in the scriptural and patristic idea that Israel's history enlarges into a cosmic history with Christ inaugurating a new creation as the New Adam, and Mary assuming a corresponding role as the New Eve. The perfection of the creature as creature—the perfection of a human person as *human*—occurs in the woman, in Mary.

Consequently, the key topics of Christian anthropology—of human nature, gender differences, the interplay of nature and grace, human autonomy, freedom, and human destiny—all find particular clarification in light of Marian thought. Likewise, current discussions of the role of women in the Church should also come under the tutelage of Marian theology.[10] What does Mary's exalted and unparalleled role in salvation history say to the reality and the dignity of women today? What might an emphasis on the Church's feminine identity offer to a world increasingly plagued by confusion on gender and sexuality? How might the Church approach reviving the ordination of deaconesses in light of the Council's Mariology?[11]

The Church can neither grasp the nuptial mystery of the Incarnation nor understand herself as the bride of Christ without considering the perfect bridal assent offered first by Mary. It is in her likeness that the Church realizes her own nature as nuptial; her mission is maternal and her structures, personal. In the person of Mary as bride and mother, the Church discovers her own tender, feminine essence. Without Mary, the Church's feminine genius risks being usurped by some androgynous conceptualization of being, or hijacked by a skewed notion of radical feminism, or suppressed by what Ratzinger calls a "masculine model that views her as an instrument for a program of social-political action."[12] Ecclesial motherhood,[13] of which

---

9. For a classic work on this topic, see Louis Bouyer's *Woman in the Church,* trans. Marilyn Teichert (San Francisco: Ignatius Press, 1984).

10. For a recent work which plays out de Lubac's perspective on Mary and the Church, see Roch A. Kereszty, "The Infallibility of the Church: A Marian Mystery," *Communion* 38, no. 3 (2011): 374–90.

11. See, for example, this constructive proposal by Cettina Militello, "Maria e la chiesa: una proposta," *Ephemerides Mariologicae* 71, no. 4 (2021): 421–44.

12. Joseph Ratzinger with Vittorio Messori, *The Ratzinger Report: An Exclusive Interview on the State of the Church,* trans. Salvator Attanasio and Graham Harrison (San Francisco: Ignatius Press, 1985), 108.

13. Pope Francis has frequently spoken of the tender motherhood of the Church; see the General Audience in St. Peter's Square on 3 September 2014, in which his exhortation especially

the sacraments and all the Church's ministries are expressions, would risk becoming a mere instrument serving a human agenda, a kind of machinery for the dispensing of divine favors.[14] Mary reminds us that the Church is Mother, and through her, redemption is experienced as nothing less than a mystical union with Christ in love (cf. Rev. 21).

There is, moreover, a unique sense in which the Church is bride. Unlike any other nuptial commitment, Christ's espousal of the Church to himself is what brings the Church-bride into being. Other brides preexist their wedding day, but the Church only exists as Church through the work of her bridegroom who "handed himself over for her, to sanctify her, cleansing her by the bath of water with the word" (Eph 5:25f). The bridal dimension of the Marian mystery brings into greater relief the fact that apart from Christ, the Church cannot be.

Vatican II bequeathed to the Church a renewed reflection on ecclesial existence in which Mary had a key place, as shown in the final chapter of *Lumen Gentium*. Yet, as noted at the outset of this study, there is a marked lack of integration of the Council's Marian theology within ecclesiological scholarship today. The ongoing reception of Vatican II's ecclesiology has yet to give sufficient attention to Mariology and to the inclusion of a final chapter on Mary in *Lumen Gentium*. De Lubac's writings, from both before and after the Council, provide an invaluable perspective into the Council's great synthesis. His writings successfully preserve the fragile conciliar consensus and enable the strange postconciliar lacuna to be addressed.

As the Church continues to reap the fruits of the Council's synthesis

---

resonates with de Lubac's ideas on the motherhood of the Church: "The motherhood of the Church is established in precise continuity with that of Mary, as her continuation in history.... The conception of Jesus in Mary's womb, in fact, is the prelude to the birth of every Christian in the womb of the Church.... We understand, then, how the relationship which unites Mary and the Church is so deep: by looking at Mary, we discover the most beautiful and most tender face of the Church; and by looking at the Church, we recognize the sublime features of Mary.... We are not orphans! The Church is mother, Mary is mother." See also the 15 September 2015 homily given at the Mass in the Santa Marta Residence.

14. Cf. von Balthasar's comment that without Mary, the Church would become "a Church of permanent conversations, organizations, advisory commissions, academies, parties, pressure groups, functions, structure and restructurings, social experiments, statistics: that is to say, more than ever a male Church.... And because in this manly-masculine world, all that we have is one ideology replacing another, everything becomes polemical, critical, bitter, humorless, and ultimately boring and people in their masses run away from such a Church"; Hans Urs von Balthasar, "Marian Principle," 110, 112. See also Rahner's comment, quoted in MC, 164: "Abstractions have no need of a mother."

and engage the modern world in the mysteries of faith, de Lubac's insights help trace and discover anew the features of Mary on the countenance of the Church. All that he ever wrote was inspired by and imbued with his love for the Church, the Heavenly Jerusalem.[15] What he says specifically on the topic of Mary and the Church all point to this final end. Gazing on her Marian countenance, let us echo de Lubac's own purpose, stated at the beginning of *Méditation sur l'Église*: "[If] anything I have to say can help anyone to a clearer sight of the Bride of the Lamb, in all her radiant motherhood, my object will have been achieved and I shall be well satisfied."[16]

15. See *Splendor*, 9, 379, in which de Lubac ends *Méditation sur l'Église* with the exclamation: "IPSI GLORIA IN ECCLESIA. AMEN" (Eph 3:21; cf. Rev 1:6; Ps 67:27; Rom 11:36).

16. *Splendor*, 10.

APPENDIX

This English translation of the main text of the draft of the "Dogmatic Constitution on the Blessed Virgin Mary, Mother of God and Mother of Men" by the Preparatory Theological Commission in 1962 is adapted from a translation by James T. O'Connor, published in *Marian Studies* 37 (1986): 198–211. Available at: https://ecommons.udayton.edu/marian_studies/vol37/iss1/16, and reproduced here with permission.

For a complete translation that includes the prefatory note and footnotes, see Joseph A. Komonchak's translation (2012) available online in the public domain at https://catholicebooks.wordpress.com/2017/10/11/online-texts-the-original-schemas-drafts-of-vatican-ii/.

Schema of the Dogmatic Constitution on the Blessed Virgin Mary,
Mother of God and Mother of Men (1962)

1. [On the intimate connection between Christ and Mary according to the will of God.] The most wise God, Creator of the immense goodness of all things, Who enjoyed complete freedom in determining the way and means by which the liberation of the human race would be accomplished by Him, in the one and the same eternal decree preordained, together with the Incarnation of Divine Wisdom, the most blessed Virgin, from whom the Word made flesh would be born in the fullness of time. Since, moreover, the Sacred Scriptures, whether explicitly or implicitly, place before our eyes, as it were, Mary as joined with Jesus by an intimate and indissoluble bond from the time of the prophetic "protoevangelium" (cf. Gn 3:15; Is 7:14;

Mt 1:23) and the virginal conception (cf. Mt 1:18–25 and Lk 1:26–38f), it is clearly fitting that the Church—which is assisted by the Holy Spirit to perceive fully and understand clearly those things which lie hidden in the Sacred Fonts obscurely and, as it were, implicitly, and which is securely led (cf. Jn 14:26f) and preserved from error (cf. Mt 16:18; 28:18–20; Jn 14:16; 15:20)—while she illustrates the mysteries of the Divine Redeemer bring into a clearer light the mystery of the Mother of God.

Moreover, this loving Parent who "has cooperated in charity that the faithful may be born in the Church" not only is a "supereminent" and completely singular member of the Church, but is also called its exemplar and mother of the same Church.

Therefore the Holy Synod, after it has spoken of the Mystical Body of Christ, adhering to previous documents of the living Magisterium of the Church which is the only authentic interpreter of the revealed Deposit, thinks it opportune to illustrate summarily and briefly the place which the Mother of God and of men occupies in the Church, as well as the privileges with which the Son has adorned His Mother and our duties toward so sublime a creature in order that Marian science and piety may fully and properly flourish and prejudicial opinions might be avoided in this matter.

2. [On the role of the most blessed Virgin Mary in the economy of our salvation.]

Since, therefore, the Word of the Eternal Father willed to take the nature of man from a woman in order that just as death came from a woman so also life might arise for us through a woman and thus the liberation would be had by the work of each sex, He did not complete that work before there would be present the free acceptance of the designated mother who was redeemed in a more sublime manner because of the foreseen merits of Christ, so that the Son of God, by His Incarnation, would be the Son of Adam, the new Adam, and the Savior of the world. By her consent, Mary, the daughter of Adam, became not only the mother of Jesus, the unique divine Mediator and Redeemer, but also associated her work with him and under him in effecting the redemption of the human race. Moreover this saving consent of the Mother of God, whence her association (consortium) in achieving the work of redemption, lasted from the time of the virginal conception of Jesus Christ unto his death, and shone forth especially when she stood next to the Cross, not without Divine plan (cf. Jn 19:25); she suffered greatly with her only-begotten; with him and through him she offered Him magnanimously as the price of our redemption; and finally she was given as mother to men by Christ as he died on the Cross. Because indeed the mystery of human redemption was not completed until the Holy Spirit, promised by Christ, would come on the day of Pentecost, we contemplate Mary persevering in prayer together with the Apostles (cf. Acts 1:14) in the Cenacle, imploring by her prayers the pouring forth of the Spirit.

Since therefore the most blessed Virgin, predestined from eternity to be the mother of God and of men, was here on earth the generous associate of the suffering Christ in acquiring grace for men—divine providence disposing it thus—she is rightly and duly greeted as also the administratrix and dispensatrix of heavenly graces.

Hence it follows that Mary, who had a part in establishing the mystical body of Christ, and who, having been assumed into heaven and made Queen by the Lord, bears toward us a maternal spirit, has obtained, through her Son, a certain primacy over all and therefore is not, as some say "on the periphery" but is placed in the very center of the Church under Christ.

3. [On the titles by which the association of the blessed Virgin Mary with Christ in the economy of our salvation is accustomed to be expressed]. Because the multiple and various titles by which the Magisterium of the Church, the Tradition, which is to be venerated and the pious sense of the faithful are accustomed to salute the most blessed Virgin rest in root and principle, as on a solid foundation, on the cooperation of the Mother of God with Christ, as of the new Eve with the new Adam in effecting the work of human redemption, it is criminal (nefas) to say that the same titles, in a sense understood by the Church, are empty and inane and, what is more, opposed to Sacred Scripture. Thus not without cause is the most blessed Virgin called by the Church Mediatrix of graces. If on this earth St. Paul the Apostle was mindful of the faithful without interruption in his prayers and insistently asked the aid of their prayers for him, how much more necessary and helpful it is that we commend ourselves to the prayers of the same most blessed Virgin Mary. For she is joined more strictly and more intimately to God and to Christ, the Son of God and her Son, than is any other pure creature, indeed in a manner unique to her alone; likewise more intimately than any other pure creature, she loves God and is likewise loved by Him. As the mother of the Savior (cf. Lk 1:31), (sic) with her soul pierced by a sword (cf. Lk 2:25) she, under the Cross, experienced in her Son, who was dying for the salvation of all, the love of God in order to reach in a certain way the highest degree in love of men (cf. Jn 19:25–27). Enriched by so many and such great titles, she intercedes with God and with Christ for us with her

continuous love, and because her intercession draws all its force and efficacy from the bloody sacrifice of her beloved Son, this her mediation in no way brings it about that the one Mediator of God and men fails to be the man Christ Jesus (cf. 1 Tim. 2:5), just as it does not follow that from His goodness God Himself as the only good ceases to be the fountain of goods for all (cf. Mt 9:17; coll. Rom 2:4).

For although among the subordinate mediators which the most wise God wished to use in the economy of our salvation, no one is able to be thought of who in reconciling God to men has ever or will ever do a work equal to that of the Mother of God, nevertheless, it is always true that She in her predestination and sanctity and likewise in all her gifts is dependent on Christ and completely subordinate to Him.

Since therefore this humble "handmaid of the Lord," whom He who is mighty has made great (cf. Lk 1:49), is called the Mediatrix of all graces because she was associated with Christ in acquiring them and since she is invoked by the Church as our advocate and as mother of mercy—because, remaining even now the associate of the glorious Christ in heaven, she intercedes for all through Christ in such a way that in conferring all graces on men there is present the maternal charity of the Blessed Virgin—in no way is the mediation of our unique Mediator obscured or diminished, according to the absolute significance of the words of the Apostle (1 Tim. 2:5): "There is one God and one mediator of God and men, the man Christ Jesus"; rather this mediation of Christ is extolled and honored. For Mary is mediatrix in Christ, and her mediation is not from any necessity but from the divine good pleasure and from the superabundance and power of the merits of Christ; it depends on that power completely and obtains all its power from it.

Therefore, the Sacred Synod exhorts theologians and preachers of the divine word to strive sedulously, cultivating the study of the Scriptures especially and of the holy Fathers according to mind of the Magisterium of the Church, to bring proper perspective the gifts and duties of the Blessed Virgin as they are joined with other dogmas, especially those which relate to Christ who is the center of all truth, of holiness and piety. In this work let there always be observed the "analogy [of faith]" as it is called, or the "unlike likeness," whenever some word or office is predicated simultaneously of Christ and the Virgin Mary: for in no way is the Mother of God to be equated with Christ.

4. [On the singular privileges of the Mother of God and of men.] The Virgin Mary has been adorned by completely singular privileges by God

Who has treated her with ineffable love: she was admirable in her origin because of the immaculate conception; admirable in her life since she was lacking in all personal sin, remained a mother and at the same time always a virgin in mind and body; admirable finally in her demise because although according to an ancient and venerable tradition she underwent temporal death by which she was more fully assimilated to her Son, she was gloriously assumed body and soul into heaven since she was by no means able to be held by the bonds of death.

These singular privileges and other gifts of grace, flowing from Christ the Redeemer, so redound to His glory that we are not able to contemplate the great gifts of the Mother without marveling at and celebrating the divinity, the goodness, the love and the omnipotence of her Son. If indeed injuries to a mother affect a son, so the glory of a mother redounds to the Son; therefore, since Mary had a singular affinity with her Son, it was fitting that from the foreseen merits of the most perfect Redeemer, the author of all sanctity—Who came into this world to destroy sin—she should be preserved immune from the first instant of conception from all stain of original sin, and should be adorned with graces and gifts far above all the angelic spirits and all the saints so that in truth the Mother of God, the daughter of the Father, the temple of the Holy Spirit, would exceed in dignity all creatures. It was completely necessary that the Son,—Who adorned his Mother with particular love and Who willed the corporeal integrity of the Mother to remain incorrupt and unstained by childbirth itself, so that "the glory of her virginity remaining she might pour out on the world the eternal light"— would not permit that most holy virginal body, the august tabernacle of the divine Word, the temple of God, completely holy and completely pure to be resolved into dust.

5. [On the cult rendered to the most blessed Virgin Mary.] Therefore since the most blessed Virgin is possessed of a singular excellence, such that she deserved to be greeted by the Archangel-messenger of God as "full of grace" (Lk 1:28) and by Elizabeth, filled with the Holy Spirit, as blessed among women (cf. Lk 1:42), it is not to be wondered at that, as she herself had prophesied concerning herself, "all generations will call me blessed" (Lk 1:48), and that she is preached, cultivated, loved and invoked with all praise by all people and by all rites, the testimony growing continually with the passage of time, so that she is proposed as an example for imitation. This singular Marian cult is so far from being a detriment to the divine cult of worship—by which adoration is shown to the Word Incarnate as well as to the Father and Holy Spirit—that

in fact it fosters that divine cult even more. The various forms of piety toward the Mother of God and of men which the Church—within the limits of sound and orthodox doctrine according to times and local conditions, the character and nature of the faithful—has approved, look to this, namely that, while the Mother is honored, the Son, in Whom the Eternal Father willed all fullness should reside, (cf. Col 1:19) is properly known, loved, glorified, and his commandments observed; and thus through Christ, Who is the "way and truth and life" (Jn 14:6), men might be led to a knowledge of and supreme adoration of the One and triune God.

This sound Catholic doctrine the Holy Synod deliberately and forcefully teaches and at the same time warns bishops that they sedulously guard that theologians and preachers of the divine word abstain from every false exaggeration of the truth as well as from an extreme narrowness of mind when treating of the singular dignity of the begetter of God.

Let the faithful of each sex remember that true devotion by no means consists in a certain feeling of a moment and that it completely rejects all vain credulity; on the other hand let them firmly hold that devotion proceeds from true faith, by which we are all led to imitation of the virtues of that most blessed Virgin who was the "handmaid of the Lord," (Lk 1:38), a most humble and most obedient handmaid who most faithfully preserved those things which pertained to the Word Incarnate, "pondering them in her heart," (Lk 2:19) and so was greeted as "blessed because she believed" (Lk 1:45). For no maternal closeness would have availed Mary "unless she had borne Christ more happily in her heart than in her flesh."

The due honor and reverence toward the Mother of the Lord and Savior with which not a few of the separated brethren, especially the Orthodox—who are moved by a certain fervent impulse to honor the Theotókos in a particular way—are adorned offers great joy and solace to this Sacred Synod.

6. [Most Holy Mary, Promoter of Christian Unity.] Mary, Mother and Virgin most holy, since she had commended to her maternal heart all men while on Calvary, vehemently desires that all cling together in faith and charity with the divine Savior and among themselves, not only those who have been given one Baptism and are led by the One Spirit, but also those who do not know that they have been redeemed by Christ Jesus. Therefore, this holy Synod, with sure hope and trust, is confident that it will happen that this Mother of God and of men—who interceded (cf. Jn 2:3) that the Incarnate Word manifest His first sign at Cana of Galilee, at which the disciples believed in him (Jn 2:11), and who assisted in the newly-born Church—will

beseech God that at the last all may come together in one flock under the one Shepherd. (cf. Jn 10:16). Therefore all the Christian faithful are exhorted to pour out prayers and supplications constantly to this Promoter of unity and Help of Christians, so that, by her intercession, her Divine Son may gather all the family of nations, and especially those who glory in the name of Christian into one people of God, who lovingly recognize as a common father the Vicar of Christ on earth, the successor of St. Peter, who was properly saluted as the "Custodian of the Faith" by the unanimous applause of the bishops at the Council of Ephesus where the doctrine of the divine maternity was solemnly sanctioned.

For a complete bibliography of de Lubac's writings, see Karl Neufeld and Michel Sales, *Bibliographie Henri de Lubac, SJ, 1925–1974, 2,* Erganzte und verbesserte Auflage (Einsiedeln: Johannesverlag, 1975).

For a further supplementary bibliography of de Lubac, see Karl Neufeld and Michel Sales, "*Bibliographie de Henri de Lubac (Corrections et compléments) 1942–1989,*" in *Théologie dans l'histoire* (Paris: Desclée de Brouwer, 1990), 408–20.

Primary Works: Selected Books by Henri de Lubac

Catholicisme: les aspects sociaux du dogme. 1st ed. Paris: Éditions du Cerf, 1938. In *Foi Vivante* series, 1965. English translation: *Catholicism: Christ and the Common Destiny of Man.* Translated from the 4th ed. (1947) by Lancelot Sheppard and Sr. Elizabeth Englund, OCD. San Francisco: Ignatius Press, 1988.

Corpus Mysticum: l'Eucharistie et l'Église au Moyen Âge. Étude historique. Paris: Aubier, 1944. English translation: *Corpus Mysticum: The Eucharist and the Church in the Middle Ages.* Translated by Gemma Simmonds, Richard Price, and Christopher Stephens. Notre Dame, IN: Notre Dame University Press, 2006.

Le Drame de l'humanisme athée. Paris: Éditions Spes, 1944. English translation: *The Drama of Atheist Humanism.* Translated by Edith M. Riley, et al. San Francisco: Ignatius Press, 1995.

Surnaturel: études historiques. Paris: Aubier Montaigne, 1946.

Paradoxes. Editions du Livre, 1945. English translation: *Paradoxes of Faith.* Translated by Paule Simon and Sadie Kreilkamp. San Francisco: Ignatius Press, 1948.

"Le mystère du surnaturel." *Recherches de Science religieuse* 36 (1949): 80–121.

"Sens Spirituel." *Recherches de Science Religieuse* 36 (1949): 542–76.

Histoire et esprit: l'Intelligence de l'Écriture d'après Origène. Paris: Aubier, 1950. English
    translation: *History and Spirit: The Understanding of Scripture according to Origen*.
    Translated by Anne Englund Nash. San Francisco: Ignatius Press, 2007.
Letter to Rev. François Charmot, dated 9 September 1950, in "Deux lettres inédites."
    Bulletin de Littérature Ecclésiastique 94 (1993): 47–55.
Aspects du bouddhisme. Paris: Éditions du Seuil, 1951. English translation: *Aspects of
    Buddhism*. Translated by George Lamb. New York: Sheed & Ward, 1954.
La Rencontre du bouddhisme et de l'Occident. Paris: Aubier, 1952.
Méditation sur l'Église. Paris: Aubier, 1953. English translation: *The Splendor of the
    Church*. Translated by Michael Mason. San Francisco: Ignatius Press, 1999.
Aspects du bouddhisme: Amida. Volume 2. Paris: Éditions du Seuil, 1955.
"Temoignage: du Henri de Lubac SJ" *Église Vivante* 10, no. 1 (January–February 1958):
    70.
Exégèse médiévale: les quatres sens de l'ecriture. 4 volumes. Paris: Aubier, 1959, 1961, 1963,
    1964. English translation: *Medieval exegesis*. Translated by Mark Sebanc. Grand
    Rapids, MI: William B. Eerdmans, 1988.
La Pensée religieuse du Père Pierre Teilhard de Chardin. Paris: Aubier-Montaigne, 1962.
    English translation: *The Religion of Teilhard de Chardin*. Translated by René
    Hague. New York: Desclée, 1967.
La Prière du Père Teilhard de Chardin. Paris: A. Fayard, 1964. Two English editions: *The
    Faith of Teilhard de Chardin*. Translated by René Hague. London: Burns & Oates,
    1965. *Teilhard de Chardin: The Man and His Meaning*. Translated by René Hague.
    New York: Hawthorn Books, 1965.
Blondel et Teilhard de Chardin: correspondance, commentée par Henri de Lubac. Paris:
    Beauchesne, 1965. English translation: *Correspondence*. Translated by William
    Whitman. New York: Harper and Harper, 1967.
"*Lumen Gentium* and the Fathers." In *Vatican II: An Interfaith Appraisal*, edited by John
    Miller, 153–75. Notre Dame, IN: University of Notre Dame Press, 1966.
"Meditation on the Church." In *Vatican II: An Interfaith Appraisal*, edited by John
    Miller, 258–66. Notre Dame, IN: University of Notre Dame Press, 1966.
Teilhard, missionnaire et apologiste. Toulouse: Éditions Prière et Vie, 1966. English
    translation: *Teilhard Explained*. Translated by Anthony Buono. New York: Paulist
    Press, 1988.
"Henri de Lubac." Interview in Patrick Granfield, OSB, *Theologians at Work*, 165–75.
    New York: MacMillan, 1967.
L'Écriture dans la tradition. Paris: Aubier, 1967. New English edition: *Scripture in the
    Tradition*. Translated by Luke O'Neill. Introduction by Peter Casarella. New York:
    Crossroad, 2000.
Images de l'Abbé Monchanin. Paris: Éditions Montaigne, 1967.
Paradoxe et mystère de l'Église. Paris: Aubier-Montaigne, 1967. English translation:
    The Church: Paradox and Mystery. Translated by James Dunne. Shannon: Ecclesia
    Press, 1969.

Athéisme et sens de l'homme: une double requête de Gaudium et Spes. Paris: Éditions du
  Cerf, 1968. Abridged English translation: "The Total Meaning of Man and the
  World." Translated by D. C. Schindler. *Communio* 35, no. 4 (2008): 613–41.
"Commentaire du Préambule et du Chapitre I." In *La Révélation divine,* edited by
  B. D. Dupuy. Vol. 1, *Constitution dogmatique "Dei Verbum,"* 157–302. *Unam Sanctam*
  70a. Paris: Éditions du Cerf, 1968.
*L'Éternel féminin. Étude sur un texte du Père Teilhard de Chardin. Suivi de Teilhard et
  notre temps.* Paris: Aubier-Montaigne, 1968. English translation: *The Eternal
  Feminine: A Study on the Poem by Teilhard de Chardin Followed by Teilhard and the
  Problems of Today.* Translated by René Hague. London: William Collins, 1971.
*La Révélation divine: Commentaire du préambule et du chapitre I de la Constitution
  "Dei Verbum" du Concile Vatican II.* Paris: Éditions du Cerf, 1968.
"Buddhist Messianism?" (1969). In *Theological Fragments,* translated by Rebecca How-
  ell Balinski, 371–73. San Francisco: Ignatius Press, 1989.
L'Église dans la crise actuelle. Paris: Éditions du Cerf, 1969. Abridged English transla-
  tion: "The Church in Crisis." *Theology Digest* 17, no. 4 (1969): 312–25.
*Les Églises particulières dans l'Église universelle, suivi de la maternité de l'église, et d'une in-
  terview recueillie par G. Jarczyk.* Paris: Aubier Montaigne, 1971. English translation:
  *The Motherhood of the Church: Followed by Particular Churches in the Universal
  Church and an Interview Conducted by Gwendoline Jarczyk.* Translated by Sr. Sergia
  Englund. San Francisco: Ignatius Press, 1982.
Petite catéchèse sur Nature et Grâce. Paris: Librairie Arthème Fayard, 1980. English
  translation: *A Brief Catechesis on Nature and Grace.* Translated by Richard Arnan-
  dez. San Francisco: Ignatius Press, 1984.
"Mystique et Mystère." In *Théologies d'occasion,* 31–76. Paris: Desclée, 1984. English
  translation: "Mysticism and Mystery." In *Theological Fragments,* translated by
  Rebecca Howell Balinski, 35–69. San Francisco: Ignatius Press, 1989.
Théologies d'Occasion. Paris: Desclée, 1984. English translation: *Theological Fragments.*
  Translated by Rebecca Howell Balinski. San Francisco: Ignatius Press, 1989.
Entretien autour de Vatican II: Souvenirs et réflexions. Paris: Éditions du Cerf, 1985.
  Abridged English translation: *De Lubac: A Theologian Speaks.* Interview by Angelo
  Scola. Translated by Stephen Maddux. Los Angeles: Twin Circle Publishing
  Company, 1985.
Résistance chrétienne à l'antisémitisme: Souvenirs, 1940–1944. Paris: Fayard, 1988. English
  translation: *Christian Resistance to Anti-Semitism: Memoires from 1940–1944.* Trans-
  lated by Elizabeth Englund. San Francisco: Ignatius Press, 1990.
Mémoire sur l'occasion de mes écrits. Namur, Belgium: Culture et Verité, 1989. English
  translation: *At the Service of the Church: Henri de Lubac Reflects on the Circumstances That Occasioned His Writings.* Translated by Anne Elizabeth Englund. San
  Francisco: Ignatius Press, 1993.
Théologie dans l'Histoire. Paris: Desclée de Brouwer, 1990. English translation: *Theology
  in History.* Translated by Anne Englund Nash. San Francisco: Ignatius Press, 1996.

"Internal Causes of the Weakening and Disappearance of the Sense of the Sacred."
    In *Theology in History*, translated by Anne Englund Nash, 223–40. San Francisco:
    Ignatius Press, 1996.
"Mémoire sur mes vingt première années." *Bulletin de l'Association Internationale Cardi-
    nal Henri de Lubac* 1 (1998): 7–31.
Carnets du Concile, tomes 1 et 2. Edited by Loïc Figoureux. Paris: Éditions du Cerf,
    2007. English translation: *Vatican Council Notebooks.* 2 vols. Translated by Andrew
    Stefanelli and Anne Englund Nash. San Francisco: Ignatius Press, 2015, 2016.
History of Pure Land Buddhism. Translated by Amita Bhaka. Accessed online at http://
    www.bdcu.org.au/bddronline/bddr12no6/bddr12no6.html.

Secondary Literature

1985 Extraordinary Synod. *The Church, in the Word of God, Celebrates the Mysteries of
    Christ for the Salvation of the World.* Available at https://www.ewtn.com/
    catholicism/library/final-report-of-the-1985-extraordinary-synod-2561.
Ackermann, Stephan. "The Church as Person in the Theology of Hans Urs von
    Balthasar." *Communio* 29, no. 2 (2002): 238–49.
Adam, Karl. *The Spirit of Catholicism.* Translated by Justin McCann. London: Sheed &
    Ward, 1934.
Alberigo, Giuseppe, and Joseph A. Komonchak, eds. *History of Vatican II.* 5 vols. Mary-
    knoll, NY: Orbis; Louvain: Peeters, 1995–2006.
D'Ambrosio, Marcellino. "*Ressourcement* Theology, *Aggiornamento*, and the Herme-
    neutics of Tradition." *Communio* 18, no. 4 (1991): 546–47.
Anderson, Floyd, ed. *Council Daybook. Vatican II.* 2 vols. Washington, DC: National
    Catholic Welfare Conference, 1965.
Antonelli, Cesare. "Le role de Mgr. Gérard Philips dans la redaction du chapitre VIII
    de 'Lumen gentium.'" *Marianum* 55 (1993): 17–97.
———. *Il dibattito su Maria nel Concilio Vaticano II. Percorso redazionale sulla base di
    nuovi documenti di archivio.* Bibliotheca Berica 14. Padova: Edizioni Messagero di
    Sant' Antonio, 2009.
Astell, Ann W. *The Song of Songs in the Middle Ages.* Ithaca: Cornell University Press,
    1990.
Auer, Johann. *The Church: The Universal Sacrament of Salvation.* Translated by Michael
    Waldstein. Washington, DC: The Catholic University of America Press, 1993.
Balthasar, Hans Urs von. "The Achievement of Henri de Lubac." *Thought* 51 (1976):
    7–49.
———. *Henri de Lubac: Sein organisches Lebenswerk.* Einsiedeln: Johannes Verlag,
    1976. English translation: *The Theology of Henri de Lubac: An Overview.* Translated
    by Joseph Fessio. San Francisco: Ignatius Press, 1991.
———. *Test Everything, Keep What Is Good.* San Francisco: Ignatius Press, 1986.

———. *The Theology of Henri de Lubac: An Overview*. Translated by Joseph Fessio. San Francisco: Ignatius Press, 1991.

———. "Who Is the Church?" In *Explorations in Theology II: Spouse of the Word*, translated by Alexander Dru, 143–91. San Francisco: Ignatius Press, 1991.

———. "Marian Principle." In *Elucidations*. San Francisco: Ignatius Press, 1998.

———. *The Office of Peter and the Structure of the Church*. Translated by Andrée Emery. San Francisco: Ignatius Press, 2007.

Balthasar, Hans Urs von, and Georges Chantraine. *Le Cardinal Henri de Lubac: l'homme et son oeuvre*. Paris: Lethielleux, 1983.

Baraúna, Guilherme, and Yves Congar, eds. *L'Église de Vatican II*. Unam Sanctam 51a-c. Paris: Éditions du Cerf, 1966–67.

Barbour, Ian G. "Five Ways of Reading Teilhard." *Soundings* 51 (1968): 115–45.

Beattie, Tina. "Mary in Patristic Theology." In *Mary: The Complete Resource*, edited by Sarah Jane Boss, 75–105. London: Continuum, 2007.

Beozzo, José Oscar. "Le Concile Vatican II (1962–1965). La Participation de la Conférenece Épiscopale du Brésil–CNBB." *Cristianesimo nella storia* 23 (2002): 121–96.

Bertoldi, Francesco. "The Religious Sense in Henri de Lubac." *Communio* 16, no. 1 (1989): 6–31.

———. "Henri de Lubac on *Dei Verbum*." Translated by Mandy Murphy. *Communio* 17, no. 1 (1990): 88–94.

Besutti, Giuseppe. "Note di Cronaca sul Concilio Vaticano II e lo Schema de B. Maria Virgine." *Marianum* 26 (1964): 1–42.

———. *Lo Schema Mariano al Concilio Vaticano II*. Rome: Marianum/Descleé, 1966.

Boersma, Hans. "Sacramental Ontology: Nature and the Supernatural in the Ecclesiology of Henri de Lubac." *New Blackfriars* 88, no. 1015 (2007): 242–73.

Boss, Sarah Jane, ed. *Mary: The Complete Resource*. London: Continuum, 2007.

Bouyer, Louis. *The Seat of Wisdom: An Essay on the Place of the Virgin Mary in Christian Theology*. New York: Pantheon Books, 1962.

———. *The Church of God*. Chicago: Franciscan Herald Press, 1982.

———. *Woman in the Church*. Translated by Marilyn Teichert. San Francisco: Ignatius Press, 1984.

Braine, David. "The Debate between Henri de Lubac and His Critics." *Nova et Vetera* 6, no. 3 (2008): 543–89.

Brown, Robert McAfee. *Observer in Rome: A Protestant Report on the Vatican Council*. New York: Doubleday, 1964.

Bulgakov, Sergius. *The Bride of the Lamb*. Grand Rapids, MI: Wm. B. Eerdmans; Edinburgh: T&T Clark, 2002.

Caporale, Rock. *Vatican II: Last of the Councils*. Baltimore: Helicon, 1964.

Cavadini, John, and Danielle Peters, eds. *Mary on the Eve of the Second Vatican Council*. Notre Dame, IN: University of Notre Dame Press, 2017.

Chantraine, Georges. "Catholicité et Maternité de l'Église." *Nouvelle revue theologique* 94 (1972): 520–36.

———. "Beyond Modernity and Postmodernity: The Thought of Henri de Lubac."
Translated by Janine Langan. *Communio* 17, no. 2 (1990): 207–19.

———. "Cardinal Henri de Lubac (1896–1991)." *Communio* 18, no. 3 (1991): 297–303.

———. "Note Historique." In *Henri de Lubac. Oeuvres complètes.* 8 vols. Paris: Éditions
du Cerf, 1999.

———. *Henri de Lubac. Tome I, De la naissance à la démobilisation, 1896–1919.* Paris:
Éditions du Cerf, 2007.

———. *Henri de Lubac. Tome II, Les années de formation, 1919–1929.* Paris: Éditions du
Cerf, 2009.

Congar, Yves. "Marie et l'Église: perspective médiévale." *Revue des Sciences
philosophiques et théologiques* 39 (1955): 408–12.

———. *Christ, Our Lady and the Church: A Study in Eirenic Theology.* Translated by
Henry St. John. London: Longmans, Green, 1957.

———. "De la communion des églises à une ecclésiologie de l'Église universelle."
In *L'Épiscopat et l'Église universelle,* 227–60. Paris: Éditions du Cerf, 1964.

———. "La personne 'Église.'" *Revue Thomiste* 71 (1971): 613–40.

———. *My Journal of the Council.* Translated by Mary J. Ronayne and Mary Boulding.
Collegeville, MN: Liturgical, 2012.

Congregation for Catholic Education. *Instruction on the Study of the Fathers of the
Church in the Formation of Priests,* 10 November 1989. *L'Osservatore Romano* (English edition), 15 January 1990.

Congregation for the Doctrine of the Faith. *Letter to the Bishops of the Catholic Church
on Some Aspects of the Church Understood as Communion ('Communionis notio').*
28 May 1992. *Origins* 22 (25 June 1992): 108–12.

Corecco, Eugenio. "Aspects of the Reception of Vatican II in the Code of Canon Law."
In *The Reception of Vatican II.* Edited by G. Alberigo, J.-P. Jossua, and J. A. Komonchak. Washington, DC: The Catholic University of America Press, 1987.

Coyle, T. William. "American Influence on Conciliar Decision Regarding BVM Schema." *Marian Studies* 37 (1986): 266–69.

———. "Development of Vatican II's Doctrine on Mary." *Social Justice Review* 78,
nos. 11–12 (1987): 176–79.

Daley, Brian. "Is Patristic Exegesis Still Usable? Reflections on Early Christian Interpretation of the Psalms." *Communio* 29, no. 1 (2002): 185–216.

———. "The *Nouvelle Théologie* and the Patristic Revival." *International Journal of
Systematic Theology* 7, no. 4 (2005): 362–82.

———. "Knowing God in History and in the Church: *Dei Verbum* and 'Nouvelle
Théologie.'" In *Ressourcement: A Movement for Renewal in Twentieth-Century Cath-
olic Theology,* edited by Gabriel Flynn and Paul Murray, 333–51. Oxford: Oxford
University Press, 2012.

———. "Sign and Source of the Church: Mary in the *Ressourcement* and at Vatican II."
In *Mary on the Eve of the Second Vatican Council,* edited by John Cavadini and
Danielle Peters, 31–54. Notre Dame, IN: University of Notre Dame Press, 2017.

DeClue, Richard. "Eucharistic Ecclesiologies of Locality and Universality in John Zizioulas and Joseph Ratzinger." *Nova et Vetera* 12, no. 1 (2014): 77–103.

De Fiores, Stephano. *Maria nel Misterio de Cristo e della Chiesa. Commento teologico-pastorale al cap. 8 della Lumen Gentium.* Roma: Centro Mariano Monfortano, 1968.

———. "Mary in Postconciliar Theology." In *Vatican II: Assessment and Perspectives,* edited by René Latourelle, 469–539. New York: Paulist Press, 1988.

Delahaye, Karl. *Ecclesia Mater: Chez les Pères des Trois Premiers Siècles. Pour un renouvellement de la Pastorale d'aujourd'hui.* Paris: Éditions du Cerf, 1964.

De La Soujeole, Benoît-Dominique. *Introduction to the Mystery of the Church.* Translated by Michael Miller. Washington, DC: The Catholic University of America Press, 2014.

De Moulins-Beaufort, Eric. *Anthropologie et mystique selon Henri de Lubac: 'L'Esprit de l'homme' ou la presence de Dieu en l'homme.* Paris: Éditions du Cerf, 2003.

Devaux, André. *Teilhard and Womanhood.* New York: Paulist Press, 1968.

Dillenschneider, Clement. *Le Mystère de la corédemption mariale.* Paris: J. Vrin, 1951.

———. "Mary, Prototype of Personification of the Church." *Marian Library Studies* 82 (1961): 1–9.

Doyle, Dennis. *Communion Ecclesiology: Visions and Versions.* Maryknoll, NY: Orbis Books, 2000.

Dulles, Avery. "Henri de Lubac: In Appreciation." *America* 165 (1991): 180–82.

———. "The Church as Communion." In *New Perspectives in Historical Theology: Essays in Memory of John Meyendorff,* edited by Bradley Nassif, 125–39. Grand Rapids, MI: Eerdmans, 1996.

———. "Mary Since Vatican II: Decline and Recovery." *Marian Studies* 53 (2002): 9–22.

Dupont-Fauville, Denis. *L'Église Mère chez Henri de Lubac.* Paris: Parole et silence, 2009.

Engen, John van. *Rupert of Deutz.* Berkeley: University of California Press, 1983.

Estevez, Jorge Medina. "The Blessed Virgin." In *Vatican II: An Interfaith Appraisal,* edited by John Miller, 301–15. Notre Dame, IN: University of Notre Dame Press, 1966.

Farkasfalvy, Denis. *The Marian Mystery: The Outline of a Mariology.* New York: St. Paul, 2014.

Feckes, Carl. *The Mystery of Divine Motherhood: A Theological Portrait of Mary.* New York: Spiritual Book Associates, 1941.

Fischer, James A. *Song of Songs.* The Collegeville Bible Commentary. Collegeville, MN: Liturgical Press, 1986.

Flanagan, Donal. "The Image of the Bride in the Earlier Marian Tradition." *Irish Theological Quarterly* 27 (1960): 111–24.

Flores, Deyanira. "Virgin Mother of Christ: Mary, the Church, the Faithful Soul— Patristic and Medieval Testimonies on this Inseparable Trio." *Marian Studies* 57 (2006): 97–172.

Flynn, Gabriel, and Paul Murray, eds. *Ressourcement: A Movement for Renewal in Twentieth-Century Catholic Theology*. Oxford: Oxford University Press, 2012.

Fouilloux, Étienne. *La collection "Sources chrétiennes": Éditer les Pères de l'Église au XXe siècle*. Paris: Éditions du Cerf, 1995.

Francis I. *Christmas Greetings to the Roman Curia* (21 December 2019). Accessed online at https://www.vatican.va/content/francesco/en/speeches/2019/december/documents/papa-francesco_20191221_curia-romana.html.

Fulton, Rachel. "Mimetic Devotion, Marian Exegesis, and the Historical Sense of the Song of Songs." *Viator* 27, no.1 (1996): 85–116.

———. "'*Quae est ista quae ascendit sicut aurora consurgens?*': The Song of Songs as the *Historia* for the Office of the Assumption." *Mediaeval Studies* 60 (1998): 55–122.

Gaillardetz, Richard, and Catherine Clifford. *Keys to the Council: Unlocking the Teaching of Vatican II*. Collegeville, MN: Liturgical Press, 2012.

Gambero, Luigi. *Mary and the Fathers of the Church: The Blessed Virgin Mary in Patristic Thought*. Translated by Thomas Buffer. San Francisco: Ignatius Press, 1999.

———. "Patristic Intuitions of Mary's Role as Mediatrix and Advocate: The Invocation of the Faithful for Her Help." *Marian Studies* 52 (2001): 78–101.

Ganne, Pierre, SJ "La Vierge Marie dans la vie de l'Église." In *Dialogue sur la Vierge*, edited by Maréchale Booth, et al. Paris: E. Vitte, 1950.

Gannon, Mary Patricia. "Mary in Vatican II: A Study of the Background for the Mariological Debate." Master's thesis. Washington, DC: The Catholic University of America, 1966.

Garrigou-Lagrange, Reginald, OP "La nouvelle théologie: où va-t-elle?" *Angelicum* 23 (1946): 126–45.

Gaurino, Thomas. *The Disputed Teachings of Vatican II: Continuity and Reversal in Catholic Doctrine*. Grand Rapids: Eerdmans, 2018.

Gavigan, James, et al., eds. *The Navarre Bible: The Book of Revelation: Texts and Commentaries*. Dublin: Four Courts Press, 1992.

Graebe, Brian. *Vessel of Honor: The Virgin Birth and the Ecclesiology of Vatican II*. Steubenville, OH: Emmaus Academic, 2021.

Graef, Hilda. *Mary: A History of Doctrine and Devotion*. New York: Sheed and Ward, 1963.

Granfield, Patrick. *Theologians at Work*. New York: MacMillan, 1967.

———. "The Church Local and Universal: Realization of Communion." *The Jurist* 49 (1989): 449–71.

Gréa, Dom Adrien. *De l'Église et de sa divine constitution*. Tournai: Casterman, 1965.

Griffiths, Paul. *The Song of Songs*. Brazos Theological Commentary. Grand Rapids, MI: Brazos Press, 2011.

Grootaers, Jan. "Une forme de concertation épiscopale au Concile Vatican II: La 'Conférence des Vingt-deux' (1962–1965)." *Revue d'Histoire Ecclesiastique* 91 (1996): 66–112.

———. "The Drama Continues between the Acts: The 'Second Preparation' and

Its Opponents." In *A History of Vatican II*, vol. II, edited by Giuseppe Alberigo and Joseph A. Komonchak, 359–515. Maryknoll, NY: Orbis; Leuven: Peeters, 1997.

Grumett, David. "Eucharist, Matter and the Supernatural: Why de Lubac Needs Teilhard." *International Journal of Systematic Theology* 10, no. 2 (2008): 165–78.

———. "Henri de Lubac: Looking for Books to Read the World." In *Ressourcement: A Movement for Renewal in Twentieth-Century Catholic Theology*, edited by Gabriel Flynn and Paul Murray, 236–49. Oxford: Oxford University Press, 2012.

Grumett, David, and Thomas Plant. "De Lubac, Pure Land Buddhism, and Roman Catholicism." *Journal of Religion* 92, no. 1 (2012): 58–83.

Hannaford, Robert. "The Eschatological Grounds of Mary's Vocation as Mother of Faith." *Maria* 3, no. 1 (2002): 5–16.

Hauke, Manfred. *Introduction to Mariology*. Washington, DC: The Catholic University of America Press, 2021.

Henn, William. "Historical-Theological Synthesis of the Relation between Primacy and Episcopacy during the Second Millennium." In *Il Primato del successore di Pietro Atti del simposio teologico*. Roma, 1996. Vatican City: Editrice Vaticana, 1998.

Hillebert, Jordan, ed. *T&T Clark Companion to Henri de Lubac*. London: Bloomsbury T&T Clark, 2017.

Hollon, Bryan. "Mysticism and Mystical Theology." In *T&T Clark Companion to Henri de Lubac,* edited by Jordan Hillebert, 307–25. London: Bloomsbury T&T Clark, 2017.

Hontiveros, Eduardo. "The Blessed Virgin Mary in the Second Vatican Council." In *Ecumenism and Vatican II*, edited by Pedro S. De Achutegui, SJ, 100–116. Manila: Loyola School of Theology, 1972.

Hughes, Kevin. "The 'Fourfold Sense': De Lubac, Blondel, and Contemporary Theology." *Heythrop Journal* 62 (2001): 451–62.

Isaac of Stella. *In Assumptione beatae Mariae, Sermo* I. PL194, 1863–65.

Jelly, Frederick M. "The Theological Context of and Introduction to Chapter 8 of *Lumen Gentium*." *Marian Studies* 37 (1986): 43–73.

John Paul II. Address to the Bishops of the United States of America, 16 September 1987. Accessible online at http://w2.vatican.va/content/john-paul-ii/en/speeches /1987/september/documents/hf_jp-ii_spe_19870916_vescovi-stati-uniti.html.

Johnson, Elizabeth. "Marian Devotion in the Western Church." In *Christian Spirituality: High Middle Ages and Reformation*, vol. 2, edited by Jill Raitt, 392–413. New York: Crossroad, 1987.

Journet, Charles. "Note sur Teilhard de Chardin." *Nova et Vetera* (Fribourg, 1958): 223–30.

———. "De la personnalité de L'Église." *Revue Thomiste* 69 (1969): 192–200.

Kasper, Walter. "A Friendly Reply to Cardinal Ratzinger on the Church." Translated by Ladislas Orsy, SJ *America*, 23 April 2001.

———. "Letter of Reply." *America*, 26 November 2001.

———. *The God of Jesus Christ*. New York: T&T Clark, 2012.

———. *The Catholic Church: Nature, Reality and Mission*. London: T&T Clark, 2015.

Kenis, Leo. "Diaries: Private Sources for a Study of the Second Vatican Council." In *The Belgian Contribution to the Second Vatican Council*. Bibliotheca Ephemeridum Theologicarum Lovaniensium CCXVI, 29–53. Leuven: Peeters, 2008.

Kereszty, Roch. "The Infallibility of the Church: A Marian Mystery." *Communion* 38, no. 3 (2011): 374–90.

———. "Toward the Renewal of Mariology." *Nova et Vetera* 11, no. 3 (2013): 779–99.

Kerr, Fergus. *Twentieth Century Catholic Theologians: From NeoScholasticism to Nuptial Mysticism*. Malden, MA: Blackwell Publishing, 2007.

Kirwan, Jon. *An Avant-garde Theological Generation: The Nouvelle Theologie and the French Crisis of Modernity*. Oxford: Oxford University Press, 2018.

Komonchak, Joseph A. "Theology and Culture at Mid-century: The Example of Henri de Lubac." *Theological Studies* 51 (1990): 570–602.

———. "The Local Church and the Church Catholic: The Contemporary Theological Problematic." *The Jurist* 52 (1992): 416–47.

———. "The Struggle for the Council during the Preparation of Vatican II (1960–1962)." In *A History of Vatican II*, vol. 1, edited by Giuseppe Alberigo and Joseph A. Komonchak, 167–356. Maryknoll, NY: Orbis; Leuven: Peeters, 1995.

———. "Modernity and the Construction of Roman Catholicism." *Christianesimo nella Storia* 18 (1997): 353–85.

———. "Toward an Ecclesiology of Communion." In *A History of Vatican II*, vol. 4, edited by Giuseppe Alberigo and Joseph A. Komonchak, 1–94. Maryknoll, NY: Orbis; Leuven: Peeters, 2003.

———. *Who Are the Church?* The Père Marquette lecture in theology. Milwaukee: Marquette University Press, 2008.

———, trans. "Draft of a Dogmatic Constitution on the Blessed Virgin Mary Mother of God and Mother of Men, by the Preparatory Theological Commission for the Second Vatican Council." Available in the public domain online at https://catholicebooks.wordpress.com/2017/10/11/online-texts-the-original-schemas-drafts-of-vatican-ii/.

Lamb, Matthew, and Matthew Levering. *Vatican II: Renewal within Tradition*. Oxford: Oxford University Press, 2008.

Lanne, Emmanuel. "L'Église locale et l'Église universelle: Actualité et portée du thème." *Irénikon* 43 (1970): 481–511.

Latourelle, René, ed. *Vatican II: Assessment and Perspectives: Twenty-five Years After, 1962–1987*. 3 vols. New York: Paulist Press, 1988.

Laurentin, René. *La Vierge au concile*. Paris: Éditions du Seuil, 1965.

———. "Mary in the New Age," *The Marian Era* 8 (1967): 27–29, 78–84.

———. *A Short Treatise on the Virgin Mary*. Translated by Charles Newmann. Washington, D.C.: Ami Press, 1991.

———. "The Virgin Mary in the Constitution on the Church." *Concilium* 8 (n.d.): 155–72.

Legrand, Hervé. "Forty Years Later: What Has Become of the Ecclesiological Reforms Envisaged by Vatican II?" *Concilium* 4 (2005): 57–72.

Lemna, Keith. "Louis Bouyer's Sophiology: A Balthasarian Retrieval." *Heythrop Journal* 52, no. 4 (2011): 628–42.

Marchetto, Agostino. *The Second Vatican Ecumenical Council: A Counterpoint for the History of the Council.* Scranton, PA: University of Scranton Press, 2010.

Marthaler, Bernard. "Henri de Lubac." In *The New Day: Catholic Theologians of the Renewal,* edited by W. Jerry Boney and L. E. Molumby, 9–19. Richmond, VA: John Knox Press, 1968.

Mattei, Roberto de. *Il Concilio Vaticano II: Una storia mai scritta* (Torino: Lindau, 2010). English translation: *The Second Vatican Council: An Unwritten Story.* Translated by Patrick Brannan, et al. Fitzwilliam, NH: Loreto Publications, 2010.

Matter, E. Ann. *The Voice of My Beloved: The Song of Songs in Western Medieval Christianity.* Philadelphia: University of Pennsylvania Press, 1990.

Maunder, Chris. *Our Lady of the Nations: Apparitions of Mary in Twentieth-century Catholic Europe.* Oxford: Oxford University Press, 2016.

McDade, John "Epilogue: '*Ressourcement*' in Retrospect." In *Ressourcement: A Movement for Renewal in Twentieth-Century Catholic Theology,* edited by Gabriel Flynn and Paul Murray, 508–22. Oxford: Oxford University Press, 2012.

McDonnell, Kilian. "The Ratzinger/Kasper Debate: The Universal Church and Local Churches." *Theological Studies* 63 (2002): 227–50.

McPartlan, Paul. "Mary for Teilhard and de Lubac." Paper delivered to the Oxford branch of the Ecumenical Society of the Blessed Virgin Mary. Wallington, Surrey: Ecumenical Society of the Blessed Virgin Mary. 8 November 1987.

———. *The Eucharist Makes the Church: Henri de Lubac and John Zizioulas in Dialogue.* Edinburgh: T&T Clark, 1993.

———. "The Local Church and the Universal Church: Zizioulas and the Ratzinger-Kasper Debate." *International Journal for the Study of the Christian Church* 4, no. 1 (2004): 21–33.

———. "Who Is the Church? Zizioulas and von Balthasar on the Church's Identity." *Ecclesiology* 4 (2008): 271–88.

———. *A Service of Love: Papal Primacy, the Eucharist, and Church Unity.* Washington, DC: The Catholic University of America Press, 2016.

Melloni, Alberto. "The Beginning of the Second Period: The Great Debate on the Church." In *A History of Vatican II,* vol. 3, edited by Giuseppe Alberigo and Joseph A. Komonchak, 1–116. Maryknoll, NY: Orbis; Leuven: Peeters, 2003.

———. *Vatican II: The Complete History.* New York: Paulist Press, 2015.

Militello, Cettina. "Maria e la chiesa: una proposta." *Ephemerides Mariologicae* 71, no. 4 (2021): 421–44.

Miller, John, ed. *Vatican II: An Interfaith Appraisal.* Notre Dame, IN: University of Notre Dame Press, 1966.

Miravalle, Mark. *Introduction to Mary: The Heart of Marian Doctrine and Devotion.*
    Goleta, CA: Queenship Publishing, 2006.

Moeller, Charles. "History of *Lumen Gentium*'s Structure and Ideas." In *Vatican II:
    An Interfaith Appraisal*, edited by John Miller, 123–52. Notre Dame, IN: University
    of Notre Dame Press, 1966.

Möhler, Johann A. *L'Unité dans l'Église.* Unam Sanctam 2. Paris: Éditions du Cerf, 1938.

Monchanin, Jules. "La Vierge aux Indes." *Dieu Vivant: Perspectives religieuses et
    philosophiques* 3 (1945): 47–48.

———. *In Quest of the Absolute: The Life and Work of Jules Monchanin.* Cistercian
    Studies Series, no. 51. Introduction and translation by J. G. Weber. Kalamazoo:
    Cistercian Publications, 1977.

Müller, Alois. *Ecclesia-Maria: Die Einheit Marias und der Kirche.* Paradosis: Beiträge zur
    Geschichte der altchristlichen Literatur und Theologie, Freiburg: Universitätsver-
    lag, 1953.

Murphy, Francesca Aran, and Christopher Asprey, eds. *Ecumenism Today: The Univer-
    sal Church in the 21st Century.* Hampshire: Ashgate, 2008.

Murphy, Roland. *The Song of Songs: A Commentary on the Book of the Canticles or the
    Song of Songs.* Minneapolis: Fortress Press, 1990.

Murphy, William F., Jr. "Henri de Lubac's Mystical Tropology." *Communio* 27, no. 1
    (2000): 171–201.

Neufeld, Karl Heinz. "Henri de Lubac SJ als Konzilstheologe." *Theologisch-Praktische
    Quartalschrift* 134 (1986): 149–59.

———. "In the Service of the Council: Bishops and Theologians at the Second
    Vatican Council (for Cardinal Henri de Lubac on His Ninetieth Birthday)."
    Translated by Ronald Sway. In *Vatican II: Assessment and Perspectives*, vol. 1, edited
    by René Latourelle, 74–105. New York: Paulist Press, 1988.

Neunheuser, Dom Burkhard. "*Église universelle et Église locale.*" In *L'Église de Vatican II,*
    edited by Guilherme Baraúna and Yves Congar, 607–38. Paris: Éditions du Cerf,
    1966–67.

———. "Adoration." In *New Catholic Encyclopedia*, vol. 1, 141–42. New York: McGraw
    Hill, 1967.

Newmann, Charles. "Mary and the Church: *Lumen Gentium,* Arts. 60–65." *Marian
    Studies* 37 (1986): 96–142.

———. "Textual Evolution of Chapter VIII of Lumen Gentium." *Marian Studies* 37
    (1986): 212–28.

Nichols, Aidan. "Thomism and the Nouvelle Théologie." *The Thomist* 64, no. 1 (2000):
    1–19.

———. "Henri de Lubac: Panorama and Proposal." *New Blackfriars* 93 (2012): 3–33.

———. *There Is No Rose: The Mariology of the Catholic Church.* Minneapolis: Fortress
    Press, 2015.

Noël, Pierre C. "Gli incontri delle conferenze episcopali durante il concilio: Il 'gruppo
    della Domus Mariae.'" In *Evento e decisioni: studi sulle dinamiche del concilio*

Vaticano II, edited by Maria Teresa Fattori and Alberto Melloni, 95–133. Bologne: Il Mulino, 1997.

Norris, Richard Alfred, ed. *The Song of Songs: Interpreted by Early Christian and Medieval Commentators*. Grand Rapids, MI: Eerdmans, 2003.

O'Connor, Catherine R. *Woman and the Cosmos: The Feminine in the Thought of Pierre Teilhard de Chardin*. Englewood Cliffs, NJ: Prentice-Hall, 1974.

O'Connor, James. "Lumen Gentium, nos. 55 to 59." *Marian Studies* 37 (1986): 74–95.

———, trans. "Schema of the Dogmatic Constitution on the Blessed Virgin Mary, Mother of God and Mother of Men (1962: in Latin and English)." *Marian Studies* 37 (1986): 198–211.

O'Malley, John. *What Happened at Vatican II*. Cambridge: Harvard University Press, 2008.

———. *Vatican I: The Council and the Making of the Ultramontane Church*. Cambridge, MA: Harvard University Press, 2018.

Origen. *Homiliae in Canticum canticorum* and *Commentarium in Canticum canticorum*. In *Origenes Werke*, vol. 8. Edited by W. A. Baehrens. Leipzig: J. C. Hinrichs, 1925.

———. *Origen: The Song of Songs: Commentary and Homilies*. Ancient Christian Writers Series 26. Translated by R. P. Lawson. London: Longman/Green, 1957.

Ouellet, Marc. "The Ecclesiology of Communion, 50 Years after the Opening of Vatican Council II." *Adoremus,* Online Edition 18, no. 6 (September 2012).

d'Ouince, René. *Le Père Teilhard de Chardin et l'avenir de la pensée chrétienne*. Paris: Aubier, 1970.

Parente, Pietro. "Nuove tendenze teologiche." *L'osservatore Romano.* 9–10 February 1942.

Paul VI. *Marialis Cultus*. Apostolic Exhortation. 2 February 1974.

Pelchat, Marc. *L'Église mystère de communion: L'Ecclésiologie dans l'oeuvre de Henri de Lubac*. Montreal: Les Éditions Paulines, 1988.

Persidok, Andrzej. "Western Sophiology? The 'Eternal Feminine' in the Thought of Henri de Lubac." *Verbum Vitae* 37, no. 2 (2020): 327–45.

Philips, Gérard. "Mariologische Perspectieven: Maria en de Kerk." *Mariale Dagen* 12 (1953): 9–78.

———. "Marie et l'Église: Un theme théologique renouvelé." In *Maria: Études sur la Saint Vierge*, vol. 7, edited by Hubert du Manoir. Paris: Beauchesne, 1964.

———. *L'Église et son mystère au IIe Concile du Vatican; histoire, texte et commentaire de la constitution Lumen Gentium*. Paris: Desclée, 1967.

Pius IX. *Ineffabilis Deus*. Apostolic Constitution. 8 December 1854.

Pius XII. *Munificentissimus Deus*. Apostolic Constitution. 1 November 1950.

Plumpe, J. C. *Mater Ecclesia: An Inquiry into the Concept of the Church as Mother in Early Christianity*. Washington, DC: The Catholic University of America Press, 1943.

Pope, Marvin. *Song of Songs: A New Translation with Introduction and Commentary*. Anchor Bible. Garden City, NY: Doubleday, 1977.

Portier, William. "What Kind of a World of Grace? Henri Cardinal de Lubac and the Council's Christological Center." *Communio* 39, no. 1 (2012): 136–51.

Prevot, Andrew. "Henri de Lubac (1896–1991) and Contemporary Mystical Theology." In *A Companion to Jesuit Mysticism,* edited by Robert A. Maryks, 279–309. Leiden: Brill, 2017.

Prévotat, Jacques. *Jules Monchanin (1895–1957) as Seen from the East and West: A Collection of Colloquium Essays from 1995.* Delhi: Saccidananda Ashram/Indian Society for Promoting Christian Knowledge (ISPCK), 2001.

Raguer, Hilari. "An Initial Profile of the Assembly." In *A History of Vatican II,* vol. 2, edited by Giuseppe Alberigo and Joseph A. Komonchak, 167–232. Maryknoll, NY: Orbis; Leuven: Peeters, 1997.

Rahner, Hugo. *Our Lady and the Church.* Translated by Sebastian Bullough. New York: Pantheon, 1961.

Ratzinger, Joseph. "The Pastoral Implications of Episcopal Collegiality." *Concilium* 1 (1965): 39–67.

———. Introduction to *Das II. Vatikanische Konzil 2,* Lexikon für Theologie und Kirche. Supplementary volumes. Freiburg im Breisgau: Herder-Verlag, 1967.

———. *Daughter Zion. Meditations on the Church's Marian Belief.* San Francisco: Ignatius Press, 1983.

———. "The Ecclesiology of the Second Vatican Council." Translated by Stephen W. Arndt. *Communio* 13, no. 3 (1986): 239–52.

———. *Principles of Catholic Theology.* San Francisco: Ignatius Press, 1987.

———. "A Response to Walter Kasper: The Local Church and the Universal Church." *America,* 19 November 2001.

———. *Pilgrim Fellowship of Faith: The Church as Communion.* Translated by Henry Taylor. San Francisco: Ignatius Press, 2005.

———. "Thoughts on the Place of Marian Doctrine and Piety in Faith and Theology as a Whole." In Hans Urs von Balthasar and Joseph Ratzinger, *Mary: The Church at the Source,* 19–27. San Francisco: Ignatius Press, 2005.

———. *The Essential Pope Benedict XVI: His Central Writings and Speeches.* Edited by John Thornton and Susan Varenne. New York: Harper Collins, 2008.

Ratzinger, Joseph, and Hans Urs von Balthasar. *Mary: The Church at the Source.* Translated by Adrian Walker. San Francisco: Ignatius Press, 2005.

Ratzinger, Joseph, and Vittorio Messori. *The Ratzinger Report: An Exclusive Interview on the State of the Church.* Translated by Salvator Attanasio and Graham Harrison. San Francisco: Ignatius Press, 1985.

Riches, Aaron. "Henri de Lubac and the Second Vatican Council." In *T&T Clark Companion to Henri de Lubac,* edited by Jordan Hillebert, 121–56. London: Bloomsbury T&T Clark, 2017.

Rivera, Alfonso. "Sentido mariologica del Cantar de los Cantares." *Ephemerides Mariologicae* 1 (1951): 437–68.

———. "Sentido mariologica del Cantar de los Cantares." *Ephemerides Mariologicae* 2 (1952): 25–42.

Rodhe, Sten. *Jules Monchanin, Pioneer in Hindu-Christian Dialogue.* Delhi: Indian Society for Promoting Christian Knowledge (ISPCK), 1993.

Rosato, Philip J., SJ "*Ad Limina Apostolorum* in Retrospect: The Reaction of Karl Barth to Vatican II." In *Karl Barth: Centenary Essays,* 87–114. Cambridge: Cambridge University Press, 1989.

Roten, Johann. "Hans Urs von Balthasar's Anthropology in Light of His Marian Thinking." *Communio* 20, no. 2 (1993): 306–33.

Routhier, Gilles. "Vatican II: The First Stage of an Unfinished Process of Reversing the Centralized Government of the Catholic Church." *The Jurist* 64 (2004): 247–83.

———. "Quarante ans après Vatican II, qu'est devenu le Mouvement marial?" *Istina* 50 (2005): 306–36.

Rowland, Tracey. *Culture and the Thomist Tradition after Vatican II.* London: Routledge, 2003.

Ruddy, Christopher. *The Local Church: Tillard and the Future of Catholic Ecclesiology.* New York: Crossroad, 2006.

———. "'In my end is my beginning': *Lumen Gentium* and the Priority of Doxology." *Irish Theological Quarterly* 79, no. 2 (2014): 144–64.

———. "A Very Considerable Place in the Mystery of Christ and the Church? Yves Congar on Mary." In *Mary on the Eve of the Second Vatican Council,* edited by John Cavadini and Danielle Peters, 113–32. Notre Dame, IN: University of Notre Dame Press, 2017.

Rupert of Deutz. *De incarnatione Domini.* PL 168, 837–962.

Russell, William C., SJ "Henri de Lubac." In *Modern Theologians, Christians and Jews,* edited by Thomas E. Bird, 183–99. Notre Dame, IN: University of Notre Dame Press, 1967.

Rynne, Xavier. *The Third Session.* New York: Farrar, Straus, and Giroux, 1965.

Sakowski, Derek. *The Ecclesiological Reality of Reception Considered as a Solution to the Debate over the Ontological Priority of the Universal Church.* Rome: Gregorian & Biblical Press, 2014.

Sales, Michel. *Der mensch und die Göttesidee bei Henri de Lubac.* Einsiedeln: Johannes, 1978.

Scheeben, Matthias. *Handbuch der katholischen Dogmatik.* 7 vols. Freiburg im Breisgau: Herdersche Verlagsbuchhandlung, 1873–78.

———. *Mariology.* Translated by J. M. J. Geukers. St. Louis: Herder, 1946.

Schlier, Heinrich. *Le temps de l'Église.* Translated by Father Corin. Tournai: Casterman, 1961.

———. "L'unité de l'Église d'après le Nouveau Testament." In *Essais sur le Nouveau Testament.* Translated by A. Liefooghe. Paris: Éditions du Cerf, 1968.

Schmemann, Alexander. "On Mariology in Orthodoxy." *Marian Library Studies* 2 (1970): 25–32.

Schnackers, Hubert. *Kirche als Sakrament und Mutter: zur Ekklesiologie von Henri de Lubac.* Frankfurt am Main: Peter Lang, 1979.

Schuon, Frithjof. *De l'unité transcendante.* Paris: Gallimard, 1948. English translation: *The Transcendent Unity of Religions.* New York: Harper & Row, 1975.

Scola, Angelo. "The Theological Foundation of the Petrine Dimension of the Church: A Working Hypothesis." *Ecclesiology* 4, no.1 (2007): 12–37.

Semmelroth, Otto. *Mary, Archetype of the Church.* Translated by Jaroslav Pelikan. New York: Sheed and Ward, 1963.

———. "The Role of the Blessed Virgin Mary, Mother of God, in the Mystery of Christ and the Church." In *Commentary on the Documents of Vatican II,* vol. 1, edited by Herbert Vorgrimler, 285–96. New York: Herder and Herder, 1967.

Shehan, Lawrence. *A Blessing of Years.* Notre Dame, IN: University of Notre Dame Press, 1984.

Stacpoole, Alberic. *Mary and the Churches.* Collegeville, MN: Liturgical Press, 1990.

Tagle, Luis Cardinal. "'The Black Week' of Vatican II." In *A History of Vatican II,* vol. 4, edited by Giuseppe Alberigo and Joseph A. Komonchak, 388–452. Maryknoll, NY: Orbis; Leuven: Peeters, 2003.

Tanner, J. Paul. "The History of Interpretation of the Song of Songs." *Bibliotheca Sacra* 154 (1997): 23–46.

Tavard, George H. *The Forthbringer of God: St. Bonaventure on the Virgin Mary.* Chicago: Franciscan Herald Press, 1989.

Teilhard de Chardin, Pierre. "The Eternal Feminine." In *Writings in Time of War,* 191–202. New York: Harper & Row, 1968.

———. *Writings in the Time of War.* Translated by René Hague. New York: Harper & Row, 1968.

———. *Human Energy.* Translated by J. M. Cohen. New York: Harcourt; London: Collins, 1969.

———. *Toward the Future.* Translated by René Hague. San Diego: Harcourt, 1975.

Thomas Aquinas. *Summa Theologiae.* 3 pars. Translated by the Fathers of the English Dominican Province. Benziger Bros., 1947.

Thompson, Thomas. "Recovering Mary's Faith and Her Role in the Church." In *Mary on the Eve of the Second Vatican Council,* edited by John Cavadini and Danielle Peters, 55–78. Notre Dame, IN: University of Notre Dame Press, 2017.

Tilliette, Xavier. "Henri de Lubac achtzigjährig." *Internationale Katholische Zeitschrift Communio* 5, no. 12 (1976): 187–93.

———. "Henri de Lubac: The Legacy of a Theologian." *Communio* 19, no. 3 (1992): 332–41.

Vatican II. *Relationes circa schema constitutionis dogmaticae de beata Maria Virgine, Matre Ecclesiae.* Typis Polyglottis Vaticanis, 1963.

———. *Schema Constitutionis De Ecclesia.* Typis Polyglottis Vaticanis, 1964.

Vilanova, Evangelista. "The Intersession, 1963–1964." In *A History of Vatican II,* vol. 3, edited by Giuseppe Alberigo and Joseph A. Komonchak, 347–492. Maryknoll, NY: Orbis; Leuven: Peeters, 2000.

Voderholzer, Rudolf. *Meet Henri de Lubac*. Translated by Michael J. Miller. San Francisco: Ignatius Press, 2008.

Vorgrimler, Herbert, ed. *Commentary on the Documents of Vatican II*. 5 vols. New York: Herder and Herder, 1967.

———. "Henri de Lubac." In *Bilan de la Théologie du XXe siècle*, vol. 2, 806–20. Tournai: Casterman, 1971.

Walsh, Christopher. "De Lubac's Critique of the Postconciliar Church." *Communio* 19, no. 3 (1992): 404–32.

———. "Henri de Lubac in Connecticut: Unpublished Conferences on Renewal in the Postconciliar Period." *Communio* 23, no. 4 (1996): 786–805.

Wicks, Jared, SJ "New Light on Vatican Council II." *Catholic Historical Review* 92, no. 4 (2006): 609–28.

———. "More Light on Vatican Council II." *Catholic Historical Review* 94, no. 1 (2008): 75–101.

———. "Further Light on Vatican Council II." *Catholic Historical Review* 95, no. 3 (2009): 546–69.

———. "Recent Scholarship on Vatican Council II." *Catholic Historical Review* 105, no. 3 (2019): 531–58.

Wilde, Melissa. *Vatican II: A Sociological Analysis of Religious Change*. Princeton, NJ: Princeton University Press, 2007.

Williams, A. N. "The Future of the Past: The Contemporary Significance of the *Nouvelle Théologie*." *International Journal of Systematic Theology* 7, no. 4 (2005): 347–61.

Wiltgen, Ralph M. *The Rhine Flows into the Tiber*. New York: 1967.

Wood, Jacob. "Ressourcement." In *T&T Clark Companion to Henri de Lubac*, edited by Jordan Hillebert, 93–119. London: Bloomsbury T&T Clark, 2017.

Wood, Susan K. *Spiritual Exegesis and the Church in the Theology of Henri de Lubac*. Grand Rapids, MI: Eerdmans, 1998.

Young, Robin Darling. "An Imagined Unity: Henri de Lubac & the Ironies of Ressourcement." *Commonweal* 15 (2012): 13–18.

———. "A Soldier of the Great War: Henri de Lubac and the Patristic Sources for a Premodern Theology." In *After Vatican II: Trajectories and Hermeneutics*, edited by James L. Heft with John O'Malley, 134–63. Grand Rapids: Eerdmans, 2012.

Yzermans, Vincent. *American Participation in the Second Vatican Council*. New York: Sheed and Ward, 1967.

Zizioulas, John. *Being as Communion*. London: Darton, Longman & Todd, 1985.

———. "The Mystery of the Church in Orthodox Tradition." *One in Christ* 24 (1988): 294–303.

The Splendor of the Church in Mary: Henri de Lubac, Vatican II, and Marian Ressourcement was designed in Arno and composed by Reflective Book Design of Durham, North Carolina.